EDUCATION AFTER SCHOOL

TYRRELL BURGESS

Education After School

LONDON
VICTOR GOLLANCZ LTD
1977

ISBN 0 575 02237 X

Printed in Great Britain by
Lowe & Brydone Printers Limited, Thetford, Norfolk

Contents

Acknowledgements

THIS book has grown from the work I have been doing at the North East London Polytechnic, first in the Centre for Institutional Studies and then in the School for Independent Study. I am very conscious of the opportunities which the Polytechnic gives for developing ideas and practice, and I must thank the Director, George Brosan; Eric Robinson, now Principal of Bradford College; and the many colleagues from whom I have learned so much. The book itself has benefited immeasurably from the criticism of particular colleagues and friends, especially Bryan Magee, John Pratt, Derek Robbins, Anne Sofer and Sir Toby Weaver.

I must also acknowledge the great kindness and patience of the publishers, especially Jill Norman of Penguin. They have not only waited for the book, but watched it change in successive drafts away from what they bargained for.

My special thanks are due to Eve Sears for typing and re-typing successive drafts and for help with research and references; also to June Sutton for help with page proofs.

I gratefully acknowledge the permission of Her Majesty's Stationary Office, the Royal Economic Society, the Ministry of Colleges and Universities, Ontario, Canada, and the College Entrance Examination Board for permission to use copyright material. ('Access to Education – A Global View' copyright © 1962 by College Entrance Examination Board.)

My family has nobly put up with my preoccupation with writing. My wife, Joan, has in particular combined encouragement, help and criticism to great effect. The book is for her so that, having read so much of it so often in bits, she might now have the chance to read it right through.

Clevancy
June 1976

CHAPTER ONE

Introduction

THIS book began as a survey and has ended as a manifesto. The original intention was to prepare a comparative account of education after school the world over. It seemed to me that this was becoming the most controversial educational issue, often for very diverse reasons. In Britain, and in Western Europe generally, we are still toying with the idea of 'mass' provision. In the United States, such mass provision has been found to be compatible with a huge minority of the comparatively uneducated, whose plight seems even more hopeless than before. In developing countries, where education after school is still the privilege of an élite, there is a growing conviction that there is nevertheless too much of it: graduate unemployment is rife. There was clearly a case for setting the educational debate in Britain in the context of what was happening elsewhere. No doubt we could learn from countries in Europe with comparable economies and comparable education systems. Perhaps a view of the United States might cheer or warn us about our own future. Nor were the rather stark lessons of developing countries negligible. I set out, therefore, to try to illuminate the British debate with experience and example from elsewhere. I had already worked in a developing country and had collaborated in an international study in Europe. I had travelled in Asia and Africa. In writing the book I visited and revisited many countries, including the United States.

Even from the beginning, however, I was determined that the book would not be a mere catalogue of systems or collection of anecdotes, however pointed. All the time I was trying to ask what were the abiding issues in post-school education. In the end it seemed to me that there were four: What is post-school education for? Who should get it? What should it consist of? How should it be organized? In writing this book I have tried to tackle these issues, drawing on international experience, but relating it to the situation in one country – Britain. Indeed I have narrowed the range even further. In asking, and trying to answer, the question of what post-school education should consist, I have avoided large curricular generalities and have tried instead to show what I think should be done. This means that at points the book swoops from the world-wide panorama to the detail of a particular programme. Without such swoops, however, the important questions can be dodged: concern with curriculum can ignore purpose; international comparisons can obscure the individual and his needs.

As the book was being completed, external events gave me an additional sense of urgency and turned the book finally into a manifesto. The British Government's reaction to an ailing economy exacerbated by an energy crisis was to attempt to control over-growing public expenditure. In education, disproportionate economies fell upon post-school education. This may not have been surprising. Indeed, the British were simply following an earlier faltering in the advance of post-school education in the U.S. The experience of the 1960s – of steady expansion in education, taking an ever-increasing share of GNP – was clearly over.

What was appalling in Britain, however, was that there was virtually no assertion, even from those engaged in it, that something of value was being lost. It seemed universally accepted that in diminishing post-school education, the Government was merely saving expenditure: not a hint that it might be destroying a contribution.

This view of post-school education as a luxury, as mere consumption, is very common. As far as most education systems are concerned, it is largely justified. But post-school education need not and should not be a peripheral frivolity: it has a job to do. Even in advanced societies people suffer from ignorance, incompetence and dependence: it is for the education system to destroy these evils. All societies, especially advanced ones, have grievous and resilient problems: it is for education to assist towards their solution. Few people in Britain in the mid 1970s saw education in that light. So the purpose of this book is to recall educators from their treason and to urge the development of post-school education.

CHAPTER TWO

What is it for?

THE first question in education after school is, what is it for? Until we can find a satisfactory answer we cannot begin to wonder who should reasonably get it, what its content should be or how it should be organized and governed. This may sound trite, but the question of what education is for is usually unasked, and if asked, unanswered. In most places the expansion of education takes place without fundamental discussion of any kind. Often those most responsible for planning are the most reluctant to articulate their purposes. There are advantages in this for the planners: if they do not say what they are trying to do nobody can tell if they fail. A good example of this was the British Government's White Paper of December 1972, *Education: A Framework for Expansion*, which said that it was specifically about matters of 'scale, organization and cost rather than educational content' (White Paper, 1972). It made a number of proposals, and had a number of additional consequences, for universities, for technical and other colleges and for teacher training institutions, but the proposals were unrelated to purpose and the consequences largely random. Another example was the reply of the Belgian Ministry of Education to a Unesco question about its educational aims (Unesco, 1971). Here it is in full:

In common with other European countries whose educational traditions go back for centuries, Belgium does not consider it necessary to set out the aims and purposes of its educational institutions explicitly. They are implicit in the level of civilization, considered in all its aspects.

This applies, in particular, to so-called general education; it is naturally recognised that the aims of technical education, teacher training, artistic and higher education are of a more specialized nature.

No doubt the tone of this reply can be attributed to the feelings of a weary civil servant filling up yet another international questionnaire, but the fact is that if there had been a handy statement of purpose in the Ministry, he could have turned it up and sent it in.

The usual objection to such a statement in something like post-school education is that it is bound to be vague. The vagueness is often itself an indication of an unwillingness to think. Even so, vague purposes are better than none at all. They are usually quite enough to reveal how far a nation or institution is failing to attain them. Without them countries might as well provide and expand at random – as indeed they mostly do. A more serious difficulty for this book is that it is the higher levels of education that have the most articulate statements of purpose. It is as if it is thought reasonable to make elaborate statements about universities and other institutions of higher education, but pretentious to do so for lesser colleges. I reject this distinction, as will become apparent throughout this book. For the moment, however, we must do the best we can.

We must start with the statements of governments or of official bodies set up by them. This is not because such statements are the most elegant or stimulating (indeed their prose can be somewhat daunting) but because they represent the nearest thing there is to a statement of the view of the particular society. In totalitarian countries we may suspect that the people, if given the chance, might express themselves somewhat differently. In democratic countries, governments and committees may be merely bland. But we have nowhere else to go for a statement of what a nation thinks its post-school education is about. Let us therefore begin with extensive quotation.

The first is from the report of the Robbins Committee, set up by the British Government, which reported on the pattern and future of full-time higher education in 1963 (Robbins, 1963). What purposes, asked the committee, what general social ends should be served by higher education? It asserted that no simple formula, no answer in terms of any single end, would suffice. Any single aim, pursued to the exclusion of all others, would leave out essential elements. 'Eclecticism in this sphere is not something to be despised,' said the committee. 'It is imposed by the circumstances of the case. To do justice to the complexity of things, it is necessary to acknowledge a plurality of aims.'

The committee then asserted four essential aims for any properly balanced system. The first was 'instruction in skills suitable to play a part in the general division of labour'. This was taken first not because it was the most important but because it was sometimes ignored or undervalued. The committee permitted itself a learned reference:

Confucius said in the Analects that it was not easy to find a man who had studied for three years without aiming at pay. We deceive ourselves if we claim that more than a small fraction of students in institutions of higher education would be where they are if there were no significance for their future careers in what they hear and read; and it is a mistake to suppose that there is anything discreditable in this.

The committee pointed out that the ancient universities of Europe were founded to promote the training of the clergy, doctors and lawyers; and 'though at times there may have been many who attended for the pursuit of pure knowledge or of pleasure, they must surely have been a minority'. Today, progress and particularly the maintenance of a competitive position depended more than ever on special skills. A good general education 'is frequently less than we need to solve many of our most pressing problems'.

The committee's second aim was that whatever was taught should be taught in such a way as to promote the general powers of the mind: 'The aim should be to produce not mere specialists but rather cultivated men and women.' There was no betrayal of values in teaching what was of practical use but the distinguishing characteristic of higher education was that 'even where it is concerned with practical techniques, it imparts them on a plane of generality that makes possible their application to many problems – to find the one in the many, the general characteristic in the collection of particulars.'

The third aim was the advancement of learning: 'the search for truth is an essential function of institutions of higher education and the process of education is itself most vital when it partakes of the nature of discovery.'

Fourth, the committee identified a fundamental if elusive function: the transmission of a common culture and common standards of citizenship. This function was to provide in partnership with the family that background of culture and social habit upon which a healthy society depends, and it was especially important in

15

an age which had set for itself the ideal of equality of opportunity. This was to be achieved not merely by providing places for students from all classes but by providing 'in the atmosphere of the institutions in which the students live and work, influences that in some measure compensate for any inequalities of home background'.

The Robbins Committee's concluding paragraph on aims summarized the traditional British view of higher education and the institutions that provide it:

Institutions of higher education vary both in their functions and in the way in which they discharge them. The vocational emphasis will be more apparent in some than in others. The advancement of learning will be more prominent at the post-graduate than at the under-graduate stage. The extent of participation in the life and culture of the community will depend upon local circumstances. Our contention is that, although the extent to which each principle is realized in the various types of institution will vary, yet, ideally, there is room for at least a speck of each in all. The system as a whole must be judged deficient unless it provides adequately for all of them.

The second formulation is from the U.S.S.R., from the 'Statute on the Higher Schools', introduced in the Khrushchev reforms of 1961 (U.S.S.R., 1961). There the purposes of higher education were said to be:

1. To train highly qualified specialists educated in the spirit of Marxism-Leninism, well-versed in both the latest achievements of science and technology, at home and abroad, and in the practical aspects of production, capable of utilizing modern technology to the utmost and of creating the technology of the future.
2. To carry out research that will contribute to the solution of the problems of building communism.
3. To produce textbooks and study aids of a high standard.
4. To train teachers and research workers.
5. To provide advanced training for specialists with higher education working in various fields of the national economy, the arts, education, and the health services.
6. To disseminate scientific and political knowledge among the people.
7. To study the problems connected with the utilization of graduates and with improving the quality of their training.

A third formulation comes from the Report of the Education

16

Commission of the Government of India (India, 1966). The commission began with a quotation from Jawaharlal Nehru:

A university stands for humanism, for tolerance, for reason, for the adventure of ideas and for the search for truth. It stands for the onward march of the human race towards even higher objectives. If the universities discharge their duties adequately, then it is well with the nation and the people.

It added that the universities could fill this role only if they were uncompromisingly loyal to certain fundamental values of life. They were a community of teachers and students where in some way all learned from one another or at least (with a flash of Indian realism) strove to do so. Their principal object was to deepen man's understanding of the universe and of himself, to disseminate this understanding throughout society and to apply it in the service of mankind. Universities were the dwelling places of ideas and idealism. Theirs was the pursuit of truth and excellence in all its diversity. 'Great universities and timid people go ill together.'

So much for generality. The commission then turned to the functions of universities, which it said went beyond the traditional functions of teaching and advancement of knowledge. These functions (seeking truth, training youth, staffing professions, equalizing society and fostering values) it identified as follows:

1. to seek and cultivate new knowledge, to engage vigorously and fearlessly in the pursuit of truth, and to interpret old knowledge and beliefs in the light of new needs and discoveries;
2. to provide the right kind of leadership in all walks of life, to identify gifted youth and help them develop their potential to the full by cultivating physical fitness, developing the powers of the mind and and cultivating right interests, attitudes and moral and intellectual values;
3. to provide society with competent men and women trained in agriculture, arts, medicine, science and technology and various other professions, who will also be cultivated individuals, imbued with a sense of social purpose;
4. to strive to promote equality and social justice and to reduce social and cultural differences through diffusion of education; and
5. to foster in the teachers and students, and through them in society generally, the attitudes and values needed for developing the 'good life' in individuals and society.

17

Finally, here is what the Carnegie Commission in the U.S.A. believed to be 'the major purposes for the total system of higher education for the period ahead' (the commission was set up by a charitable foundation, not by a government department – but it made up for this by writing like one):

Advancing the intellectual and professional capacity of individual students within a constructive campus environment

Enhancing human capability in society at large through training, research and service

Increasing social justice through greater equality of opportunity to obtain an advanced education

Advancing learning for its own sake through science, scholarship and the creative arts; and for the sake of public interest and consumption

Evaluating society, for the benefit of its self-renewal, through individual scholarship and persuasion.

(Carnegie, 1973)

Different though these formulations are, they have a number of preoccupations in common. All of them, for example, assert that one of the functions of higher education is to prepare people to do a job, both for their own good and for the general good of society. All mention research, the transmission of culture and a duty to the community. True, the emphasis differs, but (as the Robbins Report has it) there is at least a speck of each in all. The differences between them are, however, important. At one end of the range there is Robbins; urbane, orotund and essentially passive. It is no co-incidence that these aims were mentioned in the first few pages of the report and not referred to again. The rest of the report was written, and can be read, without reference to them: they were not expressed in terms of any means through which they might be implemented and they were not meant to be in any way operational. This may account for the general discursiveness. For example, the first aim wobbles rather uncertainly between the return on extra education to the individual and its contribution to the pressing needs of society. The second begs the question whether promoting the general powers of the mind is the same thing as producing a 'cultivated' man or woman. The third rests on a limited conception of research, as learning and the pursuit of truth rather than the solution of problems or the testing of hypotheses. And the fourth

18

simply ignores the dilemma it cannot avoid raising: how can a limited sector of post school education transmit at all generally the ideal of equality of opportunity? Finally, the Robbins Committee seems to have assumed that all these objectives were compatible. Different institutions would combine them differently, it seemed to say; but it showed little understanding of priorities to be defined or conflicts to be resolved. For all its nods in the direction of social responsibility, the committee saw higher education as an activity with its own values and purposes, affecting the rest of society obliquely and as a kind of bonus. This approach is in a tradition of education which can fairly be called the 'autonomous' tradition.

At the other end of the range is the Soviet formulation. Here it is quite clear that higher education has a number of socially useful jobs: the initial and in-service training of specialists, the training of teachers and researchers, research which will help to solve problems, the scientific and political education of the people, the production of text books and the better employment of graduates. Like Robbins, the Khrushchev formulation begs a lot of questions. In particular, it assumes that scientific knowledge and the kind of political knowledge accepted in the U.S.S.R. are compatible. Unlike Robbins, its platitudes conceal tyrannical direction and control. Clearly the purpose of education in the U.S.S.R., like that of everything else there, is to serve the Soviet state. The specialists must be qualified both in their disciplines and in Marxism-Leninism. The problems to be solved are those of building communism. Apart from this, the Soviet formulation explicitly lists the kinds of service which education is expected to offer. It is in a tradition of education which can reasonably be called the 'service' tradition.

In between (as is historically apt) is India. The general aims are in the autonomous tradition, the specific functions in the service tradition. Higher education is meant not only to prepare leaders and specialists but also to promote equality and social justice – though it did not occur to the commission to wonder how far higher education was an apt means for this purpose.

The United States formulation is clearly the most energetic attempt at the best of both worlds. Here we have service to the individual (with social consequences), explicit service to society, and the advancement of learning for its own sake. Characteristically, in this formulation, criticism of society is listed as a service to it – a notion absent from that of the U.S.S.R.

I believe that these two traditions, the autonomous and the service, are visible in all post-school education. Some countries lean heavily towards one of them: most have something of both. Individual countries have institutions in both traditions, and even within institutions the two tendencies can often be clearly identified. This is not surprising, because there is a tension between them, both within systems and within institutions. On the whole the tendency of institutions is towards autonomy: the tendency of society is to demand service. From time to time and from place to place the mixture of the two will vary.

All this may become clearer if we look at the experience of one country. I have chosen England, not just because I know it best, but because in England the two traditions have developed separately. From time to time, the distinction between them has been made explicit, in the creation of separate policies and separate systems of administration, financing and control. This means that they can be seen in institutional as well as academic terms. On the other hand, clarity will become parody unless one remembers that reality is never as straightforward as its descriptions: there is an element of both traditions in all English institutions, as we shall later see.

First, let us look back at the development of post-school education in England. Fortunately this does not require us to go further back in time than the nineteenth century. Before that there were only two universities in England and Wales (there were also four in Scotland) and very little systematic education of any other kind. The universities of Oxford and Cambridge were sunk in a kind of blowsy irresponsibility from which they were rescued as the century advanced only by Government inquiries and legislation. They acted very largely as finishing schools for the upper and middle classes, and their exclusiveness extended even to religious tests. Since their foundation in the twelfth century, they had induced Government to protect their independence (largely against the municipalities in which they were set) by charters and to give them control over their internal affairs and their students.

20

The first challenge to Oxford and Cambridge came from those excluded on religious grounds. A 'godless' college was established in London, to be met by an avowedly Anglican foundation a year or two later. These were then yoked together under a purely examining body, the University of London. The second challenge came from the industrial cities of the north of England. Here the pressure was for courses more relevant to the needs of the aspiring middle classes, though what strikes one is the extent of their thraldom to the older universities. They were astonishingly uneasy about the place of science and technology as university subjects, and for the most part their curricula seemed designed still for the general education of gentlemen. At first these new foundations were not accorded full university status: they were university colleges, preparing their students for the examinations of the University of London.

Nevertheless it was through these new universities that the 'modern' university approach was imported into England. Oxford and Cambridge had concentrated on the academic background to the élite professions, like law and the Church, and on the classics. The latter were held to constitute not only a liberal education but also a preparation for a career in Government and administration. This indeed had its uses: when Sir Charles Napier conquered Sind he was able to send to London a single-word telegram – 'Peccavi' – which was not only a bilingual pun but an admission that he had exceeded his brief. London (that is, that part of London that mattered) understood and was delighted.

The new university colleges, being more serious, were much influenced by the German universities and the reforms of Humboldt. In particular they embraced the idea of the academic discipline, taught by professors (who had never amounted to much at Oxford and Cambridge) in subject departments. It was here that the idea of study 'in depth' of a particular subject became the norm in English higher education. Interestingly enough, the universities still managed to aver that this too constituted a liberal education and a preparation for leadership in society. Exclusiveness became academic rather than religious, and universities began to assert the importance of 'standards'.

The developments in the universities were matched by develop-

21

ments in the schools which prepared for them. The schools for the rich in the nineteenth century were avowedly meant to educate 'gentlemen'. (Those of them which were not just privately run, but had governing bodies, were known as 'public' schools – hence the term which causes confusion today.) As the universities became more demanding, the schools became more concerned with 'standards'. By the turn of the century, municipalities had begun to set up academic or 'grammar' schools, and these schools offered the only education which was generally agreed to be secondary in character.

Parallel with these developments in academic education were others which were no less distinctive or important. One of them was a consequence of attempts to spread elementary education. This was done without help from the universities or the public and grammar schools. The teachers of the children of the poor were prepared first through a variety of monitorial or pupil-teacher systems (a species of apprenticeship) and later through training colleges established for the purpose. Another development derived from the efforts of workers, particularly artisans, to improve their economic power. Typical of this movement were the London Artisan's Club, the Trade Guild of Learning and the Artisan's Institute. Yet another arose from the efforts of individuals to bring both culture and training to working people, like the mechanics' institutes of the early nineteenth century and the polytechnics fifty years later. The mechanics' institutes were founded to teach artisans the science behind their skills. Manufacturers were jealous of the secrets of their processes, and would have preferred their workers to carry out their operations mechanically and without too much understanding. The mechanics' institutes revealed a desire among workers to master the theory as well as the practice of what they were doing, but the divorce in the instruction between theory and practice eventually proved fatal to this working-class initiative.

The institutes also became a battle ground politically. There were those who believed that workers should be taught what was then known as 'political economy', so that they could understand the economic forces shaping their lives and gain some control of them. This was not surprisingly thought to be subversive, and a

22

number of institutes were destroyed in the arguments of their members.

A major impetus in these developments in education was the growth both of science and industrialism. In the middle of the century the Government, nagged by the Prince Consort and others, made tentative steps towards founding science schools and colleges. The Great Exhibition of 1851 had seemed to show Britain as the leading manufacturing nation. The Paris Exhibition of 1867 saw that comforting pre-eminence threatened. The cause was generally held to be the British lack of scientific and technical education, and Royal Commissions reported this indefatigably. The consequence was a sudden flowering of state and municipal enterprise in the last decade of the nineteenth century with the founding and development of institutions avowedly concerned with technical and vocational education. This development had its flamboyant side. It was made possible, solidly enough, by the creation of local authorities competent and eager to found and run substantial institutions. It was vastly aided by a happy improvisation. As an Act of Parliament was being passed to dispose of the proceeds of some surplus excise duties, an enterprising M.P. moved an amendment to allow local authorities to spend them on technical education. This 'whiskey money', as it was inevitably called, built twelve polytechnics or technical colleges in London, thirteen in the rest of the country and over a hundred science schools in twelve years – amounting to nearly 90 per cent of all public expenditure for this purpose.

I believe that even this potted history is enough to display the two quite distinct traditions. Let us now look at them in more detail, as they appear today. The more familiar of them, at least to the likely readers of this book, is the autonomous tradition, typified though not monopolized by the universities. I would characterize this tradition as aloof, exclusive, conservative and academic. The independence of universities, their aloofness from the demands of society, is much prized even by people outside them. It is one of the first things that totalitarian governments attack. This means that we expect and want universities to be able to resist the demands of society, the whims of governments, the fashions of public opinion, the importunities of actual and potential students.

In England, this independence is protected. Even though most of the money which universities spend comes from the central Government, since 1919 these Government grants have been distributed through a body called the University Grants Committee. The committee has a dual function, first of arguing with the Government the universities' case for funds and second of distributing the funds made available to individual universities. The object is avowedly to set up a 'buffer' between the universities and the Government, precisely in order to prevent the latter interfering directly. This means that we do not expect the universities to respond quickly to social or industrial demand. In England, they quite simply rejected applications from the increasing numbers of qualified applicants produced by the schools in the late 1950s, until the frustration this created threatened to be politically damaging and induced the Government to set up the Robbins Committee. Nor have the universities been eager to produce new kinds of graduates or to widen opportunity for different kinds of people.

The aloofness is also expressed in academic attitudes. Universities are and claim to be engaged in the pursuit of knowledge, in the last resort 'for its own sake'. This activity is described in many different ways, all of them revealing. Some speak of the preservation, extension and dissemination of knowledge (or, in the case of a celebrated letter from several vice-chancellors to *The Times*, of 'wisdom'). Others describe their work in terms of the pursuit of truth, or excellence, and of following the truth where ever it may lead. Others claim to be upholding standards. However described, the activity is self-justifying. Indeed one of the difficulties that outsiders commonly have in talking to university people is that the latter do not seek to justify what they are doing in external terms, like that of social need. They may even assert the opposite, saying that it is their duty to do their jobs regardless of such things, and that this is in itself a prerequisite of more general freedoms and all sorts of other social good.

The approach derives from the concept of a discipline or subject of study. A discipline is an organized body of knowledge: it enables academics to speak of the structure of the subject. It encourages them to claim to spend half their academic time on research, because it is only by doing this that they can be sure they have anything worth while to teach. To keep up with the subject and to extend its frontiers is the basis of academic respectability. Publication is the key to promotion.

There are two consequences of this approach. The first is that universities are not directly concerned with professional and vocational education. This may seem an odd statement when universities can be seen to contain departments of medicine, engineering, law and the like. But the extent to which a course is vocational does not depend upon its subject matter but upon its method. The crucial question is, at the end of the course are the students ready to practise? The answer in the case of most university courses is no. The graduate requires a period of practical experience before he can be said to have qualified. This is true in the three disciplines mentioned above. What the university is concerned to do is to give a general grounding in the subject: practice comes later.

The second consequence is educational conservatism. The English universities have always had a very clear idea of what constitutes appropriate study for universities, and it is hard now to realize how resistant they have been to new disciplines. Even pure science was suspect until the 1950s. The reluctance to accept technology was a major reason why the then Government expanded and developed technical colleges in the later 1950s. Even today resistance to what the Robbins Report called 'executive subjects', like art, remains. A comparable reluctance is seen in the slowness with which universities admit novelty into undergraduate courses or give up existing elements of them. It appears again in the general failure of cross-disciplinary courses, which almost always break up into their component parts.

This conservatism is defensible. It derives from the conviction that advances in knowledge are made only with great effort, by imposing some sort of order on what previously was chaos. There is always the chance that innovators may lose what has been gained and involve their colleagues in nothing less than an attempt to teach chaos. Intellectual order is precious and vulnerable. Attempts to treat it in a cavalier fashion need to be resisted.

This concept of their role leads universities to be exclusive. Their preoccupations mean that they can responsibly accept only those students who might be held to 'benefit' from what they have to offer. Their entry requirements are rigid and over the years have become more and more formidable. There is a well recognized selection process, as we shall see in Chapter 2, which in England has begun as early as the end of primary school, with over half the population excluded from consideration by an examination at eleven plus. Most of the rest are excluded by subsequent selection at sixteen and eighteen. It is axiomatic that it is the universities themselves which decide which students they shall accept and which reject. A consequence of this is that their student body is astonishingly homogeneous, consisting largely of those between 18 and 22, who have come up from grammar schools, doing full-time courses lasting three or four years and leading to the award of an honours degree. The students are also very largely middle-class. This is mainly because the selection process, though ostensibly educational, is effectively social. Selection penalizes the children of manual workers. One of the Robbins Committees more neglected statistics was that only 2 per cent of the children of unskilled and semi-skilled manual workers (only a proportion of whom were in universities) got full-time higher education compared with 45 per cent of the children of higher professional workers. This class bias is very resilient. When Robbins reported, about a quarter of university students had fathers who were manual workers – almost the same proportion as for the whole period 1928 to 1947. Since then several new universities have been founded with a student body even less working-class than the rest. The latest figures on university entrance suggest that the same proportion of entrants are the sons and daughters of manual workers. The Open University, set up to extend opportunity through home study by correspondence, radio and television, is even less accessible. Only 10 per cent of its students can be described as manual workers (we are of course not comparing the social class of their fathers). The rest have mostly had some form of post-school education. The English universities are and always have been middle-class institutions.

It is important to be clear about the importance, the strength and the attraction of the autonomous tradition. In most societies autonomy is not easy: it may be heroic. Throughout human history governments have been more or less tyrannical, and we honour

26

those individuals or institutions who have resisted them. Very often the opponents of dictatorships have been found in universities and colleges, among both staff and students. There is a belief, all the more touching for being frequently justified, that thinking institutions are a defence against oppression. In a democracy autonomy is easier, but it is still necessary. Democratic governments can err: popular demand may be foolish. Both can be unjust, arbitrary and capricious. The health of democracy demands that there can be some individuals and institutions standing aloof from society at large, neglecting or even opposing the deepest concerns of the society around them, pursuing what no one would otherwise pay for. A democratic society is a plural society, one in which criticism is welcome and alternatives desirable.

Democracies recognize that there can be no certainty where human understanding will be next advanced. It is a commonplace that many of the most important discoveries and the greatest achievements of the human spirit have been made in the face of political oppression, popular indifference or worse. One cannot rely on even a plural society's capacity to allow for everything. What is more, the creations of the human mind themselves attain a kind of autonomy. Once a branch of knowledge exists, it imposes its own disciplines (we use the word to characterize it) and creates its own problems. It is right that there should be people with the opportunity to follow the discipline and attempt to solve the problems. Of course, the solutions may (and often do) end by destroying the bounds of the discipline, but that is one way in which knowledge is advanced. Nor need this argument be confined to those disciplines where major advances are currently being made. They can stand up for themselves. It is even more important as a defence of those areas of knowledge where few see any promise: these are worth preserving if only because one never knows when a discipline might come in handy.

The autonomous tradition, then – aloof, exclusive, conservative and academic – has many triumphs to its credit. What of the alternative, the service tradition? I would characterize this tradition as responsive, open, innovating and vocational. Its characteristics are found in what in England is called further education: that is, in a whole range of technical and other colleges provided and run by public authorities. Here is the first difference from the universities. The colleges are public institutions. They are not protected by charters and they are administered by the same local authorities that maintain schools, under regulations made by the Secretary of State for Education and Science. Their very administration encourages a response to demand. Courses are run and attract resources provided it can be shown that the students are enrolled or are likely to be, or that there is an expressed need from local industry or commerce. When the numbers of qualified applicants for full-time higher education exceeded those projected by the Robbins Committee, it was the further education colleges which took them in. In this respect the colleges of education, which train teachers, are in the service tradition. In the 1960s they enormously expanded to meet the needs of the schools: in the 1970s they will suffer a brutal contraction in the face of Government fears that there might be too many teachers.

British further education has not traditionally been concerned with knowledge for its own sake or with the pursuit of truth. It has been concerned with professional and vocational education, with the transmission of clearly defined skills. Often this has been 'mere' vocational training: that is, the narrowest possible concentration on technique to the exclusion both of a wider understanding of the job and of anything like personal development.

These colleges have been teaching institutions: not for them the demands of research, unless it be under contract for a local firm. For this latter purpose the regulations allow some respite from teaching: the service tradition is strong here too. Nor is research the basis for promotion: staff in the colleges are appointed at all levels to do specific jobs with specific responsibilities. They are chosen on the basis of some judgement that they are capable, not on the basis that they have written a number of books.

Many people who do not know the colleges will no doubt regard the claim that they are educationally innovating as simply outlandish. But this seems to me to be one of the most obvious things about them. Certainly these colleges have been the basis for two major innovations in higher education this century. The first of these was the discovery that one could give locally relevant courses a national validity. This occurred in the 1920s when, it will be recalled, new university colleges were not trusted to set their own standards but were kept in tutelage to the University of London. At this time many technical colleges were offering their own diplomas leading to professional qualifications which were often tailored to the needs of local firms. These diplomas often had no recognition beyond the locality, and might be little use if a man moved. The remedy was not to make the colleges take a national examination: that would have undermined their local relevance and responsiveness. Instead a number of joint boards were established by the Ministry of Education and the relevant professional bodies (the Institution of Electrical Engineers, for example) to monitor the courses, examinations and standards of the colleges themselves. This simple method, of local initiative externally moderated, has been astonishingly fruitful, and its potential is even now vastly underestimated. Since the early 1950s it has made possible the development first of ten colleges of advanced technology and then of thirty polytechnics, together with a huge expansion of higher education elsewhere. The principle has been extended to the schools, where a new Certificate of Secondary Education has been created which gives teachers and pupils the initiative, but gives both the assurance of national recognition.

The second innovation sprang from these developments. This was the 'sandwich' course, in which a period of practical work in a firm was made an integral part of the course. At first, sandwich courses were confined to the technologies; more recently they have been introduced into the sciences (including mathematics), the social sciences and the humanities.

It is important to realize the significance and purpose of the external validation of a local initiative. It is not, as many academics think, just a necessary check on competence. It is a process for innovation and experiment – as I hope will come clear in Chapter 5. Perhaps these claims for innovation in further education can be summed up in the discovery my colleague John Pratt and I made when we collaborated in an O.E.C.D. study on innnovation in higher education. The contributors, from half a dozen countries, were asked to study innovation under an agreed number of heads. These included coping with numbers; extending educational opportunity to hitherto excluded social groups; creating new structures of study and admitting an interdisciplinary approach; institutional management, autonomy and academic freedom; recruiting different sources of staff and linking higher education with the outside world.

When the first drafts were produced, there was a meeting in Paris at which our findings were discussed. It gradually became clear that in all the aspects of higher education that we had been asked to study the most radical and most successful innovations were in the colleges maintained by public authorities in England and Wales. Our French and Canadian colleagues even wanted to assert the principle that in higher education innovation is most likely in those institutions most closely controlled by the state.

It will be clear from all this that the service tradition implies open institutions. The technical colleges have made a habit of accepting those who have been rejected elsewhere, whether by schools or universities. As institutions they lay down no formal entry requirements. Individual courses may entail specific entry qualifications but for the college as a whole there are none. Weaker students can, and do, drop from one course to a less demanding one (instead of into the labour market, as from universities) and the stronger can, and do, aspire to courses and qualifications they had never previously dreamed of. Despite periodic attempts at rationalization, the tradition as a whole has allowed for a bewildering variety of levels and kinds of courses and of modes of study, often in the same institution. This has meant that the colleges' student body is extremely heterogeneous. The students may be of all ages, from sixteen to forty-five and more. They may take many kinds of courses (academic, vocational or recreational) at many levels – remedial, General Certificate of Education, craft and technician courses to first degree level and above. They may be studying full time, part time, by block release, in the evenings and so on. This variety makes the technical and other colleges the traditional route to further education and qualifications for working people and their children. The Robbins Committee reported that more than half of the students on part time advanced level courses had fathers who were manual workers.

In my view, both the service tradition and the autonomous tradition are visible throughout higher education in England. Of course the categories are not exclusive: there are aspects of some universities and of some technical colleges which seem to reflect the other tradition. But it seems to me that the distinction is very clear and appears in methods of finance and government, in the selection of students, in the curriculum, in the appointment of staff – in short, in all the most important activities of the various institutions.

The picture is complicated, however, by a tendency which is very nearly as observable as the two traditions themselves; that is the tendency of institutions established in the service tradition to seek autonomy. John Pratt and I call the process 'academic drift', and we have detailed its British effects first in the colleges of advanced technology and second in the new polytechnics. Broadly it consists of the aspirations to take on the attributes and objectives of autonomy. The colleges seek freedom from public control and from the discipline of external validation. They increase their commitment to research. They establish the structure of subject departments and hanker after professorships. They try to become as much like existing institutions as possible, thus eschewing innovation. Most important, they begin rejecting students they would previously have accepted and they transfer elsewhere many of the courses they previously offered. The consequence is that their student body becomes increasingly homogeneous and in particular tends to contain only the normal, university, proportion of the sons and daughters of manual workers. Perhaps one example of the process will be enough to convince. The conurbation of Manchester has founded a number of service colleges in the last hundred years, only to see them disappear with ever-increasing speed into autonomy. First there was Owens College, founded in 1851, not indeed as a technical college but in the hope that it would meet the needs of the locality. It gained its charter as the Victoria University of Manchester in 1880. The city then developed the Municipal School (later College) of Technology out of a mechanics' institute in 1902 – and this became the University College (later Institute) of Science and Technology in 1956. The neighbouring borough to Manchester, Salford (the two are only a narrow canal apart), developed its own technical college until it became the Royal College of Advanced Technology in 1956 – and then turned into the University of Salford in 1966. Two years later Manchester tried again, with the polytechnic based upon three colleges – of technology, art and commerce. This institution, in common with other poly- technics, is already well on the road to autonomy, and no doubt the time is ripe for identifying the place where Manchester will make its fifth attempt.

It may be thought that this distinction between the autonomous and service traditions, together with the principle of academic drift, is of purely local interest. Those national statements of aims quoted earlier suggest otherwise. The tensions are universal rather than merely local. Academic drift is a world-wide phenomenon. Indeed even the Soviet formulation hinted as much. The stress on the importance of close cooperation with the various branches of the national economy was apparently new – and one need not be a determined Kremlinologist to suspect that its introduction be- tokened some earlier backsliding. The Soviet authorities have always worried that education at all levels might lose contact with their view of society at large. In higher education they have devices to remind the students at any rate of their social duty. Preference for admissions, in a highly competitive situation, is given to the politically acceptable, to those who can produce references from party or youth organizations, trade unions or factory managers. Others have to have been in the forces or done at least two years' practical work in industry or agriculture. In addition students are meant to spend holidays and spare time on voluntary work for the community, and this 'social record' is said to count for as much as their academic record.

Whatever its success with students, the Soviet Government has at times expressed its frustration with its institutions. Apparently the academic approach will keep creeping in. In one of his earthy homilies, Khrushchev once said of specialists from the agricultural institutes, 'They cannot tell young hemp from nettles until they have been stung by the nettles' (Grant, 1964). The whole pur- pose of the educational law of 1958 and subsequent legislation was 'the establishing of closer links between school and life', and one of its objects has been to tip the balance of post-school educa- tion towards technical and specialized training. In schools, both at the compulsory ages and afterwards, the 'polytechnic' principle introduces manual work and contact with manual workers as a part of the curriculum. In the schools for fifteen-year-olds and over such experience may take up a third of the timetable when the schools themselves are offering general education, two thirds when they are vocational schools and more when they are trade schools. The reasons for this emphasis were partly economic and practical, and partly political and social. Let Khrushchev's memorandum on the subject explain it:

> We are striving to have our entire youth, millions of boys and girls, go through the ten-year secondary school. Naturally enough, they cannot all be absorbed by the colleges . . . In recent years, in view of the growing numbers passing out of the ten-year schools, a smaller proportion of boys and girls enter college. The greater part of them . . . turn out to be quite unprepared for life and do not know in what direction to turn . . . Owing to the fact that the secondary school curriculum is divorced from life, these boys and girls have absolutely no knowledge of production, and society does not know how best to utilize these young and vigorous people . . . This state of affairs can hardly be considered right. (Grant, 1964)

There are two distinguishable senses in which the Soviet authorities seek to emphasize the 'service' function. The first is the straightforward sense of the political and social control of a totalitarian society. The second is the sense that education should promote individual competence in a complex society. It seems that the authorities have succeeded in the first without halting academic drift from the second.

Even more remarkable is the recent experience of China. During the cultural revolution, the schools were closed for two years and higher education institutions for three, from 1966 to 1969. As they reopened it was clear that they were also reorganized. The criticisms of the old system were threefold. First, it was said to be dominated by a 'revisionist and feudal and bourgeous outlook' which tended to encourage students' alienation from their socialist environment. Second, it cultivated élitism and nurtured people who were to enjoy elevated status and act accordingly. Third, academic qualifications carried with them no guarantee of general competence. In addition, high fees and examinations excluded the children of peasants and workers from secondary and tertiary education and the length of studies was excessive and the curriculum too bookish. Apart from the revolutionary rhetoric, these criticisms do not sound oddly, even to British ears.

The changes were enormous. Control of educational institutions was taken out of the hands of professional educators and placed in those of lay committees. From 1962 middle-school graduates have been resettled in the countryside, thus effectively reducing the demand for higher education. The ideal student will now be a twenty-year-old worker who has graduated from middle school and worked for at least three years. His course will last three years instead of five. The institution he attends will try to integrate teaching, research and production. (The staff of Tungchi University, Shanghai, a civil engineering college, merged with an industrial design institute and the municipal construction bureau to form the 7 May Commune of Tungchi University.) It will also offer a variety of full-time, part-time and short courses for students from varying backgrounds.

The lessons of this story are interesting. China is a totalitarian country with an extensively expressed social purpose. Its government is in a position to demand a commitment to service from all social institutions. Yet the pressures within education towards autonomy proved so strong as to provoke a three-year closure of institutions and the forcible dispersal of students, as a prelude to a revolution in control, a re-statement of objectives and content of courses, and a complete reform of organization. There is now ground for believing that even this has failed. Academic drift in these circumstances begins to look like a movement of continental proportions.

As we have seen in the English example, academic drift occurs even in institutions specifically established to resist it. In Pakistan it was decided to found a number of institutions called polytechnics to train technician supervisors. The object was not only to man a growing industrialization but to make education useful and enhance the dignity of manual labour. Polytechnics proliferated all over Pakistan. Unfortunately, the skills for which they trained did not match the fast-growing sectors of industry. The courses were largely theoretical, and even practical experience consisted of watching demonstrations of experiments and techniques. Polytechnic graduates were generally held to be incapable of practising any skill, and they were unable to supervise either. The rate of employment of these vocationally trained young men was no better (and in some cases worse) than that of those with a 'useless' academic training. They certainly showed no more disposition to accept the need to work with their hands. This example is complicated by the fact that the polytechnics were heavily supported by foreign aid, which assisted the drift to autonomy, but it stands nevertheless as a monument to a universal tendency.

One more foreign example of academic drift must suffice, this time from Germany. Dr Jürgen Fischer, secretary-general of the West German Rectors' Conference, has described how the process began in the middle of the eighteenth century (Fischer, 1972). Then the technical requirements of the army and of the administration of the principalities led to the foundation of technical, engineering, architectural and naval colleges. Institutions in Austria and France served as models. The formula for their establishment in Austria in 1774 laid down that they were to be created 'in the interests of the political well-being of the state' and in order to make 'new discoveries in nature and invent useful machines and methods', placing them firmly in the service tradition. After 1875 these 'polytechnical schools' sought to become 'Technische Hochschulen', knowing that a change in their status would mean adopting the same admission requirements as the universities. By 1899 they had acquired university status in Prussia, when they were authorized to award doctorates. In doing so they excluded those not holding the 'Abitur' – awarded on completion of full secondary education. Dr Fischer comments: 'This obliged them to recruit their students from particular social classes and also led, within the institutions, to a weakening of the direct relationship between theory and practical experience.'

The gap created by this rise in status soon made itself felt. The growing requirements of professions not traditionally requiring a degree, the introduction of technology into trades and crafts, the need of those not holding an 'Abitur' to obtain qualifications, and particularly the new requirements of technical occupations in industry prompted the growth of new institutions at a level lower than the 'Technische Hochschulen'. On the basis of state and private initiatives, the 'Ingenieurschulen' came into being. Their students were admitted on completion of middle-level secondary education, or after primary education and some professional experience, and after three years' rigorous study they received the title of 'Graduierte Ingenieur'.

The historical process of the upward development of institutions towards the university continues today. The 'Technische Hochschulen' have after a long struggle gained full recognition as technical universities. The 'Ingenieurschulen' have, under the influence of Article 57 of the Treaty of Rome and with its help, become professional colleges ('Fachhochschulen'). Now these are all striving to introduce the 'Abitur' as the admission requirement and to establish a four-year curriculum (the shortest for university studies). By doing so, comments Dr Fischer, 'they will continue to stimulate the establishments of new institutions with lower admission requirements'.

Academic drift, then, is a normal – almost inevitable – phenomenon. Nor are its causes mysterious. Clearly, the aims of government are not necessarily those of educational institutions. It is not enough for governments to say what they think higher education is for, nor to establish institutions to fulfil these purposes, nor even to break up an old system and replace it with another. If this is all (all!) they do, the aims of the institutions themselves will prevail, whether governments like it or not. It is these institutions, after all, which are responsible day to day for what happens. Their staffs have their own goals. There may be directives and regulations, there may be a powerful board of governors or trustees, there may be all manner of devices for implementing government policy – but these must in the end be powerless against the minute-by-minute, hour-by-hour, day-by-day activity of those actually in the institutions.

Their chief object (like that of everyone else) is the good life. In unequal systems, the less favoured tend to interpret this (sometimes wrongly) in terms of the situation of the fortunate. Universities have status in the eyes of government and of the public. This status is thought to derive from various attributes, of external and internal organization. Technical colleges thus strive to take on these attributes, genuinely without considering whether or not they are apt to themselves – whether, in other words, arrangements which serve one purpose can reasonably be expected to serve another. It is quite common for institutions which have drifted academically to be genuinely astonished to find how they have changed: they can be heard asserting, all over the world, that they did not mean it.

A major study of this process is *The Academic Revolution* by Christopher Jencks and David Riesman (Jencks, 1968). In these more troubled times, the title implies student riots and staff dissension. The revolution the book speaks of, however, is that in which the academic profession in the United States freed itself from lay control. The consequence of this, at the undergraduate level, has been the growth of 'university colleges' whose avowed intention is preparation for the graduate schools of which they frequently form a part. Alongside them are 'terminal colleges' whose main purpose is to offer a final stage of education to their students. What happens, say Jencks and Riesman, is that the university colleges take the most able students, lose a few of them by wastage and send a large proportion on to graduate school. They draw their staffs from the same sources as do the graduate schools, looking for the same qualities and eschewing the same defects. They form only 5 per cent of colleges, but they are the most prestigious, attracting the most able staff and students and the most generous benefactors. In consequence, they act as a model for the terminal colleges which seek the same kinds of staff, regardless of function, who in turn seek the same kinds of students, regardless of the institution's original aims. Jencks and Riesman add:

One way to describe this change is in terms of changing reference groups. Special-interest colleges were established by laymen to serve a particular purpose, and were initially very committed to that purpose. The local college was local first and a college second: the Catholic college was Catholic first and a college second; the Negro college was Negro first and a college second, and so forth. But as time went on these disparate institutions took on lives and purposes of their own. Undergraduates thought of themselves less often as future women, Baptists, or teachers and more often simply as students, having a common interest with students in all sorts of other places called colleges rather than with girls, Baptists or teachers who were not students. Similar changes have taken place at the faculty level. Even the college president today often thinks of himself less as the president of a college in San José, a college catering to the rich, or a college for Irish Catholics

37

than as a president of an academically first-rate, second-rate or third-rate college. Such a man's reference group is no longer the traditional clientele and patrons of his institution or the trustees who still speak for them, but the presidents of other colleges, many of which had historically different origins and aims. The result is convergence of aims, methods, and probably results.

Another reason for the autonomy of academic institutions is that, especially in a time of expansion, one of their major tasks is staffing themselves and the rest of education. It is all very well for governments to insist on service to the wider society, even on the preparation of specialists, but the priority for the educational institution is self-perpetuation and expansion. The two tables (Tables I and II on pp. 40-43) show the first employment of university graduates in Great Britain in 1970 to 1971. From these it is clear that only 31 per cent of first degree graduates went into jobs in industry, commerce or public service. The comparable figure for higher degree graduates was 27 per cent. The proportions entering non-educational employment have in fact been steadily falling and in the case of higher degree graduates have been falling quite markedly.

This tendency has been worrying people for some time. For example in 1968 the Committee on Manpower Resources for Science and Technology produced the final report of its working group on manpower for scientific growth (Manpower, 1968). The report confirmed, with added statistical force, the conclusions of its predecessor. These were, first, that the careers most popular with the ablest graduates were in research, and second, that the sectors with the highest demand (industry and the schools) did not attract enough of the ablest graduates. The final report, produced under the chairmanship of Professor Michael Swann, the vice-chancellor of the University of Edinburgh, commented, 'indeed, in that there is a concentration of scientific talent in the fundamental research sector (particularly in universities) and a very significant movement abroad with a consequent starving of industry and the schools, the figures reveal a positively dangerous situation'.

Conscious that they were tackling 'only one corner of a vastly complicated situation' the Swann Committee proposed that education should take the initiative in dealing with this and made short-term and long-term recommendations. In the short term there should be a move to shorter periods of postgraduate study and new approaches to it, including matching it more closely to the needs of unemployment and moving more quickly from research to advanced course work. Its content should be reviewed in the light of the needs of industry and the schools, and more post-graduate students should follow these studies after a period of employment.

For this, industry needed to be 'intimately involved in the planning, conduct and support of postgraduate and post-experience education and training'. Industrial employers should develop 'steady policies' for research and development, while 'in applying the principle of "fair comparisons" in reviews of the pay of scientists, engineers and technologists, regard should be had to the inherently greater freedom and security in university and public service employment'. At the same time artificial barriers to mobility between various employments should be removed. Since nobody was given the job of implementing these recommendations, they remain aspirations only. The extent of educational self-concern is so great that autonomy begins to look rational. It will be noticed that the extent is much less at levels below university: the graduates of lower-level institutions do seem to get out into the community.

We come at last to the students themselves: what do they think that education after school is for? We must not overestimate the extent to which they have thought at all. They have, after all, been through a fairly thorough process of conditioning, in which success in education leads to more education. In selective systems, success at the age of eleven or twelve means transfer to a school in which pupils stay until eighteen rather than sixteen. The same pressures are at work in formally non-selective systems. Staying on at all after the compulsory school age itself involves selection. Those who do so are fortunate and successful: why question the consequences?

Many of course do so. The schools themselves lose those to whom they have not offered the chance of success. Others drop out because they or their parents feel they cannot face the economic

Table I. Destinations of first degree graduates of U.K. origin only

	Total	%	Arts based		Science based	
			Total	%	Total	%
Total graduates	50,704	100·0	25,513	100·0	25,191	100·0
Further education or training:						
aimed at higher degree – home	5,489	10·8	1,911	7·5	3,578	14·2
overseas	283	0·6	161	0·6	122	0·5
other degree studies – home	601	1·2	186	0·7	415	1·7
overseas	32	0·1	23	0·1	9	—
Other than for a degree:						
teacher training – home	7,776	15·3	5,303	20·8	2,473	9·8
Other training –						
home	3,462	6·8	2,732	10·7	730	2·9
overseas	89	0·2	71	0·3	18	0·1
Already in employment	1,202	2·4	646	2·5	556	2·2
Not available for employment	857	1·7	619	2·4	238	0·9

Gained permanent home employment:						
Doctors/dentists in pre-registration year	2,016	4·0	—	—	2,016	8·0
Public service	4,061	8·0	2,206	8·7	1,855	7·4
Schools	658	1·3	463	1·8	195	0·8
FE/technical colleges	220	0·4	145	0·6	75	0·3
Universities	416	0·8	151	0·6	265	1·1
Industry	7,495	14·8	1,148	4·5	6,347	25·2
Commerce	3,650	7·2	2,062	8·1	1,588	6·3
Others	2,241	4·4	1,454	5·7	787	3·1
Total gaining permanent home employment	20,757	40·9	7,629	29·9	13,128	52·1
Gained overseas employment (permanent and short term)	1,356	2·7	763	3·0	593	2·4
In temporary home employment	1,932	3·8	1,229	4·8	703	2·8
Employment or further study arranged	695	1·4	497	2·0	198	0·8
Believed to be unemployed	1,299	2·6	773	3·0	526	2·1
Unknown	4,874	9·6	2,970	11·6	1,904	7·6

Source: *First Destination of University Graduates 1972–73*, University Grants Committee, H.M.S.O. (with permission of the Controller of Her Majesty's Stationery Office).

Table II. Destinations of higher degree graduates of U.K. origin only

	Total	%	Arts based Total	%	Science based Total	%
Total graduates	9,994	100·0	4,057	100·0	5,937	100·0
Post-doctoral fellowships –						
home	397	4·0	36	0·9	361	6·1
overseas	160	1·6	12	0·3	148	2·5
Further education or training:						
aimed at higher degree –						
home	708	7·1	249	6·1	459	7·7
overseas	42	0·4	20	0·5	22	0·4
other degree studies –						
home	18	0·2	4	0·1	14	0·2
overseas	1	—	1	—	—	—
Other than for a degree:						
teacher training – home	175	1·8	82	2·0	93	1·6
other – home	79	0·8	53	1·3	26	0·4
overseas	8	0·1	4	0·1	4	0·1
Already in employment	1,894	19·0	925	22·8	969	16·3
Not available for employment:	106	1·1	61	1·5	45	0·8

Gained permanent home employment:	No.	%	No.	%	No.	%
Public service	774	7·7	262	6·5	512	8·6
Schools	390	3·9	202	5·0	188	3·2
FE/technical colleges	518	5·2	309	7·6	209	3·5
Universities	804	8·0	318	7·8	486	8·2
Industry	1,337	13·4	250	6·2	1,087	18·3
Commerce	284	2·8	186	4·6	98	1·7
Others	196	2·0	118	2·9	78	1·3
Total entering permanent home employment	4,303	43·1	1,645	40·6	2,658	44·8
Gained overseas employment (permanent and short term)	560	5·6	255	6·3	305	5·1
In temporary home employment	81	0·8	55	1·4	26	0·4
Further study/employment arranged	11	0·1	7	0·2	4	0·1
Believed to be unemployed	87	0·9	41	1·0	46	0·8
Unknown	1,364	13·7	607	15·0	757	12·8

Source: *First Destination of University Graduates 1972–73*, University Grants Committee, H.M.S.O. (with permission of the Controller of Her Majesty's Stationery Office).

43

burden of going on. It may be that it is among these pupils and their parents that the most serious discussions about the purposes of further education actually take place. Even among those well placed to continue, there is a lot of dropping out. When we compared earlier the proportions of the children of manual workers and of higher professional classes in British full-time higher education, it was with a view to emphasizing the disparity. But what the figures also show is that 55 per cent even of the most fortunate did not go for higher education full time.

Those who do may have three main motives. A minority become fascinated by some subject at school and wish to pursue it as far as they can. Others have a specific commitment to a vocation, for which higher education is a prerequisite. Probably more are undecided and find higher education a way of postponing choice, or of helping them to choose.

But basically no doubt Confucius (and Robbins) got it right: most young people in post-school education assume that it will lead to jobs with a higher salary and a higher status. It may not be their chief conscious motive: shall we say that at least they avoid the feeling that all this education will involve them in future sacrifice? Perhaps the best evidence for this is the outrage which the young people themselves feel when jobs of the kind they expect do not seem to be available. In countries like India and Pakistan, where the joint family can support one of its members for some considerable time in idleness, young people who have been to college will often wait years before taking a job, rather than accept one which they regard as beneath them. By and large their views are shared by their families. In Britain, similarly unemployed young people may live on social security, or take a job which is so little 'suitable' that it can plausibly be presented as a temporary expedient. They all regard education as a service, even when it does not directly serve.

What, then, is education after school for? How far can we accept the formulations with which we began this chapter? Do we have to choose between the autonomous and service traditions? There are many, like the Belgian civil servant quoted earlier, who are impatient with such questions. To them one can say that there are few human institutions with no purpose at all: a lack of explicit purposes usually means only that there are implicit ones. In general it is better to know what we are doing. Of course, many institutions, including those providing post-school education, have just grown. In so far as there was an original purpose this may well have changed. All the more reason for being clear what purposes are served now. Whether or not institutions have purposes, they always have consequences. Are these consequences what we want, and if not, what do we want instead? We cannot escape the need to determine what things are for.

Some people are not merely impatient with a discussion of purposes: they actively fear it. This is because they so abhor the purposes they see expressed that they feel safer without any. Most educators in Western countries feel that about some of the purposes of the Soviet state. But the thing to fear is the reality of totalitarian government, not its rhetoric. What is objectionable in Soviet education is the central control of people and institutions, the insistence on doctrinal orthodoxy, not the assertion that education should disseminate Marxism–Leninism. Indeed, the assertion is, in the circumstances, a sign of hope. The very worst tyrannies refuse to say what they are about. A statement of purpose makes possible an argument, limited and dangerous though it may be.

In less tyrannical societies, the demand that a government say what it is doing is the first step to accountability. A government without this discipline can easily be arbitrary. Liberties depend upon the possibility of criticism and argument: there can be argument about the expressed formulations of purpose and about the way these purposes are being pursued. It is not just against expressed policies that institutions and individuals need a defence. Danger comes quite as often from the unintended consequences of some remote action. As much evil comes from carelessness as from malice. Our social institutions should be designed to cure the former as well as curb the latter.

There are other people who fear the interventions of government less than their own formulations. They worry that if they are required to articulate their purposes they will be trapped quite as effectively as by external constraint. Is this not a recipe for stagnation? Only, I believe, if it is assumed that one thinks about purposes once and for all. The important thing to is to make both the original formulation and any subsequent changes quite explicit. It is essential to change one's *mind* not just change one's practice, leaving one's mind behind.

There is also the difficulty that this talk of purposes may be thought to beg the very question it claims to pose. It is the essence of the autonomous tradition to have no purposes outside itself, to be self-justifying – to be valued for its own sake. I think the difficulty is only apparent. There is no contradiction in *deciding* to continue and nurture an autonomous tradition and to promote institutions devoted to it. I believe we not only can do so, but must.

I have no doubt that both the autonomous and the service traditions in post-school education should be accomodated in any rational system. This may seem an unremarkable conclusion. It may recall those international symposia which seek a 'synthesis' of divergent and even opposing views for the sake of diplomacy. It may suggest an unwillingness to make the very decision I have called for, revealing flabbiness of mind, and infirmity of purpose. It may to some sound like a typically British compromise: so it is, but it is only compromise which does justice to the complexity of human affairs.

In truth, however, the conclusion is more remarkable than it seems. In the first place, the determination not to eliminate the autonomous tradition is not shared by most governments in the world, and is imperfectly maintained in the rest. Second, the determination not to eliminate the service tradition means seeking to reverse the resilient tendencies of academic drift – of 3,000 years or more of educational history. Any proposal that takes on the world's governments and the world's educators all at once has at least the merit of foolhardiness. Third, the conclusion poses immediately the question of balance. If we are to have both, how much is there to be of each? This question presupposes a democratic society. In a dictatorship, the issue is closed: in a democracy we can and should have the argument.

My own view is that the balance of post-school education in a democratic society should be heavily in favour of the service tradition. Its object must be explicitly to serve the needs of individuals and of society at large, rather than the needs either of the academic community or of individual disciplines. There is a place for the autonomous tradition, but it is a limited one. A society might well decide to support it: indeed many societies do support museums, concert halls, opera houses, art galleries and even authors. There is a case to be made for the university as a work of art. I hope to make part of that case later (in Chapter 4). The question, however, is how large a slice of post-school education should be autonomous? At present autonomy is dominant in most Western countries, both numerically and in status and resources. Its place should be more modest. The bulk of post-school education should be in the service tradition.

There seem to me to be very pressing reasons for this. The first arises from the development of democracy. In many parts of the world the attempt is being made (sometimes, as in India, on a heroic scale) to give people some say in the kind of society in which they live. This implies, first, giving them ultimate control over government and administration, and through this over social and economic institutions. Nobody believes that modern societies have yet evolved satisfactory instruments for securing to the people this overall control, still less for ensuring participation in individual decisions which affect them or a share in the government of what intimately concerns them. But the attempt is being made, and with more successes than failures. In a society organized in this way, there is no room for large and powerful corporations owing no responsibility to anyone but themselves. Democratic governments have found it necessary, for example, to tame large concentrations of economic power. The education industry can scarcely aspire to be an exception. Its avowed purpose must be the service of society and of the individuals who compose it.

Of course, like any other social institution, education will have its own interests and purposes. It will act in many ways as a pressure group. It will seek to persuade society to change. In a democratic society there will always be protection for minorities. None of this, however, undermines the general argument that education after school should be socially responsive. Indeed part of its responsiveness must lie in meeting various and conflicting demands which society may make upon it. There is room and need for diversity. As we have seen, it is the public institutions in Britain which are most diverse today, not the autonomous ones.

The argument for responsiveness seems to me to be independent of the control of finance. But the fact is that education after school is getting damnably expensive. Educational budgets are continuing to increase all over the world, both in absolute and relative terms. Unesco's *World Survey of Education* gives figures for just one quinquennium, 1960 to 1965 (Unesco, 1971). On the average countries devoted 13·5 per cent of total public expenditure to education in the former year and 15·5 per cent in the latter. For seventy-two selected countries the average *annual* increase of the budget proportions for the period totalled 14·2 per cent, and within this total the capital component increased at a higher rate than recurring expenditure.

One can also look at this rise in educational expenditure in terms of its proportion of the national income. Between 1960 and 1965 the world's average rose from 3·6 per cent to 4·5 per cent. Developed countries increased their proportions from 4·7 per cent in 1960 to 6·2 per cent in 1965, compared with rates for developing countries of 2·9 per cent and 3·8 per cent. Within this general growth there was a continuing shift of weight towards the higher levels of education. The world survey commented: 'The time seems to have gone when most countries devoted more than half of their total education expenditure to primary education.'

In democratic societies this level of expenditure cannot be sustained without proper accountability. When post-school education was restricted and did not touch most people, it was perhaps possible to defend arrangements which secured its autonomy. Expenditures were small and could be protected from scrutiny. Today's huge expenditures require that post-school education, like other public services, should welcome increased public accountability (see Chapter 5). There must be a place for an autonomous sector, but that place should be small.

CHAPTER THREE

Whom is it for?

MOST people think of education after school as a simple extension of school education. An extension it obviously is, in the sense that it follows and makes demands upon the earlier stages. But the differences are important too. Education after school is voluntary, which affects its methods and purpose. Nor is there any consensus about what it should consist of. Where, then, does education after school fit into the general provision which society makes for education as a whole? This chapter begins by describing the compulsory base on which post-school education rests. It then seeks to answer the question, whom is such education for?

For most of the world's history the upbringing of children has been in the hands of their families. The family may have been very extensive, merging imperceptibly into the wider society of the village or tribe. But it was the family which taught a child how to behave and passed on the shared traditions and knowledge which gave the society its identity. Even technical skills, often of a very high order, tended to be transmitted in this way: techniques were handed down from father to son. Where there was systematic instruction or training it was usually 'family' size: the master craftsman trained a small group of apprentices. The closest resemblance to an educational system was to be found in religious organizations or in the preparation of an élite administration – and these two often amounted to the same thing.

The growth of educational systems, in which children are corralled in institutions designed for an educational purpose, is relatively recent and is still not complete in most parts of the world. It began in those societies which became industrialized during the nineteenth century. There were several pressures at work. In the first place, industrialization tended to destroy traditional communities and their capacity for self-education. Second, it demanded a basis of skill among workers, together with habits like obedience and conscientiousness. Third, the gathering together of large numbers of people in cities revealed what may have been hidden in rural societies – the sheer extent of human misery. Ignorance came to be regarded as a scourge, along with famine and disease. It was even hoped that curing the former might help to cure the latter.

Nineteenth-century ambitions for education were relatively limited: it was common for middle- and upper-class people to fear the consequences of educating workers above their station in life. With the development of democracy, however, has come the notion that there should be a common educational experience for all children, first in primary school and then in secondary. Primary school has come to be seen as the place where basic skills are developed, not only in reading, writing and calculating, but also in social behaviour and in the activity of learning itself. These skills are thought to be indispensable for personal development in a modern society and for later education and training.

More recently, the idea of a common educational experience has been extended to secondary schools, accompanied by an extension of the age of compulsory education up to sixteen or in a few places even longer. The argument for a longer period of education at school derives from a belief in the importance of education, not just for children, but for adolescents. It is clear that the physical, mental and emotional changes at puberty have important educational consequences: it becomes possible for young people to learn things which were closed to them before. This has been well enough understood by most societies, even the most primitive. At adolescence, young people have more physical control: they are stronger and can work to finer limits. They have developed, perhaps for the first time, the power of logical thought. They have the increased understanding which comes from emotional development. In other words, a child who leaves school before adolescence can be offered an education appropriate only to children. If he stays on he can be offered an education appropriate to young adults. This extension of education is thus important for personal development, for the needs of the economy and for the health of democracy.

But why should it be compulsory? The answer is that society as a whole takes some view about the knowledge, skills and development required of its own members and feels confident enough in its capacity to provide for them. In Britain society places a duty upon parents to see that their children get suitable full-time education either in school or otherwise. In other words it lays down a demand for a minimum standard of performance from parents in the up-bringing of their children. Most societies, even primitive societies, do this, though the means they employ may be less formal and complex than our own. In order that parents may fulfil their duty, society establishes a democratic administration of central and local authorities to provide the necessary schools and to see that they are properly staffed and equipped.

When compulsion was first introduced in Britain in 1880 it was thought that most people needed an elementary education: the ability to read, write and do simple figuring. As this century proceeded it began to be argued that this was not enough and that we should offer to all young people a 'secondary' education, which was defined as being the education of the adolescent. The development has followed changes in what it is generally agreed society needs and an individual requires to take his place in it.

In this sense education is about personal power. We ask what would give people the capacity to be the masters and not the slaves of their environment, to be the collaborators and not the creatures of their fellow men. At one time, access to this power could be said to lie in the ability to read. It was this which gave mastery. But no-one can pretend that a modern industrial society is one which can be mastered by the individual through the simple capacity to read. The roles expected of modern man are too many and various.

It is right for society to insist that its young people remain to be educated to the point where their education can begin to be of use to them as adults and to their fellow men. Of course, since children develop at different rates, any single leaving age must be a very rough and ready decision. The age of sixteen is chosen because by then probably most young people are sufficiently developed for their education to be apt for adult life.

The idea of secondary education as the education of the adolescent is still far from being implemented, even in some developed countries. In particular, many countries still organize their secondary education in a number of different kinds of schools. These kinds may be academic, technical or vocational and general or 'modern', and they are based on the discredited assumption, first that it is possible to distinguish different *kinds* of children at the age of eleven or twelve, second that diversity among children requires different kinds of schools, and third that some children (and some adults) require education more than others. This kind of separate education is disappearing under democratic pressure: there are few countries with secondary education for all where it can survive for very long. So far as the ages of compulsory education are concerned, the education systems of the world are moving towards a common, general, education for everyone. And it is important to realize that these are *systems*, run for the most part by central and local government, and expressing (perhaps in a somewhat bureaucratic fashion) what is acceptable to their various societies.

Of course, there are large parts of the world where universal primary education remains a dream, and there are many others (including Britain) where the common secondary school is too. But there is no doubt about the way things are moving. Some countries have, and most countries want, an education service which provides a decent basis of primary and secondary education for all children and young people. Most either have or will have laws which make it compulsory.

Not that the consensus about compulsory education is complete. There are those who question the validity of education systems and of the institutions of which they are composed. They wish to de-school society. There are others who point out that education systems fail in many of their goals. For example, it appears that instead of mitigating inequality the best the schools can do is to stop inequalities getting worse: the service finds itself running very fast to stay in the same place, to the jeers of those who favour social equality. Even so, such objectors are in a minority: they may even be regarded as a luxury until provision for education (of whatever kind) is more universally secure. They will scarcely hold up the movement towards a common compulsory education.

This movement is a general and world-wide tendency towards a single, comprehensive system of compulsory schooling from the age of five, six or seven to fifteen or sixteen. (Because of its oddly early start, at five, Britain now has one of the longest compulsory periods of education.) For the purposes of this chapter we must concentrate rather on the differences that remain, because they account for much of the differences in what is available after school. The differences derive from the historical working out of contrasting social objectives. There are on the one hand those societies which have always sought to provide both primary and secondary education for all their children. These societies have usually had an expressed commitment to equality. On the other hand there are societies which have gradually offered primary or elementary education to all but which have had well developed secondary systems available only for a minority. These societies have usually claimed to be committed to quality and standards. Their recent movement towards the comprehensive pattern has proved more difficult precisely because a developed secondary education for the minority has been long-established.

Today, the various stages of this development are all visible in one group of countries or another. In the United States and Canada, six grades of primary school lead without differentiation to three grades of junior secondary (and then to three more grades of senior secondary). In the U.S.S.R. and Scandinavia, the nine- or ten-year compulsory school is now the pattern. In Western Europe, and in many countries which have built their systems on the West European model, four to six years of primary school lead to a variety of partly specialized secondary schools, entrance to which is by some selective process. Some of these schools have courses of six or seven years leading to higher education: others have courses of three, four or five years leading directly to work or to some sort of vocational training. The degree of differentiation varies. In some cases there are only academic and technical schools: in Britain there are academic and general or 'modern'. In others there may be up to a dozen different types of school – academic, technical, commercial, artistic, nursing, agricultural, teacher training and so on. Spain and many Latin American countries start their specialization at this junior secondary level. There are even countries where the old parallelism persists between the upper forms of elementary schools and the lower forms of secondary schools. Selected children transfer from the elementary schools between the ages of ten and twelve: the rest remain to complete their compulsory education.

These forms of compulsory education, for all their differences, are increasingly being classified as the 'first' level of education – for example, in the Unesco comparative statistics. Education after school is generally described as coming in two further levels, the 'second' and 'tertiary'; The second level covers the years immediately following the first, say between fifteen and nineteen; the tertiary level corresponds to what most people still call higher education. Not surprisingly the various systems of compulsory schooling lead to differences at the second level. In the United States and countries with similar systems, the primary and junior secondary schools of the first level lead, again without differentiation, to senior secondary schools at the second. In the U.S.S.R. and comparable systems, compulsory education is followed by senior secondary schools which are highly specialized. The selective systems of Western Europe have highly specialized provision after the compulsory school age.

There is nothing very tidy about the way in which this second level of education is provided. Some of it may simply be an additional three years of a secondary school or even of an all-through eight-year school. It may be offered in a wide variety of specialized institutions, or in single institutions for the education of all at this level. Much of it may be taken part time or in various forms of apprenticeships and on-the-job training. In the U.S.S.R., for example, second-level education is said to take place in day and evening vocational-technical schools (for one to three years), in production training for individuals and groups (perhaps equivalent to half a year), in specialized (vocational and technical) senior secondary schools, including day, evening and correspondence schools (for three to four years), as well as in those senior secondary schools providing a two-year general and polytechnic education which are the normal route to full-time higher education. In Sweden a new second-level system includes *gymnasia* offering liberal arts, social science and natural sciences (which tend to lead to higher education) and economics and technical studies (which on the whole do not); *fackskola*, offering a single specialism; and vocational schools. In India the senior classes of the schools are almost wholly academic and offer a route to higher education, but there are also polytechnics, rural institutes and training for school teachers (see Unesco, 1971).

All this may serve to set the background for the situation in England and Wales. Here, second-level education is offered both in the upper forms of secondary schools and in other institutions of further education. That offered by the schools has on the whole been academic, and has been the recognized route to university education. On the other hand, some non-academic courses have been fairly long-established in schools. These include particularly pre-nursing and commercial courses for girls. Recently the number of non-academic courses may have tended to increase. Most of second-level education takes place outside the schools, in general institutions which are variously called colleges of further education or technical colleges, and in specialized colleges of technology, art or commerce. Some of these offer the same academic courses as are offered by the schools: perhaps one in five of all those on such courses are in further education colleges. Mostly, however, they offer courses training for recognized occupations. These may be of many levels and lengths, from rather brisk training for shorthand typists or hairdressers to the first stages of a professional qualification. They prepare for various vocational certificates and diplomas, they provide a theoretical backing for on-the-job and apprenticeship training and they educate and train technicians. Many of their students are studying full time, but most do so part time and most of these do so in the evening only. So far as I know, the British system of second-level education is one of the most untidy in the world, which is to say that it is one of the most diverse: almost any attempt at an ordered description will do it an injustice. There are even some parts of it which never get into the official statistics – because these are courses not leading to the 'recognized qualifications' which is all the officials are interested in. Perhaps some idea of its variety can be gained from the figures in Table III. The colleges themselves may in effect specialize in second-level work: many of them, however, accommodate at least some third-level work, much of it part time. The continuum of these institutions includes those which concentrate on third-level work only.

So much for what is. It is possible, with a little thought, to see

Regional examining bodies	8,399	138	39,722	5,797	54,056
G.C.E. 'O' level	34,222		21,909	119,414	175,545
G.C.E. 'A' level	37,253		12,033	43,982	93,268
C.S.E.	185		299	107	591
Pre-diploma in art and design	6,099	1,750	34	25	6,158
Professional qualifications	18,381	629	26,902	35,282	82,315
College diplomas/certificates	9,136	139	2,871	3,043	15,679
Other	8,626		7,694	1,600	18,059
Total	165,574	8,286	497,667	258,039	929,566
Evening institutes (16–20-year-olds inclusive)				198,765	198,765
All establishments	598,686	8,286	497,667	456,804	1,561,443
Total population 16–20 (mid-1972)					3,337,200

Source: *Statistics of Education*, 1972 Vol. 3 and 1973 Vol. 1, H.M.S.O.

57

whom it is for. The English system provides well for those who accept the assumptions and goals of educators. The schools grow to accommodate those who are ready to take the academic courses whose main (indeed only) justification is that success in them gives access to the next stage. Only half of those who succeed do in fact go on, and the rest use their certification as a general evidence of continuing education when applying for jobs. But these students are a minority of the age group. They are given access to this part of 'second-level' education by coming through a selective process at the age of sixteen (when compulsory education ends) and by accepting and getting their families to accept the economic burden of keeping them while they are still in full-time schooling. With some exceptions, and the exceptions may be increasing, the higher forms of English secondary schools are not for those who fail to shine at the earlier stage, and not for those who need or want to go out to work – not for most people in fact.

What of the further education colleges? These accept some of those whom the schools have failed or rejected. Typically the student on a second-level academic course at a college is catching up on a qualification failed or missed earlier. But as we have seen, the main provision in the colleges is for those who are at work. Some are released by their employers for this purpose, others study in the evenings only. Nearly half the age group go neither to school nor college. Clearly these institutions, diverse though they are, are not for them.

The concentration of the upper forms of secondary schools on provision for those who do well in the schools' own terms may be explained by reference to the autonomous tradition. But what of the colleges? Are they not visibly in the 'service' tradition? What is it that determines whom they should serve and not serve? A clue to the answer to this question may be found in the history of attempts to provide for the continued education of young workers in England. In one sense, England has been well placed to do this because of its long-standing practice of part-time training for various occupations. It was a short step from this to the idea of part-time general education for all young workers, by releasing them from work for this purpose. This 'day release' has, astonishingly, been a statutory provision for well over half a century. It was embodied first in the Education Act, 1918. The date at which it would become obligatory was left to local authorities. Only one, Rugby, used this discretion and even this was ended as an economy measure. In the Education Act, 1944, 'county colleges' were promised, offering part-time education to young people between the school-leaving age and eighteen. Provision was again made for release from employment for one full or two half days a week. The date at which this was to become obligatory was left, not to the local education authorities, but to the Minister of Education. It too has remained a dead letter, and no county colleges were ever built.

In 1959 the Crowther committee on fifteen- to eighteen-year-olds urged the Minister to affirm his intention to implement the day release provisions quickly and make day release compulsory by stages. It said, 'It is the widespread lack of belief in this intention which in our view has almost stopped the growth of all part time release other than that clearly essential for technical reasons' (Crowther, 1959).

Following Crowther, the Minister of Education held talks with employers, trade unions and local authorities, and the proposal emerged that workers under eighteen should be given the right to claim release on one day a week. The Minister decided that the implications of this should be studied before taking further action, and a working party was set up with a chairman from the Ministry's further education branch. It reported that, despite unanimous agreement on the serious shortage of day release facilities as a whole and a feeling that everything possible should be done to improve them, the granting of the right to day release to all young persons under eighteen would constitute a 'heavy additional claim on the available resources of buildings and staff and would involve greatly increased recurring expenditure.' The building cost was estimated at between £65 million and £85 million (excluding the cost of sites and equipment). Another 9,000 to 13,000 teachers might be needed, involving £23 million to £32 million additional recurring expenditure. The working party's general view, which was accepted by the Minister, was 'that the right to day release could not be granted without holding back the prospects for other urgent educational developments.'

So another committee was set up under the chairmanship of

Henniker-Heaton to suggest something less – to report only on the 'maximum practicable increase in the grant of release from employment' (Henniker-Heaton, 1964). The chairman was also chairman of the industrial education and training committee of the British Employers' Confederation. Of the sixteen members only one was a representative of teachers and one came jointly from the Association of Principals in Technical Institutions and the Association of Teachers in Technical Institutions. The others were from industry, the Trades Union Congress or local authorities.

The report made twelve recommendations. The first was that

for the year 1969 to 1970, a national target should be set of at least an additional 250,000 boys and girls obtaining release from employment for further education. Our aim involves an average increase of the order of 50,000 a year for the next five years. It results roughly in doubling the present numbers

though even so only 40 per cent of those eligible would be accommodated.

The recommendation was modest enough. Even more modest were the means proposed: only propaganda, exhortation and persuasion. And this despite the fact that a Government White Paper of 1956 had also called, without effect, for a doubling of part-time day release to be achieved by propaganda and persuasion.

Compulsion to allow release could not, under its terms, be proposed by the committee. It surrendered the educational principle laid down in the 1944 Act and reaffirmed by the Crowther report. It said,

We understand from representatives of the major employers' organizations that while they oppose compulsory and indiscriminate day release there would be widespread support among their members as a whole for the view that day release should be granted as soon as national resources permitted to all young persons under 18 subject to the courses being appropriate to the individual and the industry.

Thus the 1944 promise of indiscriminate education was sacrificed to the view of employers' organizations. Even the extension of current release facilities was left to the employers' judgement about national resources. Day release, in other words, was a gift of the employer, for those workers and for a type of education of which he approved.

Not only was there no compulsion on employers but selection was also proposed. The committee's fifth recommendation was that 'efforts should be concentrated in the first place upon young people who are being trained in occupations requiring knowledge and skills with which courses in further education are associated'. This implied priority for bright boys in modern industry, against the interests of girls, commerce, operatives and general education. Some of the ensuing recommendations blandly made amends. Recommendation eleven, for example, almost contradictorily stated that 'employers should devote practical attention to the further education needs not only of those to whom priority must be given, but to all their young employees, girls no less than boys'.

The consequences of the report were predictable. The Government's acceptance of the report was, too, less than wildly enthusiastic. The written answer by Quintin Hogg, who was then Secretary of State for Education, concluded:

For their part, the Government are prepared to accept the committee's proposal but the local education authorities and industry will be closely involved, and I am consulting the national representative bodies forthwith about the action which should be taken to give effect to the report.

In the event, the number of day release students under the age of eighteen remained remarkably constant. In 1962 to 1963 the numbers were 261,400, of whom 52,000 were girls. By 1972 to 1973 (the latest year for which figures are published) they were 208,808, of whom 45,974 were girls. As a proportion of those insured, there has been no change for boys at about 30 per cent and only a marginal change for girls from 7 to 9 per cent. Indeed, a steady increase in day release since 1945 virtually ceased after the report was published. (See Pratt, 1970.)

The committee had looked to 'all public authorities, national and local, (to) give a clear lead in the granting of day release'. By 1967 to 1968, 79 per cent of those insured in public administration and defence were receiving day release: 75 per cent of those in the gas, electricity and water industry (mostly nationalized) and 46 per cent of those in mining and quarrying. Yet in 1962 to 1963 in gas, electricity and water the percentage was actually higher: 84 per cent had been released.

The committee's last recommendation was that 'the Ministry of Education and the Ministry of Labour should consider what additional statistical information is needed in order to assess the planning and development of day release and to take appropriate measures'. There still remain only two tables in the Government's *Statistics of Education* devoted to day release and the current ones are nearly three years out of date. The Ministry of Labour (now the Department of Employment and Productivity) still publishes none at all.

One of the main hopes of the Henniker-Heaton Committee lay in the then recently created Industrial Training Boards, which imposed a levy on firms and made grants to those offering training. It looked to them when 'drawing up their recommendations for training and associated further education (to) pay the greatest attention to releasing from employment for further education, which in appropriate cases should become a requirement'. The figures show how little this has happened. The board's contribution to 'statistical information . . . needed in order to assess the planning and development of day release' was negligible.

At the time, I described the report as 'the most stygian educational document since the war'. Why was day release so unfortunate? The answer was in the report itself. The central question not considered by the committee was, what is day release for? The report, together with the Industrial Training Act, pointed clearly to the assumption that day release is for the benefit of employers, not of workers. Hence the absence of compulsion, the reliance on exhortation and persuasion and the concentration on 'productive' students.

Since the report, other committees have sidled up to the possibility of compulsory day release, but no progress has been made. The lack of concern continues. There is no powerful lobby for day release, and a Government White Paper of 1972 managed to cover almost every part of the education service *except* the further education of young workers. (The other main lacuna was the further education of adults). As this book was being written there were signs that the new (Labour) Government was preparing to implement a party commitment to remedy this neglect – but we shall see.

It is interesting to compare the response to Henniker-Heaton with that to the Robbins Report on higher education, quoted in the last chapter. Both reports were published in the same year, and both recommended a doubling of provision. The Robbins proposals for expansion have been implemented and more. They explicitly assumed that all who did well enough at school and wished to do so should go on to university. The Robbins Committee explicitly rejected any 'manpower planning' approach, except in the training of school teachers. There was no disposition to allow the needs of the economy, let alone the whims of individual employers, to determine who was to get education at this level.

What is more, the expansion of higher education has been directly at the expense of the education of young workers. It was one of those 'urgent educational developments' which granting the right to day release would hold back. Day release primarily benefits the working-class school-leaver: universities, colleges of education and full-time further education mainly accommodate the middle classes leaving the sixth form. Nor can it be argued that the extension of full-time provision somehow obviates the need for part-time provision. The reverse is the case. Unless there is a dramatic and spontaneous change in the nature of the educational system, full-time further and higher education will continue to benefit the middle-class student proportionately more than the working-class for all foreseeable expansion. If the children or workers are to be equally benefited there must be more part-time provision to compensate them.

Even the costs of producing the two reports bear witness to the country's sense of priorities. Robbins cost more than one hundred times as much as Henniker-Heaton.

The lesson from this English experience is clear. If provision, powers, duties and committees for the education of workers are left to depend upon employers, further education will remain confined to a minority. It will be offered in the interests of firms rather than people, and the most powerful firms at that. The lesson has world-wide implications too. Most countries have trade, technical and vocational schools. Whom are they for? Clearly there should be a balance between the needs of society (including its industry, commerce and agriculture) and the needs of individuals. Where should the balance be struck? And what should be the relation of this to full-time education? I shall return to these questions at the end of the chapter. For the present I wish simply to assert that the balance, even in an established democracy like England, is too heavily in favour first of the academic and second on the needs of society. Second-level education is not for most young people.

So much, for the moment, for the second level of education. What about the third level, which people normally think of as higher education? Whom is that for? As long ago as 1963, Frank Bowles published his still unsurpassed study on access to higher education (Bowles, 1963). One of his major conclusions was that something that could reasonably be called an admissions process existed throughout the world. The process began when students completed primary school and entered upon a programme of study which offered the possibility of admission to higher education. It ended with enrolment in higher education. Mr Bowles went on to describe his findings in more detail. He wrote:

We actually found two forms of the admissions process, each implicit in a form of educational organization. In what may be termed the European system, secondary education proceeds in three parallel lines from the end of primary education. One line leads to the university and may be entered only by means of an examination taken some time between the ages of 10 and 12. The selection at this point is rigorous, its effect severe. In no country which follows this form of organization do as many as 20 per cent of the age group pass the examination for the university line; in some it is as low as 2 per cent. This select group is further reduced in the course of six or seven years of secondary school, with the result that about half of them drop out. There is then a final examination at the end of secondary school that is customarily passed by about two-thirds of those who still remain. These survivors are automatically eligible for university admission, and at least 80 per cent of them actually enter a university. Certain faculties – usually medicine, science, and engineering – may require students to take additional examinations; but those who fail such examinations may still join the faculties of law, philosophy, and economics, which almost never require entrance examinations of applicants.

Under this system, from 1 to 8 per cent of each age group enters higher education. Those who fail to enter the restricted secondary schools have lost their chance to enter any form of higher education. If they enter one of the other two lines of secondary education, they may go into technical schools or train to be primary school teachers. However, though the technical and teacher-training programmes parallel the university preparatory programme, they are not subject to the same requirements or standards. They do not prepare for university entrance or, indeed, for any form of higher education, since neither technical training nor the teaching of pedagogy is defined in the European system as higher education. One result of this is that the educational background and professional skills of primary school teachers and of technicians are much inferior to that of university graduates, and their status is determined accordingly.

The European system of organization prevails in most of Europe, Africa, and Asia, and in all of South America.

The other kind of educational organization may conveniently be called the American one, though it happens that at least one example of it may be found on every continent except, paradoxically, South America.

In this system there is no examination for entrance to secondary schools, and all primary school graduates can move into a general secondary programme. Students may be drawn out of this programme into specialized courses – technical training and teacher-training – or continue to the end. If, after finishing secondary school, they wish to enter higher education, they usually must take an entrance examination, since admission to a college or university is not automatic. In this system, from 70 to 90 per cent of the students in each age group enter secondary school, and perhaps half of them drop out before completing it. About half of the secondary school graduates – that is, from 10 to 35 per cent of those in the age group – continue on into higher education. The countries other than the United States which follow this form send between 15 and 20 per cent of their students on to higher education, about twice the percentage that occurs under the European system.

Countries which follow the American system – though with marked differences in detail – are Australia, Canada, Japan, New Zealand, the Philippines, the Soviet Union, the Union of South Africa (with respect to the white population), and, of course, the United States. In most of these countries, teacher-training and technical training are offered as higher education, and graduation from the general secondary course may be accepted as meeting the requirements for admission to any programme of higher education, provided the student shows evidence of the requisite ability and preparation.

He added:

> The real difference between the systems lies not in the nature of the education they provide, for both systems deal with the common body of the world's knowledge and both teach in the way men have always taught. The difference lies in the fact that one system eliminates most of its students and fully educates only those who survive, while the other retains all of its students as long as possible to give each one the opportunity to develop at the highest level possible for him.

Since Mr Bowles wrote, we have all become more sophisticated about such phrases as those which make up the end of the last sentence quoted. The offering of opportunity is no longer held to be enough. But there can be no doubt that broadly Mr Bowles was identifying what have come to be characterized as an élite and a mass system of higher education.

He himself made the point explicitly:

> The eliminations are interesting to an observer because no one pretends that the students who survive are any better than those who were eliminated, nor that the passing of the examination means that they will succeed in university work, nor even that the repeated examinations serve any important educational purpose. But they continue, nevertheless, for a combination of reasons. For one thing, facilities are inadequate to accommodate all the candidates for higher education and many of them *must* be eliminated. For another, the failure rate has remained constant for many years in most European countries and is now maintained in the name of 'standards'. And finally, the students have no alternatives . . .
>
> Those who succeed in the European system become members of a privileged élite. Those who fail at any point have nothing to show for their pains. And those who pursue the other types of opportunity available will find that these opportunities are illusory and that they can hardly achieve more than a rudimentary qualification.

There is no doubt that in 1960 Britain stood firmly in the élite tradition. According to Frank Bowles' study, about 4 per cent of the relevant age group went into higher education. There is room for argument about this figure. The British Government has claimed that for 1961 it was 7 per cent, but this included teacher training, which was there by convention rather than comparability, and 'advanced' further education, some of which would certainly have been excluded from the Bowles figures. Both Bowles and the Government excluded part-timers. The point is that, even taking the Government's inflated figure, Britain was simply favourably placed among the élitists. If we take Bowles' figure, the British were mediocre élitists. They even earned a mention in his account of the way in which places in higher education could be artificially restricted and expansion opposed. One of these ways was a refusal to bring teacher training and advanced technical training into the established structure of higher education. As an example Mr Bowles mentioned the British universities' refusal to take responsibility for developing advanced technical education and their opposition to extending degree-granting powers to the colleges of advanced technology which were established to do the job instead. The CATs did get to grant degrees, ten years after their establishment, but by a decision of the Government, not the universities. Another (this time un-British) method of restriction was to resist the enlargement of existing university programmes, largely to protect the authority of the professor over the teaching of his subject. Although university enrolments had risen by 50 per cent in the preceding decade in Western Europe, only eight university institutions had been founded in the region, four of which were in England. Yet another method of restriction derived from the desire of professional bodies to safeguard their status. Mr Bowles' example has drawn from Latin America, but he could equally well have pointed to Britain, where the activities of the professional institutions have been increasingly restrictive.

Even those who were prepared to agree that the British system was élitist in 1960 might well have assumed that it had since ceased to be so. Did not the Robbins Committee (1963) recommend a great expansion of higher education? Indeed it did, but by means which ensured that it was simply the expansion of the élite. In particular it quite specifically sought to retain the 'standard' of entry to higher education, and its institutional proposals were for increased homogeneity rather than diversity. The committee regarded higher education almost as synonymous with universities and proposed to eliminate the anomalies (like teacher training colleges and advanced further education) by bringing, or turning, them into universities. The numerical proposals of the report would have meant that by 1980 or so, between 10 per cent of the age group (on the Bowles definition) and 17 per cent (on the Government definition) would be getting higher education. In the event, the Government is now planning to accommodate 9 per cent (Bowles) or 18 per cent (Government) – and rising 'standards' in non-university institutions should probably lead us to accept something very near the higher figure. (Presumably, however, 'standards' have not ceased to rise elsewhere in the world, so Britain may still be comparatively unimpressive.) All this means, however, is that Britain in 1980 will have the same proportion of young people entering higher education as countries with the alternative process had twenty years previously. It will be on the brink of mass higher education, but not yet over it.

During the 1960s, there was the chance that things might have gone differently. One of the essential features of the élitist system was the selection process which took place between primary and secondary school. In England and Wales, the eleven plus procedure sorted children into grammar schools, which could prepare them for higher education, and secondary modern schools, which on the whole did not. After 1965 the local authorities, which maintain the schools, were encouraged to end this process and reorganize their secondary schools on 'comprehensive' lines. A consequence was that by 1972, about a third of the eleven-year-olds of England and Wales avoided a selection procedure at eleven plus. Similarly, after one false start, the age of compulsory education was raised in 1972 to sixteen, thus keeping all children in school until the time of the first major external examination which begins to lay the foundation for qualification for university entry. (The crucial examination for this, however, is two years later.) The effect of these changes is not yet easy to see, and in any case the Government is planning on the assumption that they will make no difference.

We do, however, have the chance to see how expected and unremarkable the British performance is, both in this respect and in access to higher education in general. In an appendix to the Bowles Report, Mary Corcoran set out to predict developments in the future (Corcoran, 1963). Among these predictions was that by 1970 the world-wide proportion of these entering secondary programmes which prepared for higher education would double, because of greater success in keeping children in primary schools. Even further increases were expected to come from widespread changes in secondary-school organization. Can it be argued that the still incomplete British reorganization has itself doubled the proportion entering a course which prepared for higher education? The British performance in higher education itself is equally predictable. Dr Corcoran predicted that in élitist countries between 8 and 15 per cent of the age group would enter 'some form of higher education' – this time including technical and teacher training. The British Government's figure for 1971 was 15 per cent. Since Dr Corcoran appears to have underestimated world trends, the British comparative performance may again be rather worse than it looks.

We can now turn to look at the consequences of the Western European systems of second- and third-level education for people in Britain and comparable countries. The most obvious consequence is that relatively few people get such education at all. In Britain few people think this is either remarkable or important. But this is because they are used to thinking of education as something in itself, which people are fit to use or not, if they can measure up to its demands and choose to do so. Things look different if we regard education as a service. Looked at in this way, it immediately becomes significant that half of all adolescents leave education as soon as they legally can, and most of the rest leave soon after. They do so for good reasons: they find education both useless and boring. The reaction of educators, however, is normally to explain that such a rejection of education is caused by unsatisfactory home backgrounds. I am perpetually amazed at the arrogance of this diagnosis, at the fact that so few people share my amazement and that, on the contrary, there still exists a vast academic sociology industry confirming in detail the famous working-class insight that 'It's the poor what gets the blame.' The truth that educators have to grasp is that to most people education offers little. That is why they reject and scorn it. As things stand, they are right.

One reason for the failure of the education service to be a service is that an élite system not only accommodates very few people but it effectively dominates the education even of those whom it excludes. This tendency is evident throughout. The curricula and examinations of the upper forms of secondary schools are dominated by the universities, in the interests of their entry requirements, even though most of the pupils are not in fact destined for university. This dominance extends down through the secondary schools and, in Frank Bowles' analysis, even to the transition from primary schools. Even the British further education colleges, which are much less rigid, are organized in a way which favours minorities. As we have seen, most of their students are part-timers; but staffing, accommodation and resources are all calculated on the basis of full-timers or conventions of full-time 'equivalence'. (One full-time student equals five part-time day and ten evening-only students.) In other words, the education of most people is organized on the basis of their assumed equivalence to a minority whose needs are actually quite different. It has simply not occurred to the authorities to determine what part-timers need and to accommodate full-timers either under different conventions, or, if administratively they must be the same, under some convention of part-time equivalence. Most of them would not even understand that there is an issue involved, and the frequency with which they refer to full-time and full-time equivalent students interchangeably suggests that they are indifferent to the number of actual people involved.

The domination of education by the requirements of the élite means that it is very hard to make it useful or attractive to most people. Teachers in British primary schools were among the first to see this. They realized that the reforms which have produced the 'open' primary school (one of Britain's educational claims to fame) depended upon minimizing the influence of the eleven plus procedures and then upon abolishing them altogether. Primary education for all has come by minimizing the influence of the grammar schools: secondary education for all will come when Britain has minimized the influence of the universities. Of course, the way in which élite education dominates the rest does not depend solely on status, or even on human wickedness. It does so because in a competitive situation, any one stage of education must necessarily concentrate on the next. In my view it is much safer to treat each stage of education as a terminal stage, and to ask what it is that can be offered to these pupils and students and what good it will be to them. Of course, one should be careful not to do anything that positively unfits people for further education, but this is the most one should need to do. The concept of education as little more than a continuous opener of doors seems to me to be mindless and destructive. It quite certainly leads to the neglect of most of the people whom educators are dealing with at any one time. It renders the system unable to offer service, except to itself and to a clambering minority. What it offers, in short, is mobility, not competence.

If status is not the root of this deficiency, it is at least a very persuasive symptom. The provision which is made at various stages of education powerfully implies the notion of higher education as a reward. One has only to contrast the provision made for students at this level with that available for others to realize what social attitudes are enshrined in it. A student at a British university, and at most others in the world, has available to him an extraordinary variety and combination of intellectual talent. He has access to libraries, laboratories and quantities of expensive equipment. Much of this can be said to be essential to study, but there is a great deal more that cannot be explained in this way: subsidized clubs, societies, sport and other activities, even subsidized meals and residence. None of this can be said to depend on the needs of academic study, but rather on the background to the development of the full man. But such provision is thought to be appropriate only to university students. It is not made for those in technical colleges, especially those studying part time. And it is especially not offered to those who are unconnected with formal education at all. Can it be said that their need is less? Is it acceptable that they should be less than full men? The answer to both these questions is 'yes' – in an élite society.

I have left until last the aspect of British higher education which is most familiar to academic commentators: that is, the heavy bias of the class composition of its students. The facts are summarized in Tables IV and V. Perhaps the most significant table in the Robbins Report was the one showing the percentage of undergraduates with fathers in manual occupations over a period. This is reproduced as Table VI.

Other European countries show comparable figures, though some are more egalitarian than others. Stephen Jessel quoted in

Table IV. Highest course of education: by father's occupation. Great Britain. Children born in 1940–41

Percentage

Father's occupation	Higher education			'A' level or S.L.C.	Other post-school course or 'O' level	No post-school course nor 'O' level/S.L.C.	All children	Weighted sample numbers (= 100%)	Un-weighted sample numbers
	Full-time		Part-time						
	Degree level	Other							
Higher professional	33	12	7	16	25	7	100	376	128
Managerial and other professional	11	8	6	7	48	20	100	2170	651
Clerical	6	4	3	7	51	29	100	946	262
Skilled manual	2	2	3	2	42	49	100	6165	1176
Semi- and un-skilled	1	1	2	1	30	65	100	3418	479
All children	4	3	4	3	40	47	100	15000	3008

Source: Robbins, 1963, Appendix 1, Part II, Table 2

The Times on 6 October 1971 a document prepared for restricted circulation by the Organization for Economic Cooperation and Development. Allowing for the difficulty of comparing educational and social systems it appeared that the proportion of university students who were of 'working-class' families was as follows (the percentage of the total population classified as 'working-class' is in brackets): France 29 per cent (from 74 per cent of the population); Germany 35 per cent (from 70 per cent); Norway 35 per cent (from 79 per cent); Sweden 34 per cent (from 75 per cent); Denmark 39 per cent (from 75 per cent); and the United Kingdom 27 per cent (from 71 per cent) (Jessell, 1971).

The most frequent explanation for the social class distribution in higher education, as we have seen, is the pervasive influence of family background. All manner of remedies have been suggested, beginning with the compensatory provision of nursery schools. Radicals who have noticed the long-drawn-out selection process described by Mr Bowles have concluded that it is this which excludes the children of working people. They have heavily supported moves to abolish selection at eleven, are in general opposed to differentiation (that is streaming, or in American 'tracking') within schools and will shortly be girding against selection at sixteen or even eighteen.

I am afraid that the international facts are disappointing to such people. One of them will do: in the United States, which has the most open educational system in the world, 87 per cent of all high school graduates whose families earned $15,000 a year or more entered college in 1967, compared with 20 per cent of those whose parents earned less than $3,000. To be sure, the absolute number of workers' children going on were proportionately higher than in Britain – but so were the numbers of children of the well-to-do. The disparities have remained enormous. British experience in the last fifty years should have been enough to warn us: remember the consistency of the proportion of university students whose fathers were manual workers. I am persuaded that, because educational institutions reflect social inequalities rather than cause them, no increase in equality is to be expected through existing educational institutions. The short point is that equality of opportunity, which has been a non-partisan goal in British education for some time, is

Table V. Social class (father's occupation). Great Britain 1961–62

| | Non-manual | | | Manual | | | | Percentage | |
	Higher profes-sional	Other profes-sional and mana-gerial	Clerical	Skilled	Semi-skilled	Un-skilled	Not known	All students	Sample numbers (= 100%)
Undergraduates									
Men	17	40	12	19	6	1	5	100	2641
Women	20	43	11	16	6	1	3	100	1084
Students on three-year courses in teacher training									
Men	5	27	16	32	13	2	5	100	s286
Women	8	35	14	28	8	2	6	100	937
Men and women	7	33	14	29	9	2	6	100	1223

74

Full-time students in further education by method of study									
Continuous	14	36	11	25	7	2	5	100	1409
Sandwich	10	24	19	33	9	2	4	100	1361
All students	12	32	14	28	8	2	4	100	2178
Part-time students in further education by method of study									
Part-time day	6	20	16	39	12	4	3	100	837
Evening	5	22	14	39	12	3	4	100	921

Source: Robbins, 1963, Appendix 2(B), Part I, Tables 5, 81, 102 and 135

Table VI. Percentage of undergraduates with fathers in manual occupations

	Men	Women	Men and women
1928–47	27	13	23
1955	27	19	25
1961	26	23	25

Source: Robbins, 1963, Appendix 2(B), Part I, Table 6

meaningless without equality – or at least something like comparability.

I believe the ideal of equalized access to existing institutions is mistaken, and attempts to attain it are chimerical. We shall do much better if we assume that people avoid existing institutions for good reasons and seek instead to create the kind of institutions which might be of some use to them. It is for these reasons that I regard the present debate about the expansion of higher education as far too limited.

Broadly speaking, the debate is between the view of the Robbins Report, which seems to be shared by most academics, and that of Anthony Crosland (the Secretary of State for Education and Science in 1965 to 1967 during the 1964 to 1970 Labour Government). Within the limitations of the argument the difference between them is important. We have seen how the effect both of the Robbins proposals and subsequent Government policy was to perpetuate the élite system. Robbins was particularly élitist, and it is worth explaining why. The Robbins Committee recommended a relatively large expansion of numbers in higher education: from 216,000 students in 1962 to 1963 to 309,000 in 1973 to 1974 and about 560,000 in 1980 to 1981. But the expansion was not to be accompanied by change. The Robbins Committee saw the future of higher education dominated numerically and academically by the universities. For example, the universities were meant to offer 350,000 out of the total of 560,000 places for 1980. To do this existing universities should grow and six new universities should be founded. The colleges of education (for the training of teachers), offering about 145,000 places, should be brought administratively as well as academically under the aegis of universities. A further 20,000 university places were to be found by giving university status to non-university colleges. All this would have left about 65,000 places to be provided by non-university colleges in 1980–81.

The Robbins Committee's proposals were essentially a 'holding operation', designed to maintain the existing system in all its essentials. The committee itself had been set up because numbers emerging from the traditional grammar school route were growing faster than the numbers of university places and it was getting increasingly difficult for 'qualified' school leavers to get to university. The élitism of the system was becoming more obvious and more burdensome. What Lord Robbins and his colleagues did was to offer some relief, so that the proportion of 'qualified' school-leavers getting higher education would rise again to the level of the 1950s. But at no point did they seek to counter élitism, as their preoccupation with the 'qualified', or what Mr Bowles would call 'standards', made clear.

The Robbins Committee's administrative proposals were consistent with its élitist view of numbers. There was to be a separate Minister for higher education working through a grants commission and the research councils. These bodies, being extensions of the existing University Grants Committee and Research Councils, were to distribute public money in higher education on the well established 'buffer' principle. The UGC has had many admirers in Britain and abroad as a device for distributing government money while protecting individual institutions from a direct relationship with the state. Academically, the preparation of non-university colleges for university status was to be undertaken through a Council for National Academic Awards; another extension, this time of the National Council for Technological Awards, which assessed and moderated degree-level courses in the former colleges of advanced technology. But these non-university colleges, like the rest of post-school education, were to be administered quite separately from the universities – in fact through the local education authorities.

The trouble with all this is that the Robbins Committee took a very partial view of what constituted higher education. This was due in part to the committee's composition (it was heavily domi-

77

nated by the universities) and in part to its terms of reference. These defined higher education in terms of full-time students working at degree level, with a concession to include students in colleges of education working below this level. The committee's reference excluded from serious view more than 100,000 students on part-time courses at degree level and another 100,000 students in non-university colleges on courses below that level, but above craft level. Few people thought this odd at the time, as it reflected the general 'educated' consensus. Even Frank Bowles missed the significance of the British non-university colleges.

This vision of the Robbins Committee, which seemed to most people at the time to be inevitable (built as it was on six volumes of statistics), soon turned out to be quite impracticable. Indeed it was detached from reality at several important points. In the first place, most academic commentators assumed that the committee's recommendations implied a 'unitary' policy for higher education, in contrast with the 'binary' policy invented, as we shall see later, by the Department of Education and Science. But the Robbins Committee recommended no such thing. In the first place, even after the colleges of education had been corralled by the universities, 65,000 full-time students, or one in nine of all students in higher education, would in 1980 be in non-university institutions. The committee expected that the growth in numbers of part-time students in higher education would be relatively modest, but even so that there would be very nearly 200,000 part-time students on advanced courses by 1980. These too would be almost entirely in non-university institutions. And as we have seen, the committee's definitions precluded it from considering technical college courses which could be said to be of 'training college' level; that is, courses which would not demand A level as an entry qualification but whose final qualification approached a university pass degree. Nor must one forget that in framing its recommendations the committee forced itself to ignore the intimate connections between advanced courses in technical colleges, which it accepted as higher education, and those courses below advanced level which were preparatory to it.

This division of higher education into two kinds of institutions (the universities taking mostly full-timers and the technical col-

leges taking mostly part-timers) was to be confirmed by the external
administrative arrangements which the committee proposed. For
the autonomous universities there was to be a grants commission,
but not for the rest. There was to be a separate cabinet minister
responsible for the university sector, but not the rest. In other
words, the Robbins Committee was proposing a 'binary' system
of the most rigid kind. That they and subsequent academic commentators have assumed they were doing the opposite derives
from their assumption about the identity of higher education and
universities. On the needs of students inside those technical colleges
waiting for university status, of students in other colleges and of
students on non-advanced courses the committee had nothing to
say.

   This failure was especially staggering in the light of the committee's numerical recommendations. Sometime early in its delibera-
tions, the committee decided to offer one set of projections of
future demand, rather than a range of such projections. It equally
decided that the projection it offered should be a *minimum*. These
decisions were taken on reasonable 'political' grounds. The committee felt that it had been asked to make recommendations and
that its recommendations should be as definite as possible. Further-
more, it believed that in choosing a conservative estimate for the
demand for places, its recommendations about expansion would
be relatively unassailable. Looking back on it, most members of
the committee probably felt that these decisions were right. Perhaps its major achievement was to make the British universities
'expansion-minded', when the instincts of most of their staffs were
then and are still anti-expansionist. The committee's arguments,
based on what it called a 'bedrock' of projections, were intellectually and politically unassailable.

   On the other hand they did represent a minimum recommendation, as members of the committee realized and asserted. But it is in
the nature of government and administration to fasten upon concrete recommendations rather than an expression of principle,
especially when the former requires the smaller use of resources.
The Government has been prepared to expand the universities
roughly along the lines suggested by the Robbins Committee, even
though Robbins estimate of demand has turned out to be too low.

The Government has failed to meet the Robbins requirement that competition for university entry should get back to the 1950s level. So the expansion of higher education outside the universities has been spectacular. In the first place, the expansion of colleges of education, tied not to student demand but to the schools' demand for teachers, has exceeded the Robbins expectations, though during this decade it will be cut back again. In the second, the increased numbers of 'qualified' applicants for whom university places have not been provided have flooded into the technical colleges. In the half dozen years since the Robbins Report, the universities had taken 50 per cent more students, but the colleges of education and technical colleges had much more than doubled their numbers. There are now as many students in full-time higher education outside the universities as inside them. The technical colleges alone accommodate one in four of all such students. And this excludes part-timers.

Something of this sort might have been predicted by the Robbins Committee, precisely because its numerical recommendations were minima. It was more than probable that they would be exceeded. But the committee did not ask itself what would happen to its administrative recommendations if the numbers were greatly exceeded, let alone what *should* happen to them. The failure to discuss what kind of higher education would be appropriate, given a more substantial expansion, was accompanied by a failure to discuss what kind of system was needed. It is now impossible even for university people to regard higher education as synonymous with universities. The principle of academic drift no longer seems inevitable, or even sensible. But the Robbins Committee did not question it and considered as an alternative only the establishment of 'liberal arts colleges' on the American pattern, a solution which it rejected. It did not consider the possibility that British higher education might develop upon different lines, based upon an alternative, though native, educational tradition and taking the country out of the European attitude to higher education into the American. The committee did not evolve a *policy*: what it did was to accept historical trends and institutionalize them. In all this it was not only conservative: it was reactionary.

The question which the Robbins Committee should have asked

80

and answered was which of these two traditions was the more apt for the expansion of higher education. It did not do so, but saw higher education as a kind of club, with the universities as full members, the colleges of education (training colleges) as associate members and a few technical colleges always on a gratifying waiting list. It was recommending the modest expansion of an élite system of higher education. Whether consciously or not, it proposed to expand higher education in such a way as to make it more accessible mainly to the same kinds of people who had been successful in getting there in the past.

Anthony Crosland had many reasons for suspecting the Robbins approach, as John Pratt and I have detailed elsewhere (Pratt and Burgess, 1974). In a speech at Woolwich he made a particular defence of the service tradition – and to this he added a specific commitment to try to widen the social base from which applicants to higher education would in future come (Crosland, 1965). He began by accepting the fact of 'the twin traditions which have created our present higher education institutions'. He said:

These are broadly of two kinds. On the one hand we have what has come to be called the autonomous sector, represented by the universities, in whose ranks, of course, I now include the Colleges of Advanced Technology. On the other hand we have the public sector, represented by the leading technical colleges and the colleges of education.

He went on:

The Government accepts this dual system as being fundamentally the right one, with each sector making its own distinctive contribution to the whole. We infinitely prefer it to the alternative concept of a unitary system, hierarchically arranged on the 'ladder' principle, with the Universities at the top and the other institutions down below. Such a system would be characterized by a continuous rat race to reach the First or University Division, a constant pressure on those below to ape the Universities above, and a certain inevitable failure to achieve the diversity in higher education which contemporary society needs.

He offered 'four basic reasons' for this preference for the dual system. First, the ever-increasing need and demand for vocational, professional and industrially-based courses could not be fully met by the universities. It must be fully met, and required a separate sector with a separate tradition and outlook. Second, a system based on the ladder concept

must invariably depress and degrade both morale and standards in the non-University sector. If the Universities have a 'class' monopoly of degree-giving, and if every College which achieves high standards moves automatically into the University Club, then the residual public sector becomes a permanent poor relation perpetually deprived of its brightest ornaments, with a permanently and openly inferior status.

Third, it was desirable that 'a substantial part of the higher education system should be under social control, and directly responsive to social needs' and it was also desirable 'that local government, responsible for the schools and having started and built up so many institutions of higher education, should maintain a reasonable stake in higher education'. Fourth, in a highly competitive world Britain could not survive if 'we ... alone downgrade the non-university professional and technical sector'.

Mr Crosland also went on to describe the threefold role of the technical colleges as institutions of higher education. First they would provide full-time and sandwich courses of degree level for students 'who are attracted by the more vocational tradition of the colleges, and who are more interested in applying knowledge to the solution of problems than in pursuing learning for its own sake'. Here the Government's policy would be supported both by the 'background' distinction and by the creation of the Council for National Academic Awards, which had ensured equal awards for equal performance. The second function of the colleges fell outside the scope of normal university work: the provision of full-time and sandwich courses below degree level. Third, there were the 'tens of thousands of part time students who need advanced courses either to supplement other qualifications or because for one reason or another they missed the full time route'.

In a later speech at Lancaster Mr Crosland emphasized the 'historic and invaluable FE tradition of providing opportunities for educational and social mobility' (Crosland, 1967). The colleges, he said, had always catered for students who could not on entry show that they were of university calibre and for those who could profit from a university course but could not give their whole time to it. Technical college teachers could quote hundreds of examples of such students who had been helped by good teaching and their own strong motivation to tackle a full-time degree course.

Mr Crosland went on to describe these students. 'Perhaps they left school early, perhaps they were late developers, perhaps they were first generation aspirants to higher education who were too modest at the right moment to apply to a university, perhaps they had started on a career and thought that a technical college course would more directly improve their qualifications for doing it.' All this was, among other things, an extended circumlocution for 'working-class students'. The important thing for the leading technical colleges was that they gave such students a chance not only to tackle degree-level work part-time or full-time but also to develop their latent capacity to do so. 'This range of opportunity is a precious part of our educational heritage that we would be mad to abandon.'

In the event, the chief means which Mr Crosland chose to carry out his policy were at variance with the ends he so clearly stated. He 'designated' thirty polytechnics as 'comprehensive academic communities of higher education', and at a stroke set them off on the path towards autonomy. There is already evidence that as a consequence the polytechnics are accommodating students with much the same social background as those in universities. Academic drift is under way. Oddly enough, the argument is not yet dead. In the White Paper of December 1972 the Conservative Government, which had taken over the binary policy and the polytechnic proposals intact, announced its plans for the future of higher education (White Paper, 1972).

In contrast to the Robbins recommendations, the Government expected that half of all those in full-time higher education would be in non-university institutions. The colleges of education (much diminished because of a descried fall in demand for teachers) would mostly become further education, rather than university, institutions. A new award, the Diploma of Higher Education (Dip. H.E.) would be available for those following a two-year course. And there was even an indication that colleges offering higher education would be expected to go on providing at lower levels. There is clearly still a possibility that the social imbalance of British higher education will be to some extent redressed.

A further weakness of Mr Crosland's proposals was that although they paid lip-service to the importance of part-time students and those studying at below degree level, the numbers of these were never quantified and thus never specifically planned for, and those outside higher education were even more seriously neglected, as we have seen.

It is time to take stock of what this British debate has been about. On the one hand, the Robbins Report represented perhaps the high water mark of the autonomous tradition and the élite system of higher education. Universities were to expand to offer, and to accommodate, more of the same. Their standards, particularly of entrants, were to be maintained. Their administration, finance and control were to be consistent with this vision, and were in particular to be divorced from those of the schools and other post-school education. They were to continue to exclude most people. According to Robbins, higher education was for the few.

Anthony Crosland, on the other hand, was at least moving towards a 'mass' system, in Frank Bowles' sense. He sought an alternative tradition and a system that could accommodate more people. The expansion he had in mind would offer different educational experiences and accommodate different kinds of students. To do this he stuck to the public administration, finance and control that had historically provided the schools and both second- and third-level education together. Crosland's vision has survived two changes of Government, and there seems little doubt that it will officially prevail. The present Government is explicitly giving priority to the 'public' sector of post-school education.

It is important to realize, with all this, what Crosland was *not* doing. He was not extending higher education very far. True, he sought to include those studying part-time and educational programmes below (but only just below) British degree level. But he was still concerned, in the main, with eighteen- to twenty-one-year-olds, and his successors have emphasized that concern. Even then, most eighteen-year-olds were excluded. And other adults, those who had passed their early twenties, were quite neglected. Crosland's move towards 'mass' higher education was still to be for a minority.

But even here we have been dealing with post-school education in the sense of what is available, full time or part-time, to those who have recently left school. What of those who left school some time ago? What about the education of adults? Has Britain begun to take seriously the idea of recurrent education? The answer to this question is equivocal. As we have seen, there is a very great variety of provision, both full-time and part-time, in colleges of further education and evening institutes. But it is bedevilled by a damaging division between 'vocational' and 'non-vocational' courses. Vocational is interpreted narrowly and non-vocational is held to mean leisure time and cultural activities. The British system is inhibited from meeting some of the deepest problems of most adults because they cannot be fitted into these tidy categories. A Government committee set up to consider non-vocational adult education simply missed the opportunity of making any contribution here. Its recommendations were structural ('A Development Council for Adult Education should be established . . .') or hortatory ('The Secretary of State should use the many ways open to her to stimulate the development of adult education . . .'). In so far as it made any positive recommendation it was for more of the same (Russell, 1973).

I hope it will be clear by now what is the status of the debate about the expansion of higher (or third-level) education. Even the most optimistic discussion is still about minorities. Since Frank Bowles' report it has become fashionable to talk about 'élite' and 'mass' higher education, and it is generally assumed that the difficulties of countries in Western Europe (including Britain) stem from the transition from one to the other. There is no doubt that increasing the percentage of the age group getting full-time higher education in Britain from 7 per cent in 1961 to 18 per cent in 1981 will make a very great difference. But we cannot call the latter mass higher education without losing our grip on the meaning of words. What it means after all is offering a particular kind of three-year full-time course to one in five of eighteen-year-olds – and ignoring all other adults. I do not think it is unfair to claim that what Britain is doing is gradually enlarging the élite, rather than accommodating the mass.

A similar cavalier attitude to words characterizes American

educators. There it is fashionable to say that the system is in transition from a 'mass' to a 'universal' provision of higher education. In this context universal means that about 40 per cent of high-school graduates enter some kind of college. In other words more than half of the relevant age group does not get this 'universal' provision, and again we are not counting other adults.

The whole discussion about education after school is bedevilled by this kind of facile description. Liberal optimism can be relied on to conceal the point. And the point is that world-wide experience suggests that as countries get richer, more people get education. The minority getting anything out of the education service is gradually enlarged. But even the very richest of modern societies still accommodates a minority of young people and still ignores very nearly all other adults. In other words, education systems do not begin to offer a service for most people.

It is for this reason that I regard the usual debate about education after school as rather frivolous. Of course it would be a staggering achievement to shift Britain from the European tradition into the American tradition. The question is, when we have done it, will it be worth it ? If the American experience is any guide, the social effects will be very limited. I think we must approach the discussion in a quite different way. In the past our society offered education after school very largely to the rich. More recently it has sought to accommodate the clever – or at least the trainable. The school system has gradually enlarged the 'pool' from which clever and trainable people can be drawn. Bodies like the Robbins Committee take the greatest pains to reassure us that any expansion they propose is not meant to embrace anyone who is not clever. Opponents of expansion believe they have a knockdown argument when they assert that 'more must mean worse'.

In school education most societies have come to see that this kind of limitation is unacceptable. They have asserted that first primary education then secondary education should be for all. It seems to me quite clear that education after school must be conceived of in terms of education for all, and the task is to start imagining the provision which could accommodate everybody.

We need to take seriously the principle that all adults are equally important. They all have needs and aspirations which an education service can seek to meet. Most countries' present arrangements imply that clever eighteen-year-olds have some sort of priority, and subsidies are lavished upon them so that they can continue their education. When they think of doing more they think of increasing the number, roughly in line with the growth of GNP, who benefit in this way. So far as I can see the expansion of post-school education throughout the world operates on this principle, even when attempts to legitimize it by imagining 'demands' for skilled man-power can be clearly seen to fail.

The question to be discussed in Britain seems to me to be – not whether 20 or 25 per cent of eighteen-year-olds embark on a three- or four-year course leading to a degree, nor indeed whether these students should be accommodated in universities or polytechnics – but whether we should offer this kind of course to eighteen-year-olds *at all*. Should we not start by planning an education service for everyone? It is quite clear that such a service will be different from the one we have now – because the one we have now excludes most people and will continue to do so until well into the next century. What is more, even if it attracted people it would scarcely offer them anything which they would regard as being of much use. The question of what education after school should consist of is the subject of the next chapter. It is enough to point out here that discussing it in terms of élites is a way of avoiding discussing its content. If once we take seriously the idea that the education service is a *service*, and one which seeks to serve everybody, we are committed to fundamental changes.

I would go further. It seems to me that the gradual expansion of an élite system is the enemy of post-school education for all. In the first place it is very expensive, and is inclined to swallow up all available resources. We have seen the fate of the Henniker-Heaton proposals and the way the post-school education of most people was explicitly shelved in the interests of other parts of the service, particularly of full-time higher education. In the second place, the expansion of higher education 'on demand' has meant that such education has been made available to the same sorts of people who were getting it already – that is, the relatively advantaged. It is sobering to realize that in this way Britain could be offering higher education to something over one third of the age-group without mitigating educational inequality at all. Indeed we could be making matters worse. The larger the minority getting higher education, the more they come to take jobs from the less educated who could earlier have gained them. The more higher education comes to confirm social inequalities, the less likely is higher education itself to change to accommodate the excluded. The lesson is that in the future it will not be enough to expand higher education as hitherto. We shall need to find ways of extending opportunity in higher education to those who have hitherto lacked it. This cannot be done merely by expansion; indeed it may be prevented by it.

We must make up our minds to a universal provision of post-school education. For convenience, we can divide it, as international surveys do, into two 'levels', meaning simply two age groups. The first accommodates those over the compulsory school age and under eighteen, the second all adults of eighteen and over. There will no doubt be different provision possible for those under the age of legal majority and those over it. But both 'levels' require a continuum of provision of all kinds, offering education in full-time, part-time, day release, block release and evening courses, so that they have the capacity to meet the needs of all and are ready to take the initiative in doing so. What such education should consist of and how it should be organized are the subjects of the next two chapters.

CHAPTER FOUR

What is it?

Part One: Conformity in Diversity

EDUCATION after school appears in a bewildering variety of
forms. This chapter will follow the same plan as the others in
describing and analysing what there is and in suggesting a view of
what might be. But every description is an interpretation, so I must
confess at once that I believe the surface diversity of post-school
education the world over is misleading. For all the differences, the
activity of education remains the same. As an anonymous school-
leaver said, when invited by his former headmaster to admire his
old school's new buildings, 'It could all be of marble, sir, but it
would still be a bloody school' (Newsom, 1963). Or as Frank
Bowles more soberly put it, 'Both systems deal with the common
body of the world's knowledge and both teach in the way men have
always taught' (Bowles, 1962). I shall seek, therefore, to make the
case that diversity conceals conformity and that this is mistaken,
to suggest a genuine alternative, and to show how this might work
out in practice.

DIVERSITY

Systems

We know that systems of education can differ. In some countries
secondary schools are simply extended for two or three more years
to provide a general academic education, leading in turn to colleges or universities. In others, the second level consists of separate
academic and general vocational schools. There are others where
vocational education takes place at a variety of specialist schools or
colleges. Some organized vocational education takes place in
industrial and commercial firms, with or without assistance from
the formal education system. There are some countries, including
Britain, in which second-level education takes place in all of these

kinds of institutions, and even in institutions which accommodate people at both the second and third levels.

A similar diversity characterizes the third-level. Again, institutions may be comprehensive or specialized. One country may tend to accommodate liberal and general education at first-degree level in the same universities or colleges as professional education in law, medicine, engineering and the like. Indeed the term university has been held to mean a concern for all human knowledge, and this is the general British view. On the other hand there are respectable systems where professional education takes place in specialized institutes, often for one profession apiece, but sometimes, as in the Technische Hochschulen, for a group of allied professions. Sometimes third-level institutions accommodate both undergraduate and graduate programmes and preparation for higher degrees as well. In others, undergraduate education goes on in distinct institutions, and students later transfer to admired graduate schools. The balance between general and specialist education, between the academic and the otherwise vocational, between various levels of study, may differ not only between systems but between institutions in the same system – and even within individual institutions. To this variety of type and level of course there is variety of mode of study. Some institutions accommodate only full-time students, others have part-timers as well – or chiefly. Others, like the British Open University, operate mainly by correspondence. It is presumably of no significance that of all advanced countries, Britain and the U.S.S.R. seem to go in most for part-time higher education.

The extent of variety within any particular country seems to be connected with the scale of provision. In comparing Western Europe with the United States and the Soviet Union the Robbins Report asserted that in spite of the many differences between Britain and Europe there was a common sense of hierarchy, which stemmed from their past, and a certain resistance to fundamental change. 'New types of institution', it said, 'may establish themselves in time, but they have a difficult road, and universities as such continue to be regarded as sharply distinguished from them.'

To this the systems in the United States and the Soviet Union were said to present a sharp contrast. Much as they differed from each other, they shared a more variegated pattern of institutions. Professional training was provided within both systems in far more forms than in Europe. The report attributed their variety partly to the individual history of each country and partly to the scale on which higher education was provided: 'the nature and functions of institutions change imperceptibly as the numbers of students in higher education grow' (Robbins, 1963).

It is worth following the report's contrasts between the American and Soviet systems. In the United States, it said, there had never been fixed lines of demarcation between institutions of different kinds. Although it was possible to distinguish the private and the state universities, the liberal arts colleges, the land-grant colleges, the teachers' colleges or the professional schools, now, as the tide of numbers advances, distinctions between categories of institution were becoming even less clear. There were large differences in the prestige and academic standing of individual institutions, but this did not prevent colleges formerly devoted to one or two specialisms from developing to cover wider fields of knowledge; and many liberal arts colleges, formerly offering courses leading only to the first degree, were now developing postgraduate work.

The Soviet Union offered an alternative method of achieving a varied pattern of institutions. Here again there was no caste-system among institutions of different types, although Moscow and Leningrad Universities stood out in prestige. The universities proper accommodated only some ten per cent of enrolments in higher education: additional needs for qualified people were met by the spread of specialized institutions, of which many now equalled the universities in repute. 'Colleges like the Leningrad Polytechnic Institute are very similar to the German Technical High Schools in this respect, but the process of building up special colleges has in Russia been carried very much further, so that universities are now devoted mainly to arts and science in their "pure" forms and mostly exclude fields such as law, medicine and economics' (Robbins, 1963).

Size and shape

Even allowing for contrasts of balance, level and purpose, there is an enormous variety in the size and organization of institutions. Organization is discussed in more detail in Chapter 5: for the present it is enough to notice that, given a particular number of students, they may be accommodated all together on a vast campus, on a number of campuses within a city or more widely scattered, or in a number of quite separate institutions. The University of California has 95,000 students on nine campuses. The Royal University of Malta has 1,000 students on one.

What is not generally realized is that Britain probably contains all the contrasts of scale – except perhaps giants of the Californian kind. The University of London has 35,000 students in over forty colleges, institutes and medical schools – and it still offers external degrees to students who do not belong to any of its institutions. The University of Wales has six campuses spread around the principality, including St David's College, Lampeter, with only 400 students. The major industrial cities have universities at or near their centres, each accommodating between 3,000 and 9,000 students. There are a number of smaller, newly established, universities with campuses outside pleasant county towns, and a dozen small universities which are heavily biased towards technology. Oxford and Cambridge are quite large by British standards (11,000 students each) and are the only two universities in England which are older than the oldest universities in the U.S.A. and the U.S.S.R. The Scottish universities are also mostly oldish and display similar disparities of size. And the Open University, which has its headquarters in a new town, presumably regards the whole country as its campus. The variety among non-university institutions is even greater. There are polytechnics with many thousands of students, some of them with 'precincts' scattered over a number of towns. Colleges of education may have anything from a few hundred to nearly 2,000 students. Technical and other colleges may accommodate 10,000 or more, full time and part time. Some colleges of art may have as few as 300.

Buildings

Another contrast is in the extent to which institutions are residential. The question is partly a practical one: the students have to be housed somewhere, and the local housing 'market' may be inadequate. But often residence is regarded as part of the educational experience, and it is interesting that this argument is more often advanced and accepted at the third level than at the second.

Physically, the differences between institutions seem very largely to depend upon age. For an Englishman, Oxford and Cambridge exercise such charm that it is hard to realize that there are not many places like them in the world. The combination of integration with a medium-sized town (rather than dominating or being dwarfed by it) with the fact that, since the thirteenth century, each generation seemed to add buildings, without ever needing to pull others down, makes for a mellowness which is much sought after elsewhere. The most successful seekers were perhaps the 'ivy league' universities and colleges of the United States, and their success is all the more remarkable for having been meant. In the industrialized nations of the West, the nineteenth century saw a great boom in university, college and school building of all kinds. These buildings often present a happy combination of wealth and self-confidence, with a flamboyant eclecticism of style. An English technical college of the later part of the century could be described as 'a handsome building in Ruabon brick in a subdued Victorian Renaissance style'. The 'renaissance' was a North European one, and implied bright brick with stone courses, steep roofs, cupolas, bow windows, mullions, gables – and statues of eminent scientists in niches along a frieze.

A consequence of this and the short but vigorous period of European colonization in Asia and Africa was that all over the world there are even more happy examples of these buildings, often combining the gothic, the classical, the renaissance, together with an interpretation of indigenous styles at least as authentic as Verdi's *Aida* was to ancient Egypt.

In the 1920s and 1930s there also emerged in Europe a formal grandiloquence in the educational building of the totalitarian states, the most famous of which was the thirty-six-storey tower of Moscow University.

However, since the major expansion in education after school, in all countries, has taken place in the last thirty years, most educational buildings are new. A very few of them are recognizably both modern and architecture. Many, especially colleges in rich countries, are intended and often successful pastiches of past styles, or, less successfully, attempts to make an artistic statement without being quite sure of what it is that should be said. Mostly the new building relies on the cheeseparing application of new technique. The four-square steel and concrete construction houses every kind of educational institution. If you set off north from Rawalpindi in Pakistan, along the grand trunk road that leads to the Khyber Pass, you will pass on your left a serried set of two-storey cuboids and a parabaloid hall with some other plain buildings dotted about. A board outside tells you that this is the Rawalpindi Polytechnic, but it could equally well be a trade school in Iran, a university college in East Africa, a college of home economics in Madras, a technical institute in the Congo, a law school in Egypt or a hospital and medical school in Timbuktu. To say this is not to sneer at it or them. The buildings are decent and apt for their purpose. They are often flexible in use and are easily maintained. I mention the similarity only because there is no very great mileage to be got, even in a book which compares educational provision, out of the elaborate physical description of recent institutions.

The Campus

There is a general tendency which heightens this effect of sameness. Within cities land is scarce and dear. Those who establish educational institutions have to think not only of present needs but also of the likelihood that the institutions will have to expand. They even hope that they will do so. They therefore go for plenty of space. The greater the importance attached to the institution the more space they feel they have to go for. This means that new educational building tends to take place on the outskirts of towns and cities, and this development is new. The medieval universities of Europe were in the centres of towns; so were the colleges and technical institutes of the nineteenth century. They were recognizably part of the communities they were established to serve. This was also true of the first American universities. As the thirteen states colonized the West, however, land was more plentiful – and so there became established the concept of the campus (the derivation is significant): in other words, the self-contained institution established from scratch apart from the rest of the community. Today the tendency towards the campus ideal is general. It is not only new institutions which are founded on 'green field' sites. Older institution seek them when they expand. For example, if the University of Dijon were to grow without bulldozing a town in which even the unromantic can still feel the presence of the Dukes of Burgundy (to say nothing of the wine and the mustard) it had to go outside. The new university buildings there might well be a rather grand polytechnic in Pakistan.

Paradoxically, even those institutions which have managed to remain in the centres of large cities (like many civic universities in Britain) have been able to do so because the city centre (or at least the people in it) has very largely left them. Leeds, Manchester, Liverpool, Aston in Birmingham, all have campuses based upon slum clearance. In New York, Columbia tried it before the local people were really ready to go: and that caused a riot. I do not think it fanciful to regard the growing popularity of the campus model as yet another example of the impulse towards autonomy in academic institutions. When decisions had to be made, the need for growth, for the convenience of a single site, for better working conditions – all weighed more heavily than the opportunity to serve a locality. Nor were governments guiltless: they too were quite ready to think of academic institutions as self-contained entities for which a far-off field was an appropriate situation.

CONFORMITY

There are of course other reasons why educational institutions built in any age tend to look alike. They are engaged in very similar activity. They need classrooms, staffrooms, laboratories, workshops, libraries and perhaps dining rooms and kitchens, halls, sports tracks, gymnasia, theatres, student unions . . . The physical context of education is similar, because the very activity of education is the same the world over. We shall come to this in more detail later.

The 'structure' of knowledge

Similarly ubiquitous is the normal form of academic organization. This is the subject department with a professor at its head – even if these are sometimes grouped in 'faculties' of allied departments. The department presupposes an organized body of knowledge, which is understood by some people (professors, and to a decreasing extent assistant professors and lecturers of various grades) and passed on to others. The teachers possess something which it is their duty to impart: their job is to initiate the young into the mysteries of a craft. In this respect vocational and general education are very similar. The difference is that vocational education usually makes fewer intellectual claims for itself, particularly at the lower levels.

The dominance of the subject department is a more recent phenomenon than most people think, though it has generally been more resistant to change than academics believe. Jencks and Riesman say (Jencks, 1968) that it was not until the 1880s that anything like a modern university really took shape in America. Johns Hopkins and Clark were founded as primarily graduate universities. Eliot instituted the elective system at Harvard which was important both in its own right and in easing the assemblage of a more scholarly and specialized faculty. The 1890s saw the founding of Chicago, the reform of Columbia,

and the tentative acceptance of graduate work as an important activity in the leading state universities. This was also the period when national learned societies and journals were founded and when knowledge was broken up into its present departmental categories ('physics', 'biology', 'history', 'philosophy', and so forth), with the department emerging as the basic unit of academic administration.

Johns Hopkins and Harvard led the way in establishing medicine and law respectively as serious graduate studies.

The process of conformity is described by Jencks and Riesman as follows:

These universities have long been remarkably similar in what they encourage and value. They turn out PhDs who, despite conspicuous exceptions, mostly have quite similar ideas about what their discipline covers, how it should be taught, and how its frontiers should be advanced. (This does not mean that there are *no* differences of opinion on these matters within the academic profession. It means only that when contrasted with trustees, administrators, parents, students, or the present authors, the outlook of PhDs in a given discipline seems quite uniform.) These men were not only like-minded at the outset, but they have established machinery for remaining like-minded. National and regional meetings for each academic discipline and subdiscipline are now annual affairs, national journals publish work in every specialized subject, and an informal national system of job placement and replacement has come into existence. The result is that large numbers of PhDs now regard themselves almost as independent professionals like doctors or lawyers, responsible primarily to themselves and their colleagues rather than their employers, and committed to the advancement of knowledge rather than of any particular institution (Jencks, 1968).

The strength of the subject department was well put by J. R. Gass in a preface to an OECD study of 'interdisciplinarity' (OECD, 1972). The universities, he said, were often conservative in what and how they taught. The reason, he thought, lay in the fact that academic disciplines were the basis for the organization of knowledge for teaching purposes: 'The disciplines are not only a convenient breakdown of knowledge into its component parts, they are also the basis of the organization of the university into its autonomous fiefs, and of the professions engaged in teaching and research.' To meddle with the disciplines, he concluded, was to meddle with the whole social structure of the university.

The dominance of the subject department expresses itself in many ways. First among these is the need to establish the subject with an organized body of knowledge and a structure of its own. This is normally simply assumed by academics, because they are seldom under pressure to make themselves explicit. This is how the Vice-Chancellor of a British university, Sir Robert Aitken, interpreted his university's charter (Aitken 1966): 'The Charter declares . . . the university . . . "shall be both a teaching and an examining university, and shall further the prosecution of original research in all its branches". The branches of research, which are the branches of knowledge, determine the organization of academic study.' The last sentence is extremely revealing.

In his university, like so many others, academic organization is divided broadly into faculties (of science and engineering; arts; medicine and dentistry; commerce and social science; and law) and then subdivided into departments. With their constituent departments the faculties form the framework of teaching and research 'and therefore of academic administration'. Organizationally a department is subordinate to a faculty and a faculty to the university senate. This subordination may be embodied in regulations. For example, 'the pattern of courses leading to a degree is often devised in a department, but requires the approval of the faculty and of the senate, whereas the content and the method of teaching of a subject-course are left to be decided by the head of the department, in consultation with his departmental staff'. The teaching activities of a department are coordinated by the faculty, since a given student may be taught in more departments than one. The examining activities of a department are regulated by the faculty and the senate, in the interests of 'reasonably uniform standards'.

Sir Robert also offers this interesting contrast: 'Even problems of the timetabling of classes sometimes have to come to the Senate to be settled. By contrast, the research activities of a department are almost entirely its own affair; they are determined by the interests and ideas of the head of the department, and his staff (with his approval) . . .' Could even fiefdom go further? The central activity of research is independent: there is horsetrading over timetables.

Most teaching and research programmes can fit into and be administered in this framework, says the Vice-Chancellor, but a few *refuse to conform* with it. (His italics.) The solution is the extra-faculty department. Administrative problems also appear with degree courses taught in departments in more than one faculty: they are met either by cross-membership of the faculties concerned or by the establishment of joint boards or committees.

Departments are headed by professors to whom their staffs are responsible. Larger departments may have two or more professors, each responsible for teaching and research in a division of the subject, each with his academic staff. Departments not only grow, they divide. Sometimes a completely new department is formed, its subject forming a separate new degree programme. Sometimes new departments, separate for their administration and post-graduate work, remain associated in a 'school' for undergraduate teaching. There are also 'personal professorships' – for professors, so to speak, without portfolio. All professors, in Sir Robert's university, were members of the senate . . .

Perhaps the most blatant consequences of the organizational control of the subject can be seen in Italy (Boston 1971), but the Italian situation is I believe merely a grotesque parody of the universal dominance of the subject. In Italy, the professors are generally and aptly called 'barons'. They are a small, powerful, privileged, conservative, and mutually-selecting élite. They control jobs and promotions, teaching and examining. This leads to toadyism among staff and students: the former extol professors in footnotes, the latter reproduce lecture notes in examinations. The lecture notes are an additional source of income and are revised annually, thus reducing the second-hand value. Absenteeism is common: jobs in industry, banking, politics and government are all compatible with professorships. (Richard Boston wonders whether the efficient running of the country or the universities has suffered most from this.) The student riots which this system has provoked have encouraged a certain elementary politeness from professors and even some changes in teaching methods, but the system remains intact.

It is not surprising that, even in less extreme situations, subject departments are very resilient. There is an enormous intellectual and personal vested interest in the existing ones. When it inconveniently appears (as it frequently does) that advances in knowledge are taking place between rather than within existing subject boundaries, as when researches into the origins of life found themselves between biology and chemistry, the academic reaction is, first to suspect the new knowledge, then to absorb it into the existing framework, and then to set up another department. In the example just mentioned the new departments have been in molecular biology. All this takes time, so the academic organization of knowledge changes slowly.

Interdisciplinarity

Sometimes this causes unease. It may occur, even to academics, that the single-subject discipline may not chime too well with the needs of students, particularly as they leave college and enter employment. The solution offered, however, is usually the joint honours degree, which may consist of two or three subjects. Here, however, it is normal for the individual subject departments to retain their autonomy and indeed to squabble over the amount of time the students should spend with them. An example of how an attempt to do better foundered on the resilience of subjects is given by Harold Perkin in his study of the new universities in England and Wales (Perkin, 1969). These institutions were established in the 1960s with the specific object of encouraging innovation. They were also meant to accommodate the growing numbers of students, but their immediate contribution to this was recognized to be small. (It would have been quicker to expand existing universities even further.) The new universities were expected, however, to develop new ideas. Professor Perkin noted that their biggest contribution was to experiment with new structures of organization. Both the collegiate structure of York, Kent and Lancaster and the schools of studies of Sussex, East Anglia, Essex, Ulster and, to a less extent, Warwick, were designed 'notably to escape from the straitjacket of departmentalism of the older civic universities'. They allowed growth to take place more easily and flexibly, 'not only in mere size but in more academic directions, than in the traditional departmental universities'. He concluded: 'Within this freer structuring for growth we have seen that the cellular or collegiate system offers more flexibility in social organization, the schools system more in academic organization. Neither system, however, has completely overcome, nor perhaps should it, the tendency towards departmentalism which is both the strength and the weakness of the academic profession.'

Professor Perkin detailed some of the new academic structuring Keele attempted 'in a crowded four-year course to trace the evolution of the earth in space and of man in the context of Western civilization . . . [to give] every student some understanding of both science and the humanities, and to produce broad specialists in a combination of at least two subjects'. The others attempted less. Most preferred to provide 'a much broader base of cognate studies than in the traditional honours degree, on which the student could build in the second and third years a narrowing pyramid of specialization. The breadth of the base and the narrowness of the peak differ considerably, from a wide base and a high and narrow peak at Sussex and Kent, through a moderate base and a broad, flat peak at Lancaster and Stirling, to a narrow base and a high, narrow peak at York and Warwick.' In addition, several of them emulated Keele 'with cross-disciplinary courses such as the "breadth subject" or "distant minor" at Lancaster, the Arts–Science scheme at Sussex and the Open Courses at York'.

The new universities were not remarkable in introducing new subjects of teaching and research. This, said Perkin, was not their function. 'New subjects grow within or at the margins of old ones, and are not created at the behest of institutions.' Their main function was to introduce new approaches to and combinations of old subjects. The new multi-disciplinary schools, of area studies, social studies and comparative studies on the arts side, and of physical, molecular, biological and of engineering sciences on the other side, were, in Perkin's view, 'sufficiently innovatory'.

His conclusion was sombre. Soon, he said, the new universities of the 1960s would become older ones and would be committed to existing systems. If they could not do better than previous new universities in remaining flexible, innovating and experimental, then 'for the health of the university system, to prevent hardening of the academic arteries and stagnation of the scholastic and scientific bloodstream, there ought to be once in every generation the founding of a wave of new universities as numerous and experimental as those of the United Kingdom in the 1960s'.

Nothing could better have summed up the subject departments' resistance to change than the stated conviction that the only remedy is to start again every generation with some new institutions. It simply does not occur to academics that existing institutions can be organized for change, responsiveness and flexibility.

This experience is not at all unusual. Further attempts to encourage 'interdisciplinarity' have been made in many Western European countries, but a survey of such developments (OECD,

1972) reported general failure; its causes – inadequately defined goals; rigidity among teachers, especially professors, 'who all too often cling to their lecturing role and remain cloistered in their discipline', fearing challenges to their discipline or their status; absence of individual or collective leadership over the teachers and over those institutional means which make a team experiment possible; difficulties of coherence and of avoiding a simple juxtaposition of disciplines and the encyclopedic approach; resistance of the traditional structures at all levels – separations among disciplines, examinations, diplomas, jobs for graduates; disarray of students faced with confused, incoherent and arbitrary teaching and the lack of any professional goal; operational difficulties of scheduling, budgeting and the like. 'In summary, there were problems involving goals and curricula, problems involving personnel, problems involving institutions, problems involving facilities.'

This commitment to the subject discipline does not of course preclude differences in the way in which subjects are treated. I am persuaded that one of the major differences between education in the United States and in Europe is that the former tends to value synthesis and the latter analysis. This has been well put by Bryan Magee in his book *Go West Young Man*:

... the bent of higher education in the United States is away from analysis and towards synthesis. The habits of mind formed at, say, Oxford, are essentially critical. No evaluation without a careful examination of the facts, which will usually be found to incorporate grounds for a dissenting judgement; no statement without its exception; no clause without its qualification; no generalization. 'We must make a distinction ...' This emphasis on precision, clarity and analysis gives rise not only to an acute awareness of the *sort* of statements one is making but also to a brand of intellectual caution that makes one reluctant to commit oneself, and makes many people unwilling to say anything at all. At American universities the tendency is quite the reverse. The more elements a man can throw into a generalization the cleverer he is thought to be, and statements of fact, value judgements, definitions, tautologies, historical allusions and literary quotations get thrown in without much discrimination. To the end of what he is currently saying an American is likely to add whatever saying it reminds him of. This way of associating ideas can go on indefinitely (Magee, 1958).

Bryan Magee also quoted contrasting questions, the first from the final history examination at Yale which he invigilated and the second from the history paper he took as an undergraduate at Oxford. The Yale question was:

State the leading conception of the primitive world-outlook, often designated the 'daemonic universe', and at least five of its correlative ideas. Comment on the relation of this outlook and its correlative ideas to the subjective orientations of the great traditional civilizations as these exist today.

The Oxford question was:

How far did British investments abroad influence British foreign policy between 1830 and 1854?

He comments:

It is entirely unthinkable that the Yale question should appear in an Oxford examination except as a practical joke. These two questions illustrate better than any description of mine the diametrically opposed tendencies of the two educational systems – and, infinitely more important, the opposite ways in which educated Englishmen and educated Americans think.

This contrast appears even in less 'general' subjects than history. In a report for the Council for Science Policy Mr M. C. McCarthy made a comparative study of the employment of highly specialized graduates in the U.K. and the U.S.A. (McCarthy, 1968). The study distinguished between science-based 'specialists' and science-based 'generalists', and in the light of this distinction analysed the content of university curricula, the patterns of employment of graduates, the structure of their subsequent careers and the amount and distribution of the education and training in the two countries. The major difference was found to be that the proportion of American scientists and technologists who were generalists was strikingly higher (between 65 and 70 per cent) than in Britain (less than 15 per cent). What is more, education and training in Britain was concentrated in the early years of a career, so there was an obvious risk that British scientists and engineers would get out of date and inflexible. There was much less in-career training in Britain. That British engineers would scarcely lose, from the point of view of employment, by approaching the U.S. pattern was shown by the finding that only exceptionally did the nature and extent of specialization in education match that in employment.

Modules

The American approach encourages a great deal of eclecticism, particularly at the undergraduate level. The whole notion of 'majors' and 'options' suggests that the student may choose from among the widest variety of subjects. A version of this is the 'module' approach to education, in which the student may make up a programme out of a number of choices, with at each moment of choice the guarantee that his chosen module will count for the same in the final evaluation as any other. The approach is presented as being more liberal than the insistence on a single subject for a degree. I am not persuaded that it is. Indeed it offends against the well-established principle of family life that the baby should not be expelled with the bathwater. The general attempt to mitigate the disadvantages of the single-subject honours degree seems likely to destroy what it valuably offers.

The objection to the single-subject honours degree is that it requires a commitment to a subject. The practitioners in the subject determine what is appropriate for its study at undergraduate level and make demands on applicants to universities and colleges. These demands in turn virtually determine the preparation of applicants in the two years before entry and in many cases in Britain in the two years before that as well. Effectively the single-subject honours degree requires the student to specialize in one discipline for three or four years, to study it and related subjects for two years before that, and at the least to drop some 'irrelevant' studies even earlier. The education thus offered is extremely narrow, at least so far as its subject matter goes, and academics have been wont to say that it is the other aspects of university and college life – the residence, the sports and societies, the contact with one's peers – which provide the wider 'education'.

There is of course a long history of attempts to combat this narrowness, particularly in those ancient universities in Britain which resisted longer than most the reforms of the late nineteenth century which elevated the claims of the subject discipline and its professors. 'Greats' at Oxford offered a number of recognizable disciplines, albeit held together by their limitation to the ancient classical world. 'Modern greats' offered the admittedly disparate disciplines of politics, philosophy and economics. Another method of broadening the single subject was to make subsidiary demands for other subjects: historians and English students were required to be literate in other languages. Since 1945 the movement has gathered strength, as we saw earlier. Keele students were required to take more than one subject for an honours degree and in particular to bridge the divide between arts and sciences. The new universities which started in the 1960s have attempted 'new maps of learning' offering a broad base of 'cognate' studies and a narrowing pyramid of specialization. 'Interdisciplinarity' has become a vogue topic for international conferences and projects.

More recently the James Committee on the education of teachers (James, 1972) recommended a Diploma of Higher Education, to be awarded at the end of a 'first cycle' of preparation for teaching which was to be a combination of 'general' (or broad) and 'special' (or narrow) studies. In the White Paper *Education for Expansion* (White Paper, 1972) the Government quite specifically stated that the Dip.H.E. should be developed on a unit basis offering a programme which could be modified as students' interests and career plans unfolded and making it possible for them to earn credits towards other qualifications including degrees and professional status.

A study group set up by the University Grants Committee and the Council for National Academic Awards to draft 'guidelines' for these diplomas went further (Guidelines, 1973). In its preamble it said that modular teaching programmes offered 'advantages of flexibility of choice and operation' and were thus 'cautiously commended'. The guidelines themselves urged that diploma programmes should be composed of defined courses which would allow the student's record of achievement to be presented comprehensibly. All diploma holders, and even those who failed to get a diploma, should be offered a 'transcript' listing all the courses in which they had been successful, using descending pass grades A to D. The accompanying example of a form of transcript showed an imaginary student getting grades A, B, and C respectively in courses of mathematics, statistics and economics which had occupied in turn 40, 30 and 30 per cent of his time. This is clearly the kind of academic world which is more familiar in North America than it is in Europe – where a student may be presented with a vast range of units (modules, options, majors) from which he may choose enough courses to build up a required number of 'credits'.

Even the study group's preamble reflected a sense of unease about all this. It said that modular teaching programmes, if used unwisely, may lack coherence. And it is precisely at this point that one has to recall the virtues of the old single-subject degree. The first of these is the visible responsibility of the academic for the whole curriculum which a student follows. This sense of personal responsibility is not wholly fulfilled by the notion of pastoral care: it needs to extend to intellectual responsibility. The second virtue was coherence. The student had some kind of guarantee that all his work, in breadth or depth, was contributing to an experience with some intellectual design. A subject discipline may be narrow, but it can be grasped: that is its advantage. A third virtue, which may seem paradoxical, is the freedom it offers. Two students reading for a single-subject degree may cover very different ground, depending on their own strengths, weaknesses and interests. By contrast a student on a modular programme may choose his individual modules, but be forced by the demands of time and organization to work within each module in a general and standardized way. The opportunity to skip some areas and to pursue others deeply is available in the single-subject degree without jeopardizing the final qualification. A fourth virtue, often unacknowledged, is that the single-subject degree could be seen to be in some sense a vocational preparation, even though large numbers of students enter vocations for which their degrees have been irrelevant.

If we accept that the single-subject degree leads to excessive specialization and inflexibility we must surely try to replace it with something that mitigates these disadvantages but retains its virtues.

Unfortunately the modular approach is ill designed to do this. It undermines intellectual responsibility, coherence, individualized learning and vocational relevance. It suggests a frivolity about the total experience that the student may undergo as a result of his programme. There is indeed no guarantee that the experience will be educational in any obvious sense – unless it be the absorption of different snatches of knowledge. On the other hand it retains, in its individual modules, most of the disadvantages of subject specialization. It is not too much to say that in going from single subjects to modules, we are in danger of dispensing with the baby and retaining only the bathwater.

It is easy to see how the notion of the liberality of modules arises among those committed to subject disciplines. How modest to be able to say that a student may of course choose to study a discipline that is not one's own. But real radicalism would consist in wondering whether a subject discipline is really a vehicle for education at all. Academics are precluded, by their training and by the very organization of their work, from raising this question, let alone taking it seriously.

What then is to be done? Clearly, if we are to reject the single-subject degree yet retain its major advantages, it will not be enough just to offer multi-subject degrees. We have to start from something other than the subject, otherwise all coherence is lost. We have to start instead from the student. Later I shall elaborate what I mean by this, but in summary I believe that it implies creating a programme which enables him to formulate his problems (personal, social, educational, vocational), to propose his own solutions and to test them. A student entering such a programme needs help in discovering what strengths and weaknesses he brings to the task. He needs to be able to say what capacities he will carry away at the end of it. And his programme, which he must help to devise, will be a way of getting from the one to the other. In this way his tutors can offer intellectual responsibility for his programme; his studies have some basis for coherence; he is offered not just choice between options but the chance to take the initiative in planning a programme; and he can seek the vocational relevance he needs. To point the contrast perhaps too starkly, such a student will gain not so much knowledge as competence. The fear is that in a modular programme he will get neither.

Levels

The dominance of the subject discipline has other consequences, notably the deference paid to the 'demands of the subject'. Foremost among these demands is the level at which the subject may be studied. There is an all-pervasive sense of hierarchy here. There are subjects which are studied at schools, but not in higher education; there are subjects suitable for higher education and not for schools; and there are subjects suitable for both. This kind of distribution is vigorously defended by academics at any one time, though it tends to shift quite markedly over time and in different places. For example, reading and writing are thought to be the business of the schools, rather than higher education – until one realizes that courses in how to read better and faster are common in colleges in the United States. For a long time, economics was thought to be more suitable in higher education than in schools. In the subjects which are held to be apt at both levels, there has often been a firm division between school and third-level work. In the early part of this century the differential calculus was part of the British first degree in mathematics. By the time I was at school it was in the syllabus for sixteen-year-olds. My children tackled it in primary school.

The notion of levels is particularly strong in vocational education, with its concern for training operatives, craftsmen, technicians and technologists. Typical is this description of engineering technology:

Engineering Technology is that part of the technological field which requires the application of scientific and engineering knowledge and methods combined with technical skills in support of engineering activities; it lies in the occupational spectrum between the craftsman and the engineer at the end of the spectrum closest to the engineer (Lohmann, 1968).

The preoccupation with what is and what is not a suitable level for this or that stage of education leads to the imposition of formal entry requirements for courses and institutions. In British universities it is widely believed that one cannot do university work in mathematics, physics, chemistry or biology without already knowing a certain stated amount of the subject. Subjects like these are cumulative: you cannot go on to one stage until you have completed the one before. In the arts subjects, like native and foreign languages, history and geography, there seems to be no requirement for a certain body of knowledge to have been attained. What is required is that students should have had *some* previous knowledge, or, more precisely, that they should have shown that they can work at university level before they get there. There are yet other subjects. largely in the social sciences, where there is no requirement of this kind at all – simply because the subjects are not widely taught in the schools. Needless to say these departments exert pressure on the schools to get them to do so. Meanwhile, they do not of course waive formal entry requirements: they insist on performance in *something*, however irrelevant.

These requirements are often very stringent: in Britain they imply pretty limited specialization for two or more years beforehand. Of course, the universities then complain that their entrants are uneducated. They know too little about the wider social, political and cultural movements of our times. Why, some of them can scarcely read and write. To this the schools can only reply that they did not know that this too was a requirement.

The point of mentioning these various demands is to suggest that we treat with suspicion the claims that the subject demands this or that from those who are to study it at some level or other. Looked at together they appear to be arbitrary and capricious. They stem, however, directly from the idea of the subject as perceived by its practitioners, and it is these academics who interpret demands of the subject they have to such a large extent created.

They seem to underestimate the extent to which even a specialist degree course contains elements which can be regarded as alien to or of a significantly lower level than the main subject. Arts courses commonly involve a smattering of modern languages; social science courses commonly require elementary mathematics or statistics; science courses may include history and languages. The view seems to be that these lower-level studies are ennobled by the purpose to which they are put: that is, the study of the subject at the required level. But if this view is right, it underlines the notion of a subject as a construct – something that turns out to be whatever its practitioners say it is – and opens the door to the discovery that we might imagine some organization of studies which is entirely different from subject disciplines.

This point is worth labouring. I am not arguing that present courses of higher education do not require some prior level of performance. Most of them do, and it is nearly impossible to make much of them unless one has completed the prior study. Indeed efforts to 'open' entry to such courses to the unqualified normally founder on the failure of the unqualified to keep up. My argument is rather that there is nothing inevitable about present courses. If their subject matter were different, or were presented in a different way, they would make different demands on entry. They could in principle be designed to make no demands at all. If one wishes to open entry to the unqualified, they must be so designed. I am not claiming, either, that subjects as a whole make no prior demands. Those working on the problems of a discipline need to know at least enough to know that there are problems. The question is whether this kind of knowledge is required of undergraduates – or whether it is the kind that is in fact demanded of them. What I am arguing is that most academic discussion of level is somewhat parochial, ignoring not only the theoretical possibility that things might be ordered differently but the actual differences that exist, from one discipline to another, from one course to another and from one decade to another.

Standards

Perhaps the most familiar defence of entry requirements is the need to maintain standards. We have already seen that it is doubtful whether entry standards exist at all. Frank Bowles pointed out that there was nothing to choose between the applicants accepted in European systems of higher education and those excluded. It all boiled down to supply and demand. Certainly in British universities standards rise with an increasing number of applicants, and fall when applicants are scarce. There is a minimum entry requirement on which standards may be said to rest, but it is not certain that this represents the same level of performance from one year to another.

As a consequence of all this, there is very little agreement about objective standards. When the Robbins Committee came to compare the amount of higher education in Britain and in other countries, it worried a good deal about comparing like with like: what could be regarded as equivalent to a British first degree? Faced with the fact that the courses leading to these degrees were shorter than degree courses almost anywhere else in the world (normally three years as against four or five), the committee decided that it must take into account the quality of instruction. This it did by comparing staff–student ratios, which turned out to be as follows:

Table VII. University student–staff ratios in selected countries 1960

	Ratio
Great Britain	8
France	30
Germany (F.R.)	35
Netherlands	14
Sweden	12
U.S.A.	13
U.S.S.R.	12

Source: Robbins, 1963, Table 16

The committee concluded, without too much confidence, that brevity and more generous staffing might be said to cancel each other out. What happens in practice is that no serious attempt is made to equate standards. A political decision is made that certain standards are equal, and there's an end of it. Degrees in British universities are held to be equivalent, as are the degrees awarded by the Council for National Academic Awards. There are extensive lists of foreign institutions kept by the Department of Education for the purpose of deciding whether or not their degrees are held to be equivalent for the purpose of awarding qualified teacher status. The universities of the Commonwealth have agreed which of the degrees of their various countries can be said to be equivalent to which. And now the European Economic Community is doing the same with both degrees and professional qualifications.

It is held to be particularly important to maintain standards when dealing with professional qualifications: one would not, certainly, like to be in the hands of an ill-prepared doctor or live in a block of flats built by an inadequate engineer. (Both situations do, of course, occur.) Unfortunately there is more than a suspicion that professional requirements are designed as much to exclude as to qualify. The best evidence for this is that they are usually expressed in terms of the number of years of training needed and the syllabus to be covered. They do not rely on a clear statement of what the qualified person should be able to *do* or of what would definitely disqualify him. This chimes with their attitude to later failure: in Britain professional associations defend incompetent colleagues, but tend to expel immoral ones. At all events, comparability of professional qualifications (for example in the EEC) are decided through political haggling rather than through any genuine notion of standards.

Excellence

Another version of the notion of standards is the claim to be pursuing excellence. I have recently found myself in two discussions about excellence. The first was for one of the television programmes early on Sunday evenings, which are known in the trade as the 'God slot', because only He watches. This particular programme was about the universities. It was introduced by the Vice-Chancellor of Durham, with (as he admitted) unfairly mellow pictures of Durham's cathedral, castle and city, a quietly confident plea for living and learning together as a community, and all set to the harpsichord. My role was that of 'specialist critic' – so I wondered whether the Vice-Chancellor might not have told us what the universities were for, what contribution they should make to society, how many people should go to them and what they should be doing once they got there. The ensuing discussion, with a former student, a lady and a statutory reverend, took its predictable course through personal reminiscence, 'education for leisure', recent changes at Cambridge and so on – until the point when the chairman, Bernard Levin, announced suddenly that what I was overlooking was 'excellence'. Both he and the rest of the panel seemed convinced that there was such a thing, that it ought to be pursued and that universities were and should be places where you pursued it. At this point our programme gave way to community hymn singing.

The second discussion was in the office of a large charitable foundation, where I was trying to explain the idea of studying institutions to see whether they were apt for their purpose. Here again one of the foundation's officials intervened. Might not such an approach to educational institutions be positively dangerous?

Even to ask an institution to define its purposes might turn out to be destructive – let alone to judge its performance. The example of All Souls, Oxford, was oft cited as an institution whose duty it was only to exist: further definition, of aims or purpose, was a positive danger.

What these two conversations had in common was an attitude which has seeped through education from the universities downwards, that there are abstractions, like truth, excellence, knowledge, which are to be pursued 'for their own sake'. This pursuit is self-justifying and by definition good. Arrangements must be made and paid for, so that selected people can engage in it, unshackled by accountability, social responsibility or even criticism. Those of us who question this are uncouth, destructive and lacking in sensitivity, imagination, and even the intelligence to understand truth or excellence when we see it. I want to argue, on the contrary, that it is precisely this attitude, not the assaults of the uncouth, which does and will condemn education to mediocrity, error and incompetence – and that this is a very real danger if we uncritically expand the universities.

But let us take seriously the idea of excellence. The tendency to do so has a long intellectual history. All those young men who kept hopping into bed with Socrates were fascinated by the question of what is Truth, Good and so on. Much academic debate, then, in medieval times and since, has been concerned with definitional problems of this kind. But the venerability of the arguments and their lack of conclusiveness should by now have alerted us to the fact that they are sterile. Definitions are no help at all: they settle no arguments (except trivial ones), they tell us nothing and they do not enable us to make any progress. If two people cannot agree on the meaning of a word, they should stop using it and find another one.

There is no such *thing* as excellence, which is visible and attainable. It is just one way of saying which way we want to go. We want to improve, to excel; and it is not a quibble to recognize that excelling and excellence are comparative states. We can break records, and then break the new records thus established. The 'pursuit of excellence' is a way of saying that we give a high priority to doing as well as possible. But we have to be doing something other than merely pursuing excellence, and we have to have some ground for judging how well we have done. Nor can we ever be sure that we have eliminated all faults, flaws, defects, mediocrity or inferiority. And once this is recognized we have to leave the heights of abstraction and generality, because in talking of eliminating defects we are in the concrete world. We identify defects when some particular thing goes wrong. We similarly need to demand that claims for quality of any kind are couched in terms which we can test.

The confidence trick which the pundits seek to pull on us is that we should accept their claims to 'excellence' because these are expressed in terms which we cannot test or argue with. We are all in favour of excellence – all, that is, except the uncouth – and so there is no more to be said. Academics cannot be expected to defend their activities, procedures, influence. What they are doing is done for its own sake. Criticism retires baffled: if an acitivity has no purpose outside itself then there is no ground for claiming that it has succeeded or failed.

This immunity to criticism is built into British academic education. In research, academics run the gauntlet of their professional peers, and science proceeds by trial and error, by publication and criticism, by hunches and tests. In education and organization, academics have no such check. They are 'autonomous' (shielded, in universities, by the University Grants Committee); they effectively govern themselves; they admit – and they pass or fail; they decide what and how to teach; they choose their staffs; they determine their own development. And they are used to doing this by reference only to themselves, not in relation to yardsticks which people outside can use. They are pursuing excellence, and the rest of us must be silent because neither they nor we can tell whether they have found it or not.

But why should we not take the academics' word for it? They say they are pursuing excellence, so why not take the will for the deed? Why not take the excellence on trust? One answer to this is that in terms of part of the academic's job, his 'research', we do not. We insist that he publish and lay himself open to judgement. Another answer is that when we do seek to test the claims we are not encouraged.

Take again the question of standards. This is central to the question of excellence, yet it is clear that academics have no real standards. Their admission requirements are a matter of supply and demand. Their final degree results are related more to the method of teaching and examining than to the quality of the students. They are indifferent to the need for competence, let alone excellence, in their teaching. Faced with this sort of evidence we can be forgiven for supposing that the reluctance to test their claims stems at least partly from worry about the likely results of testing.

All this, of course, is of more than 'academic' interest. Universities cost money. They are being expanded to accommodate more students – without being required to show that they are places to which more and more students ought to go. If they have their way, the rest of us will never be able to discuss whether the expansion was right or wrong. What is more, they are being expanded on their own assumption that teaching should occupy only a minority of their staffs' time. There may be an argument regarding the universities as instruments of public patronage: places where able people are kept in relative comfort and underemployed, so that some of them may produce worthwhile work. But we need to know what the argument is. And we need to be convinced of the numbers involved. No doubt we need as many as possible (because one cannot have too much excellence), but there are other claims on public resources (we cannot have too little poverty) so we need to be offered a justification for multiplying sages. It is surely a coincidence that the numbers of the latter needed by the nation rises in proportion to the number of undergraduate students.

And if we are to be told that every teacher of undergraduates must necessarily have an opportunity for research, are we not entitled to ask the grounds on which we are to regard many teachers of undergraduates outside the universities as inferior? If it is simply that they have fewer research opportunities, the judgement is tautologous, and worthless. The point of all this is not to assert that the universities and colleges are valueless or fraudulent or worse, but to argue that they make it hard for us to judge *what* they are.

Student impotence

The main defect of the dominance of the subject discipline, however, is that it is profoundly anti-educational. In the first place it is authoritarian. It is the staff which knows what the subject is, indeed decides what it is. This gives them the whip hand in dealing with colleagues and students. As the Balliol rhyme put it:

> First come I, my name is Jowett:
> If there's knowledge then I know it.
> I am the master of this college,
> And what I know not is not knowledge.

The academic decides not only what the subject is, but the grounds on which it is to be discussed. Indeed, it is normally held that an academic study is self-justifying. There can be no other way of justifying it. This has one precious advantage: it renders academics immune from criticism, except on their own terms. Again, this renders the student particularly powerless.

I believe that it is the self-justifying nature of academic work which leads students to discard it as irrelevant. On the face of it, the criticism is trivial: most of what one does at any one time is likely to be irrelevant to most other things. Nor is there any agreement among students as to what their studies should be relevant to. The cry is often simply for 'relevance'. And academics have no difficulty in showing that such a cry is absurd. What they miss, however, is the sense of frustration that gives rise to it. This derives from the inability to get a satisfactory answer to the question, What is it all for – apart from itself? What purposes outside itself does academic study serve? It really is very unnerving to find that there is no very good ground for being where one is – apart from the fact that it is good to be there.

The demand for relevance has a number of sources and takes a number of forms. Some students complain of courses over-crowded with detail and giving little time to think. Others see their activities as 'tricks and dodges' and the course as consisting of anything that could attract a twenty-minute question in the final examination. Many students come to fear that their courses are directed to no vocational end. Those on supposedly vocational courses may see the relevance as spurious, because they seem to get no nearer to the *practice* of their specialism. Yet others complain of narrowness and stultification. All seem to hanker for more command over their educational experience, preferring project work or

116

requesting more options. The preference for discussion over lectures is another expression of a desire to be heard as well as to be
taught. A few students, identifying with the 'deprived', demand
'black studies' or 'working-class studies'.

Most of these complaints from students are as permanent as the
failure of academics to heed them. Even the large-scale distur-
bances in Western colleges and universities at the end of the 1960s
brought little serious change. 'Some attempts are being made', said
Ruth Beard in summarizing student complaint and the response to
it, 'to modify courses comprehensively ... As yet, however, the
majority of new courses incorporate modifications of a less ambitious nature' (Beard, 1970). This is not because academics are
wicked, or hate students. It derives from their unexamined assumptions about knowledge, teaching and learning.

Learning and teaching

Clearly we must look more closely into the activities of teaching
and learning. What is done in educational institutions is not only
consistent from place to place all over the world, but has been so,
I am told, since Aristotle. Young people in formal education
attend lectures, seminars or tutorials. They read books, write
essays for their teachers' judgement, watch demonstrations. They
may carry out 'experiments'; that is, they go through prescribed
procedures in order to see for themselves some established process
at work. They may get to do project work. In relatively rich places,
the students may get a lot of individual attention: elsewhere they
are dealt with very much in groups. In large institutions there may
be a wide choice of subjects and of teachers; in smaller places
there may be no choice at all. Usually, but not always, the higher
the level, the more independence the student may have. Usually,
though unnecessarily, arts students have more independence than
science students. Throughout, the object of all these activities is to
cover a set amount of knowledge (the course, curriculum, syllabus)
and then convince the examiners that one has done so.

These are the externals of education, the name we give to the
events we arrange. But what is happening? What takes place when
the student learns and when the teacher teaches? I confess that
when I first came to consider this I was shocked at how little was

117

known. For example, almost nothing is known about the development of the brain after the age of two, yet one theory of learning postulates maturation of the brain and another the linking of 'cell assemblies' within it. Most of the current theories themselves are based upon the learning habits of those pigeons, rats and circus apes that have had the misfortune to be captured by learning theorists. The theories are many, and they conflict. In this situation the best one can do is to set them out as clearly as possible. Fortunately that is enough for the purposes of this book.

One group of theories, associated with 'gestalt' or 'field' psychology, regards learning as the imposition by the learner of order or pattern upon his experience. The first gestalt psychologist, Max Wertheimer, suggested five ways in which a learner imposed this order: similarity, where similar items were seen as groups; proximity, since this grouping was easier with adjacent objects; closure, or the completion of incomplete outlines; continuation, or the extension of straight lines or curves; and membership character, in which characteristics of parts of a whole are derived from the whole. The field psychologists have emphasized the learner's whole experience. If a new experience makes the learner reorganize his 'field' it is said to give 'insight'.

A second group of theories has been developed by 'associationists', or those who accept the notion of learning as stimulus and response. The learner gets a stimulus from the environment, he responds, this changes him, he gets new stimuli which lead to similar change – and so on. A positive stimulus (or reward) which follows a response 'reinforces' the response. The famous 'conditioning' experiments by Pavlov suggested that if two stimuli (food and a bell) were presented together often enough, the response (the dog's salivating) could be produced by one of them (the bell) alone. In contrast to the field psychologists, the associationists concentrate on discrete steps in learning: on each stimulus and response.

A third group of theories, those of the 'functionalists', explain learning in terms of solving problems. The functionalists assert that purposive activity of this kind is itself an innate human characteristic, and is not a mere by-product of other needs, like hunger.

These three groups of theories are all still current and attract adherents. There are two more which are discredited among professional psychologists, but still (as is often the case with exploded theories) remain as unstated assumptions among many teachers and students. The first derived from 'faculty psychology', or the idea that appropriate exercises would develop 'faculties' of the mind. Latin, for example, would develop the logical faculty which would be transferred to other studies. Boring or distasteful work would develop 'character'. It was, however, apparent that more usually logic and character remained undeveloped, while boredom and suspicion of learning grew apace. Many teachers do still talk, and more often act, as if this theory held.

The second discredited theory was that of 'natural unfoldment', deriving at some remove from Rousseau. The idea was that since human beings were naturally good, it was enough to create an environment for their natural self-determination. It is now clear that in these circumstances there is no guarantee that anything will be learned at all. At least it seems hard to say clearly *what* has been learned. Much of the pressure, from students and others, for the abandonment of formal instruction and syllabuses seems to be based implicitly on an idea of natural unfoldment.

These, then, are the broad theories of learning. What of the detailed ways in which learning takes place? These, too, have been categorized. They include 'signals' – gestures, words or facial expressions which encourage or discourage a response; 'chaining', or linking together a sequence of actions or words; 'discrimination' between and within groups or classes; the creation of concepts and principles; and problem-solving. In all this the learner may not be acting consciously. He may impose order or pattern on his experience without being aware that he is doing so. He may be simply 'conditioned' on the basis of reflex actions. He may not be aware that he has learned something until the opportunity arises to act, when his 'latent learning' is made overt. He may be influenced by suggestion, imitation or identification with another person. It is clear, too, that individual differences affect learning, differences of perception (for example visual and verbal perception, or synthetic and analytic problem solvers), of personality (extrovert and introvert, dominant and submissive, independent and dependent, convergers and divergers), and of 'ability'. Most people, of course, do not tend to any extremes in all this, but are placed somewhere along each of the dimensions of difference. Nor are the measures which have been developed to place them equally acceptable. Even the best developed, like those of 'ability', are vulnerable to the criticism that they are measuring experience as much as any innate individuality.

So much, in outline, for theories of learning. What of the practice of teaching? The traditional method is the lecture. Both staff and students in higher education agree that this is a good method of giving a clear and orderly synopsis of a subject, particularly to introduce a new and difficult topic and to set it in context. It is an economical way of presenting new material that is not yet to be found in books. It forms a base for later discussion. In particular it is a method which can reach large numbers of people at once, and is more economical than other methods of staff time. The television and radio programmes of the Open University are simply a nationwide extension of the lecture.

There can be many kinds of successful lecture: the intellectual *tour de force*, the thinking aloud, the dramatic exhibition, the evocation of a situation, the informal account, and so on. Nor is there any great disagreement on the qualities of a good lecture. The content should be neither too dense nor too abstract; it should be well organized; the delivery should be audible and undistracting; the non-verbal signals (facial expressions for example) should be appropriate. There are now many examples of attempts to evaluate lectures, largely through questionnaires to students. These cover surrounding factors (like noise, ventilation, hunger), the lecturer himself (audibility, speed, grooming, manner, rapport), the content and presentation (amount, clarity, usefulness interest) and the use of audio-visual materials (blackboards, slides).

Interestingly enough, these questionnaires rarely seem to inquire into the effects of the lectures on the students. It is as if the performance can be evaluated without reference to them. Indeed, it is seldom asked what the students are doing while the lecture is taking place. Even with the best lectures, some students are bored, others baffled. Even when all are attentive, what will they carry away afterwards? What most students are doing, of course, is taking notes, well or ill as the case may be. The evidence is doubtful, but it appears that the most students get down is half of what the lecturer considers important. And what will they do with the notes once they have them?

It is questions like these which have led to the supplementation of lectures by small group discussion. These may include tutorials for one or two students, seminars for half a dozen or more, or what are in effect small meetings. Usually these are arranged rather more informally than lectures. Again both staff and students seem to agree that these smaller groups are best thought of as a chance to get a better understanding – of lectures, books and other material. They offer more personal contact between staff and students. They promote critical and logical thinking, through the presentation of material and its criticism. They enable students to present and discuss their work, to get help with expressed difficulties and to learn about problem-solving. The best small group discussions avoid being simply a lecture in disguise, and start instead from the students and their work. In this way intellectual, oral and literary skills can be deployed, and the students can combine to cover some piece of work (like surveying a new area of study) and be brought to change their attitudes.

Of course, different students make differing contributions to the groups, but there are a number of simple techniques for coping with this. Dominant, talkative members can be stilled; shrinking, silent members can be encouraged. On the whole students appreciate the small group situation. But, as with the lecture, it is not clear what they take away from it. Many staff seem unsure of this, and seek to counter their insecurity by requiring follow-up work, to see what learning has taken place. They seldom seek to discover whether the other claimed advantages of small groups (working together, oral presentation, greater clarity) have also been attained.

A third teaching method is practical or project work. This may typically be seen in a laboratory or workshop, and this kind of method is a staple of courses in the physical sciences and engineering. More recently it has entered the social sciences, in the form of field work and project work. What is claimed for the method is that it gives practice and experience. It enables students to relate their theory to the 'real' world. In addition, the laboratory or workshop activities themselves give an appreciation of the significance, importance and difficulty of precise measurement, make equipment familiar, develop practical skills, improve accuracy in observation, inculcate scientific method – in the recording of observations, evaluation of results and the presentation of findings. In order to be sure that the work contributes to the whole course, the teacher sets the experiment or project, often with precise and detailed instructions, and the students work it through. In a few places, the experiments may be genuinely open-ended and give the students the chance to make their own discoveries. Often, when pressure on time and laboratory space is heavy, the teacher will demonstrate an experiment or technique to a large group of students, who will then note it down and write it up.

There are two other teaching methods which are often overlooked, the first because it is new-fangled and the second because it is very old indeed and taken for granted. The first is programmed teaching, perhaps by the use of machines. In this method, the material offered is broken down into its successive steps. In 'linear' programmes, the student proceeds by the gentlest means through a series of correct answers to a mastery of the whole. In 'branching' programmes he is led to different material depending on whether his answers were right or wrong. It is claimed for this method that it can teach students simple concepts, facts and techniques economically – because the student can go at his own pace without affecting the pace of others.

The second of the overlooked methods is the book. It is odd how seldom this appears in studies of teaching methods, how much it is taken for granted. Through books the teacher can present his material in permanent form. The lecture is fleeting: a book can be kept by the student for the rest of his life. What is more the good teacher can reach thousands, perhaps millions, of students. There are some brilliant text books and introductions to disciplines which have taken a teacher's influence across a country or a continent. A book has the merit that it too can be adapted to the student's own pace. He can go back and read a passage again. It has the disadvantage that it does not respond to the student's questions: the student has to take it or leave it.

In discussing these various teaching methods, I have taken pains to assume that they are all done well. There are many complaints from students and teachers about incompetent lecturing, careless group discussions, boring and repetitive laboratory work, trivial programmed texts and unreadable books. There is a substantial literature on the good and bad practice of various teaching methods (see Beard, 1970). Clearly anything can be done well or ill. My purpose here, however, is not to criticize bad practice, but to try to understand what happened in education. For this purpose it is best to assume that what is done is done well. If there is then any doubt about its effectiveness, we shall know we have a genuine problem, not a local difficulty that can be put right with conscientiousness, better organization or more practice.

We have now seen something both of theories of learning and of the practice of teaching. The first thing that strikes one is how little connection there is between the two. Only programmed teaching is based directly on any learning theory – that of stimulus-response – which is the justification for its more usual name of programmed learning. But its application is confined to the more routine parts of education. For the rest, where does the lecture stand in relation to *gestalt* or field psychology, or the set experiment to functionalism? How do the practices outlined above accommodate the varieties of individual 'abilities', perceptual capacities, personalities? It may be argued that some do – that, for example, a group discussion allows for different kinds of contributions. But is it well designed to do so, or is it rather an opportunity for students to demonstrate their differences (and some not even that) rather than build upon them to make learning more likely? The very combination of lectures, group discussions and student presentation, orally or in essays, displays a certain lack of confidence in the methods. The lecture is meant to promote understanding. But in order to promote understanding of the lecture, there have to be group discussions. And in order to secure even then that there has been understanding, there has to be a presentation by the student. Why not, one might wonder, start with the student's presentation and go on from there? In all the kinds of learning outlined earlier, it was clear that the various activities – the reflex actions, practice, chaining, verbal association, discrimination, concept- and principle-learning, problem-solving – were required of the *learner*. Most of the activities of higher education in effect require these things of the *teacher*. Consequently it is he, if anyone, who learns, not the student.

Perhaps the most reliable kinds of learning in post-school education are those described as 'incidental learning' – that is, by suggestion, imitation and identification. This is implicit in the practice of many teachers, in much of their performance in lectures, discussions and laboratory work. Some of them make it quite explicit.

The simple question this discussion raises is – are the actual practices of teachers in post-school education consciously designed to make the best use of what is known about learning? To my mind the answer is visibly, no. Teaching and learning are largely disconnected. Indeed I would say that there appear to be two kinds of need in the world, the need to learn and the need to teach. These two needs are at war. The one is incompatible with the other. The fact that it is so derives very largely from the acceptance of subjects, disciplines, bodies of knowledge, which the teachers have, and the taught do not; which the teachers have to present, and the taught 'acquire' and then reproduce. In these circumstances, learning is genuinely incidental, and what is learned is different from what the teachers intended.

All this is intermittently understood. It is known, for example, that the pretensions of academics are different from the experience of students. Academics typically claim that the experience they offer gives the student a body of knowledge, it is true. But they add that it inculcates a critical attitude of mind and gives a grasp of underlying principles a higher priority than the accumulation of facts or the acquisition of technique. At the end of their courses the students will (it is asserted) not only understand the extent and significance of their own subject but will show they can handle it, welcome what is new in it, explore it eagerly and above all work confidently on their own. They will have undergone a rigorous intellectual discipline which leaves them able to collect evidence for themselves and make a balanced judgement. They can think for themselves, and resist received opinion on the basis of reason (see Mountford, 1966).

The students typically report, however, that everything in their courses tends towards the accumulation of knowledge and the acquisition of skill. They find that having the knowledge does not itself enable them to apply it. Even when theory and practice are integrated, students may not be able to either apply the theory or to describe and defend their practice. (My whole argument asserts that teachers in post-school education cannot themselves defend their practice by relation to any theory.) The final examinations frequently demand little more than memory. As for the general intellectual gains attributed to this education, all one needs to do is to point to the way in which decisions are taken in educational institutions. It cannot be claimed that the most highly educated best display the attributes claimed for education. Nor is any of this surprising, since little in the student's' experience is explicitly designed to achieve the stated ends.

Some teachers in higher education have sought to meet these difficulties by stating the ends more clearly. The most elaborate example is the attempt of Benjamin Bloom and his colleagues to create a 'taxonomy' – that is, a classification – of objectives. These included knowledge (terminology, facts, methods, principles), comprehension (interpreting, extrapolating, determining con-sequences), application (general ideas, rules, procedures), analysis (reducing to parts and understanding their relationships, detecting unstated assumptions, distinguishing fact from opinion, recogniz-ing form and pattern), synthesis (communicating and planning, testing and deduction) and evaluation (judgement of value and methods) (Bloom, 1956).

Unfortunately this does not do the trick. You do not make the connection between learning and teaching merely by particulariz-ing what the teaching is for. You are still left with the question of whether or how the various activities of post-school education (the lecture, the discussion and so on) do ensure the attainment of understanding, analysis, synthesis and the rest.

There should, of course, be a sure way of discovering whether this is happening or not, in the form of assessment or evaluation which determines whether or not the student gets his degree, diploma or certificate. Unfortunately this is not so. The bulk of examinations are of the traditional type in which students have to give written answers to a number of questions within a specified time. These examinations appear to test mostly the very lowest category of performance, that of 'isolated recall', or plain memorizing. They test little of the understanding of concepts or principles, the ability to generalize or synthesize, or unfamiliar application. The students discover this very soon, and they distrust, as a consequence, those claims made for their education which suppose it to be otherwise. They assent that the examinations act against the very ends which academics claim to be serving. They describe them as 'irrelevant' (again), arbitrary, and unstandardized. So indeed they are. The marking of examinations is notoriously unreliable: different examiners differ widely. The failure rates are equally varied and cannot be seen to relate to the abilities or even the diligence of students. 'Standards' thus vary within institutions and from one institution to another. We return to the question, what has been tested? The students' cynicism over this derives from their experience that the clever and fluent student, working only in the last term before the examination, can gain exactly the same mark or classification as the diligent plodder who has done little else for three years. Nothing could reveal more brutally the fact that academics do not care about what they profess to be important. Neither do they show interest in the consequences of their teaching activities. They do not know and do not want to know what, if any, learning is taking place. They are all professors indeed – professing what they do not practise.

If I am right in this, it may help to explain the authoritarianism of most education. In a sense this needs no explanation: it is a question of power. The teachers possess the power, and the students do not. The teachers determine what the subject is and how it shall be presented. They arrange, before the students arrive, the course, curriculum, syllabuses, and the detail of timetables. The students must take it or leave it. The teachers also wield the power of awarding success or failure. But they are also intelligent people and could defend their activities if a defence were possible. It is not. So teachers in post-school education fall back upon authority. What is to be done shall be done in the way they say, because they *know* and because they say so.

Part Two: The Logic of Learning

It has been the argument of this chapter so far that this sorry state of affairs derives from the organization of knowledge in subject disciplines and its presentation to the students in this form. I now come to the most serious objection of all: that it is all based upon a view of knowledge which is quite simply mistaken. Its assumptions are pre-scientific, or at best rooted in a wrong view of science. Educational institutions have continued to act as if the most momentous intellectual developments of the world had not taken place. Most academics, and most scientists, have not yet understood the meaning of science or its implications for education.

This is a large claim, and I should be very hesitant in advancing it if it were mine alone. Indeed, left to myself I should no doubt have stopped this part of the book round about here, with expressions of irritation at a view of knowledge, and thus of education, which is authoritarian, cumulative, exclusive and arcane. Education, I have long felt, cannot mean an ever deeper initiation into the mysteries of a subject, nor research the gradual extension of a body of knowledge. If it is this, then it cannot serve anybody except academics. If education is to mean increasing mastery of their circumstances for most people, it must be differently based.

To anyone caught in this sort of unformed dissatisfaction the work of Sir Karl Popper comes as a stroke of liberation. In what follows, it will be clear that I have based myself very much on a Popperian view of knowledge, though explicit application to post-school education, as well as any failure of understanding, is of course my own.

What Popper has done is to assert the priority of logic over psychology in understanding the way in which we learn, think and discover. He himself has described the process of 'giving up the psychology of discovery and thinking' in two separate sections (10 and 15) of his autobiography (Popper, 1976). Later still (in section 29) he sets out his increasingly familiar schema for the logic of scientific discovery, which accompanies his substitution of falsifiability for induction as the criterion of science. One of the most startling and attractive things about Popper's writing is the integrity of his thought (and the autobiography is movingly honest about the time it took to achieve it), but it may help readers who are unfamiliar with it to separate what he has to say about learning and about science.

He early on distinguished three main types of learning, of which the first was fundamental. These were learning in the sense of discovery, learning by imitation, and learning by repetition. From his observation of young children he asserted that they needed discoverable regularities, settled routines and expectations, and unchanging 'things'. The learning process (in the sense of discovery) begins by forming these regularities and expectations, these theories, and this is its 'dogmatic' phase. It continues when these dogmas are tested against experience, in a 'critical' phase. Disappointed expectations, or refutations of the theory, create problems and lead to the trying out of other theories. It is an explanation of learning in terms of continuous trial and error. He sums it up as the '(dogmatic) formation of theories or expectations, or regular behaviour, checked by (critical) error elimination'.

Both dogmatic and critical phases are necessary to learning. Without dogma there is nothing for criticism to work on. Without criticism, no progress is made beyond dogma. It was this that led Popper to the view that there is no such thing as unprejudiced observation or passive experience. All observation has an aim, it is guided by problems and the context of expectations. Experience is the result of active exploration, of the search for regularities. Theories come before perception, and all learning is a modification of prior knowledge.

For Popper, learning by imitation is a special case of learning as discovery. And learning by repetition, or practising, differs from it in 'automatizing' certain actions so that they can be performed without attention.

These theories of learning are recognizably in the same world as the psychological theories described earlier. *Gestalt* psychology postulates the creation and modification of regularities. Functionalism postulates an inborn need to solve problems. The main difficulty is with some of the associationists: 'I came to realize that the theory of conditioned reflex was mistaken' (Popper, 1976). But Popper's theories are less limited: they seem to accommodate more of the learning process. They apply from the start to human beings, rather than to laboratory and circus animals. Above all, they are couched in logical rather than psychological terms. This latter characteristic is central to Popper's formulation of his theory of scientific discovery. He sets it out as a schema, or formula, the importance of which has been overlooked by people who feel that if something is clear it must be trivial. This is it:

$$P_1 \rightarrow TT \rightarrow EE \rightarrow P_2$$

What this schema summarizes is a view of scientific discovery akin to his view of learning as trial and error elimination. Scientific discussions, he says, start with a problem (P_1), to which we offer a tentative theory (TT) or solution, hypothesis or conjecture. The theory is then criticized, to try to eliminate error (EE) – whereupon the theory and its critical revision give rise to new problems (P_2). As Popper puts it, 'science begins with problems and ends with problems'. But it does not begin and end with the same problems: P_2 is always different from P_1 – which is why we can speak of scientific progress.

Each step in this formulation, and its place in the sequence, have important consequences. It asserts, for example, the primacy of problems. The beginning of an inquiry is *not* the attempt to solve a problem (the tentative theory comes second, not first): it is the problem itself, and it is important to work as hard as possible on the formulation of problems before searching for solutions. This is because success in the latter often depends upon success in the former. An enormous amount of time and energy is wasted in the world by people who jump straight into solutions, and concentrate upon the difficulties of these – without pausing to consider whether they are apt for the problem formulated or even without formulating a problem at all. (It is also misleading to talk of 'identifying' problems, as if the problems were sitting there waiting for us. They are not. Problem-formulation is a creative activity.)

Nor should one be misled by the word 'tentative'. A theory is tentative because it has to be tested: it does not have to be half-hearted. Indeed, the bolder and more definite it is the better it can be tested. What we need are theories with a high informative content, because the more information they contain the more likely they are to be false – but if they survive our best efforts to falsify them, they have enabled us to make a correspondingly large progress in understanding. The best theories are the most daring leaps of imagination, and science, like art, is an expression of the human spirit.

Error elimination is this process of expressing our theories in ways which can be tested. And the object of the test is to falsify the theory. This step is nearly as often neglected as the first – or is widely misunderstood. Neglect resides in the uncritical acceptance of theories, and in the unwillingness to consider what would falsify them. Misunderstanding arises because people think that the object of tests (or experiments) is to confirm a theory. But no amount of confirmation can make a theory more secure, and our knowledge remains as it was. But one falsification can destroy a theory – and our knowledge advances. We are ready to formulate the new problems.

With the introduction of falsifiability we reach Popper's criterion which demarcates science from non-science. This is itself one of those bold leaps of imagination whose consequences are only now being slowly realized. For example, it means that all knowledge, including scientific knowledge, is provisional, and always will be. We cannot prove that what we know is true, and it may turn out to be false. The best we can do is to justify our preference for one theory rather than another. Disciplines, even scientific disciplines, are not bodies of established fact: they are changing all the time, and not by the accumulation of new certainties. Of course, we assume the 'truth' of our existing knowledge for practical purposes and are quite ready to do so; but we must be ready for it to be superseded. What Popper has done is to replace the notion of certainty in science, and in all human knowledge, with the idea of progress. We cannot be sure that we have the truth: we can, however, systematically eliminate error. The way we eliminate error is by testing. In particular, observations are not used as the basis of a theory, but are derived from a theory and are used to test it. He says 'that observations, and even more so observation statements and statements of experimental results, are always *interpretations* of the facts observed; that they are *interpretations in the light of theories*' (Popper, 1959).

To readers not familiar with these ideas, it may help to say what it is that Popper is arguing against. Ever since Francis Bacon, scientists have been trying to say what it is that demarcates science from other human activities, and scientific knowledge from other kinds. Most have accepted that scientists base their activity upon observation, carefully controlled and measured observation. They record their findings, publish them and accumulate data. From this they may formulate hypotheses which fit the facts and explain the causal relations between them. They then seek evidence to support the hypothesis, and if the latter is thus verified they have established another law or theory. Science on this view, is the accumulation of certainties based on observation and experimental evidence. (If we had a formula it might be:

$$O_n \rightarrow H \rightarrow V \rightarrow L;$$

or numberless observations lead to a hypothesis which when verified is established as a law.) This method of basing laws on accumulated observations is known as induction, and has for centuries been seen as the hallmark of science. I am convinced that Popper has shown it to be mistaken. As he says: '. . . there is no induction, because universal theories are not deducible from singular statements. But they may be refuted by singular statements, since they may clash with descriptions of observable facts' (Popper, 1976).

It appears to me, however, that the organization and practice of higher education, both academically and institutionally, rests upon an implicit acceptance of induction; in other words upon a fallacy. It is impossible to speak, as academics do, of the preservation, extension and dissemination of knowledge unless one has in mind the gradual accumulation of certainties. The whole idea of the preservation of knowledge is alien to scientific method: what we should be seeking to do is destroy our present theories. The organization of subject departments is defensible if they are small groups working on the problems of the subject, but not if they are (as they are) bureaucracies for the issue of established bodies of fact. It is accepted that one needs to have a first degree before one can do research: as if to say to the students, when you know enough you can start to think. The whole activity of teaching, in lectures, seminars, tutorials or what you will, is explicable only on the basis that knowledge exists and can be imparted. The presence of courses, syllabuses and curricula assumes that knowledge is independent of problems: does anyone ever ask, to what problem is this degree course a solution? – and if he does, is the answer ever other than the problem of getting a degree? And what of the examinations at the end of these courses? Do they test more than the accumulation and manipulation of knowledge? Are the problems they pose any more serious than the problem of passing the examination? Does the ideal of a community of scholars survive in practice the division between the teachers and the taught – the one with the duty to know and impart, the other with the duty to accept and to learn?

Of course there have been many people with this sense of unease about the practice of education. More important, there have been many teachers who have either instinctively or after worrying thought tried to organize learning rather than teaching. They have encouraged 'discovery methods', project work and independent learning. But they have been under attack, partly because these methods still sit uneasily in the rest of the system (how, for instance, does one examine such work?) and partly because they have been unable to give as coherent an intellectual account of themselves as is claimed by traditional academics. This insecurity is no longer justified. It is the traditional academic practice which needs to be defended.

What we have, in fact, is a continuum of learning, whose logic is the same, from the new-born babe (indeed from the amoeba) to the research worker on the frontiers of knowledge. Each is engaged in the formulation of problems, in solving them and in testing the solutions. Most people will formulate problems that have been formulated many times before. Their proposed solutions will be familiar; their tests commonplace. But they will *learn* by this activity. They will not learn better or faster if we parcel up received solutions to problems formulated by others: indeed this is an anti learning process. Moreover it inhibits the possibility of progress, because it is always possible that someone will formulate a common problem differently, will propose a different solution or a more effective test.

At the other end of the continuum are those people engaged on formulating problems which have remained unformulated in the past, who are leading the attack upon ignorance at its strongest. They may indeed be working in a discipline, upon the problems of the discipline, though it is a commonplace of scientific discovery that the successful formulation of problems may involve breaking through the limits of the discipline. The leap of imagination required of them may be enormous. But the nature of their activity is not arcane. We are all learners: in logic we are equals.

There is, I think, something more to be said about problems and their formulation, if only because in my experience the idea of problems gives people trouble. In Popper's formulation of the logic of discovery he uses, interchangeably and often all together, a number of words for the second term of his schema – theory, solution, hypothesis, conjecture. This practice presumably derives from his impatience with discussions of meaning, which he regards as trivial. He does not wish understanding to be limited by definitions. What is more, it is part of what he is arguing that theories are solutions to problems and solutions, even to practical problems, are theories. But I find that for many people (indeed for me) it is useful to distinguish two kinds of problem: the first consists of problems of what is so, and why. The second consists of problems of how to get from one state of affairs to another. The first of these are commonly thought of as scientific problems, the second as problems of engineering. In everyday speech we are used to distinguishing between scientific theories and engineering solutions. The reason for mentioning this is that in confusing the two kinds of problem, people often inhibit the search for solutions. For example, the problems of explaining the physical world are met, in part, by the theories which make up the discipline of physics. The problem of getting to understand physics, or getting to be a physicist, may or may not be solved by learning or trying to learn all of physics. There are certainly more economical ways. Yet probably most people, and most physicists in post-school education, believe that the way to become a physicist and to put yourself in the position of solving the problems of physics is to learn everything that someone has decided constitutes (for the moment) physics. It is at least plausible that a capacity to formulate problems, of any kind, is at least as important. This is just one way in which existing theories may be mistakenly regarded as a solution to quite different problems, unless we are clear what kinds of problems we are dealing with.

What, then, are the consequences of the logic of learning and of discovery for the practice of education? I believe them to be shattering. In the first place, what is important is not a particular fact or even a particular ordered collection of facts, but *method*. It is method rather than information which gives mastery, and it is method which must be the chief business of education. Nor is there any need to insist upon a particular field of human interest in which scientific method can be understood: an educator can use any interest of the student as a vehicle.

Second, it is clear that existing subject disciplines are ways of organizing knowledge from particular points of view. They were so organized to solve the problems of their practitioners. But these problems may no longer actually be those even of existing practitioners, let alone those of students and potential students. The presentation of knowledge as bodies of organized facts is a way of ensuring its unhelpfulness to most people.

Third, the provisional nature of knowledge suggests caution in regarding education as involving the accumulation of it. This is recognized increasingly as educators and their students find that it is possible, indeed normal, for the knowledge painfully acquired to become quickly out of date. Unfortunately the educators' solution is to offer 'refresher' or 'up-dating' courses, so that the students can have his obsolete knowledge replaced by some more – which will itself become obsolete in turn. There can be no sense in this process.

Fourth, since criticism is of the essence of the method, education must offer opportunities for students to be critical and to use criticism. It cannot, even (indeed especially) for the sake of instruction, ask the students to accept the greater knowledge, experience, wisdom of the teacher.

This implies, fifth, that it is the students who must take the initiative in planning their own education. There can be little justification for the prior imposition of curricula and syllabuses. Such curricula must necessarily presuppose purposes which may not be the students'.

Sixth, in testing the efficacy of the education provided we shall need to examine what it is the student can *do*, rather than what he knows. The latter always was a somewhat arbitrary proceeding, since even if the most successful undergraduate were to know all that an undergraduate *could* know – his knowledge would still be infinitesimal. Since we can know so little (and since what we know is provisional) we can at least learn how to do something – and what we can most sensibly do is tackle our own problems.

Most important, perhaps, this view of education cannot exclude people, on the ground that they do not know enough, or have not had so many years' previous education, or do not show an aptitude for a subject. These educational arrogances have a place only in a superseded view of knowledge.

We are in short face to face with the chance of a creative revolution in education. For almost all its history and in almost every place education has tended towards the autonomous and the élitist. It has done so for what have been thought to be good 'educational' reasons. It is now clear that these reasons are not good: there is nothing to prevent education tending towards service and towards accommodating everyone. It can do so by accepting the logic of learning: by organizing education explicitly round the formulation of problems, the proposal of solutions and the testing of these solutions. It is to examples of such problems that we must now turn.

Part Three: The Problems of People

It is easy when discussing the practice of teaching or the logic of learning to lose sight of the practical problems to which education for all could be a solution. But educators ought to be able to move with elegance from high theory to mundane practice: that is their task. Educational ideas, however intellectually sound, must survive contact with reality. Indeed it is in the mutual stimulus of theory and practice that educational advance is to be sought. Let us therefore consider those people and those problems to whom education at present offers little or nothing. Take people trapped in what some people call a ghetto. They are poor, they are often desperately ill-housed, they are frequently unemployed, their children are ill-educated: the picture is familiar enough. Their handicaps are daunting: the amount of self-help needed to better their lot would overtax even the most fortunately placed and energetic. The reaction of society is to provide intermittent palliatives. These are not only inadequate, but in so far as they are prescribed from outside are often both inappropriate and stultifying. (There are innumerable examples of how the first efforts of a family in difficulties to help itself lead to a swift end to outside help. People who try may be worse off than people who do not.)

The reaction of educators to this has hitherto been peculiarly narcissistic. Faced with families in poverty and other difficulties, they have almost universally concentrated on the fact that the children of such families are not very good at education. This is on the whole true, and some money and effort has gone into improving their performance. Headstart programmes in the United States, nursery schools in England, are all designed to get a better educational performance out of the children of the poor. To do educators justice, they have argued that equalizing educational performance will help to avoid wide disparities of circumstances in the future.

Unfortunately it is now clear that the education system does little to equalize performance, let alone equalize social circumstances. But even had there been more success along these lines, the attempt still seems to me to be misconceived. More, it appears nothing less than frivolous to tackle the pressing problems of the present in ways that can affect them at the earliest a generation hence. In concentrating on the children, educators have shown that they are concerned more with education than with people. What has education to offer adults in difficulties?

The answer, regrettably, is that it has very little, because the adults do not see any help in educational programmes or institutions. The institutions themselves make it perfectly clear that entry to them depends on previous success in education – which is exactly what most people, and especially most poor people, cannot show. But cannot an education service begin to think of what it might do for men who are unemployed, for mothers with children in deplorable houses, for those who need to manage the forbidding social services, for communities surviving in the detritus of the industrial revolution? Or must its only service be to a minority who by some quirk of character or circumstances can 'profit' from what it has to offer? This degree of service was tartly characterized by R. H. Tawney as the tadpole philosophy: the unhappy lot of tadpoles is held to be supportable because a few tadpoles do go on to be frogs.

Education after school, then, is education for adults, all adults. And the job of the education service can be briefly stated. It is to go to adults, and help them to formulate their problems, to try solutions, to test them – and thus to build up a mastery of their circumstances. The accumulated wisdom of the ages is little use to an idle man with a depressed wife and two small ricketty children contemplating the damp pouring down the wall of their one room. But education need not be so impotent.

Touchingly enough, most people do have expectations of education, and these chime with the idea that it should be of some use to them. One of the most thoughtful inquiries into these expectations was carried out for the Schools Council by the Government Social Survey, in order to help schools to prepare for raising the school leaving age to sixteen in 1972. The inquiry was into the interests and motives of pupils between thirteen and sixteen and their views on what schools were doing to prepare them for adult life. One of the questions which it asked, of pupils, parents and teachers, was what a school is for. A representative number of fifteen-year-old school-leavers and their parents were asked which of a number of objectives of schools they considered very important. Very broadly speaking, most fifteen-year-olds thought objectives concerned with careers to be very important. Slightly fewer of them gave priority to other practical aspects of everyday life, like money management and running a home. Slightly fewer again rated highly the objective of self-development

137

(becoming independent, making the most of one's self and so on). Only about one in three of the children rated highly the objective of broadening the mind and developing interests and awareness.

To take some more detailed examples, when asked which school objectives were very important, 86 per cent of the boys and 88 per cent of the girls plumped for 'teaching things which will help you to get as good a job or career as possible' and 81 per cent chose 'teach you things which will be of direct use to you in your job'. Other career objectives were chosen as most important by 60 per cent or more of both boys and girls. Similarly, 78 per cent of boys and 83 per cent of girls picked as very important 'teach you how to manage your money when you are earning and about things like rates and Income Tax'. Some 78 per cent of girls picked 'teach you things that will be useful in running a home, for example, about bringing up children, home repairs, decorating'. Of both boys and girls 72 per cent chose 'teach you to put things in writing easily'. In all, over one half of the fifteen-year-old school-leavers chose help in these practical aspects of everyday life as very important objectives of schools.

Among the self-development objectives 66 per cent of boys chose 'help you to become independent and able to stand on your own feet' and 'teach you about what is right and wrong'. More of the girls chose these objectives: 76 per cent for right and wrong and 75 per cent for independence. Overall one half or more of both boys and girls thought self-development an important objective of schools. The contrast with the arousal of interests and awareness is stark. Neither of these was rated as very important by as many as half the children. Some 45 per cent of girls and 38 per cent of boys picked 'teach you plenty of subjects so that you can be interested in a lot of things'; 32 per cent of boys and 23 per cent of girls chose 'give you interests and hobbies that you can do in your spare time'. Only 4 per cent of boys and 8 per cent of girls chose 'study poetry in school and read and learn poems'.

There is some evidence in the inquiry that these views change as the pupils themselves grow older and have more experience of the world. In particular, nineteen-to-twenty-year-olds were less likely to feel direct use in jobs was very important and would have rated higher the development of their own capabilities and interests.

The opinions of parents on the whole backed up those of the pupils – except that 91 per cent of parents of both boys and girls put 'teach you to be able to put things in writing easily' as very important, and 90 per cent of girls' parents chose 'teach you to speak well and easily'. Similarly as many as 68 per cent of boys' parents and 69 per cent of girls' parents chose 'run clubs that you can go to out of school hours' – one of the interests and awareness group so neglected by their children. On the whole more parents thought that all school objectives were important than did their children!

The views of teachers, on the other hand, were the direct reverse of both parents and pupils. Most of them claimed aspects of self-development as very important, and many of them chose from the interests and awareness group. Only a half or fewer thought that school objectives related to careers were very important. For the rest both heads and other teachers stressed the schools' contribution to personality and character, independence, confident behaviour and moral training. Some parents would be astonished to discover that few heads or teachers put examination achievement high on their list of important objectives. Only 19 per cent thought exams very important.

What all these figures suggest is that schools and pupils are far from being at one in their estimate of what school is for. Both the fifteen-year-olds and their parents thought that school ought to provide knowledge and skills to enable young people to get the best jobs and careers. Teachers on the whole did not accept the achievement of vocational success as a major objective of education. What most of them thought important was the development of character and personality, the inculcation of ethical values and their maturing of personal relationships. The school-leavers and their parents generally supported this except that neither saw personality and character development as a main responsibility of the schools. The fifteen-year-olds also normally approved of instruction in the practical aspects of living, like managing money, being able to spell well and to put things into writing. Many fewer of them attached importance to the development of their interests and increasing their awareness of what was happening in the world.

These views were also reflected in what the pupils thought of their school subjects. The inquiry had an interesting table classifying school subjects under 'useful' and 'useless', and dividing each of these into 'interesting' and 'boring'. More than half the boys found metalwork, woodwork and English both useful and interesting. Only slightly fewer of them made the same judgement on mathematics, science, physical education and commerce, technical drawing and geography. Between 20 and 40 per cent thought the same of current affairs, art and handicraft, foreign languages and history. Between 10 and 20 per cent thought maths, foreign languages and English useful but boring. Just over one in ten thought art and handicraft useless but interesting. Between 10 and 20 per cent thought history, art and handicraft and current affairs useless and boring, and the same judgement was given by 30 and 26 per cent respectively for religious instruction and foreign languages. The accolade for uselessness and boredom went to music, judged to be so by half the boys.

The judgements of the girls were not significantly different overall. More than half found English and practical subjects like housecraft, commerce and needlework both useful and interesting. A similar number to the boys found maths and foreign languages useful but boring, and art and handicraft useless but interesting. With them too the accolade for uselessness and boredom went to music, though only a third of them judged it to be so. The major oddity with the girls was the finding that one in five of them regarded religious instruction as useful and interesting. Perhaps the most cheerful sign in all this for the schools is that very many more of the children were prepared to say that their school work was interesting than claimed it to be boring. Many more regarded their school work as useful than useless.

Parents tended to agree with their sons and daughters. More than two thirds of the parents of boys thought that English, mathematics, technical subjects and physical education were important at school, and over three quarters of the girls' parents plumped for domestic subjects, English and mathematics. One of the most constructive replies from the children was to questions about the subjects they wished they were better at. Substantial proportions of them wished they were better at mathematics and English. A number of them offered suggestions for helping this improvement, including more lessons in the subjects they considered important, more practical work and so on. But an appreciable number of them simply blamed their own lack of ability and assumed that nothing could be done to help them – a quiet but damning indictment of their education.

Asked what additional subjects they would choose if they became available, the largest proportion of boys (say one in six or seven) went for engineering subjects and foreign languages. Interestingly enough, nearly a quarter of the older nineteen-to-twenty-year-olds said they would like to have learnt foreign languages. Among the girls foreign languages were mentioned as an additional subject by about a quarter, about the same number as for commercial subjects.

It is the disparity between what people think education can do for them and what educators choose to provide that leads so many young people to leave school as soon as they can – and not to present themselves for the second and third levels of education. Yet a response to people's expressed needs would not lack for subject matter. Nor would the creation of competence. Let us look at these notions a little more closely.

It is beginning to be a desperate need for modern societies as a whole to become competent in managing themselves, in changing and in formulating and tackling their problems. This is necessary at both the national and international level and involves large questions of politics, economics and social organization. It is necessary at the more local levels, in firms and organizations, in local government, in voluntary societies and the like. Modern societies are complex organizations, and they are not obviously universally successful. But it is surely not too ambitious to suggest for the education service the role of the creative critic. By this I mean that educational institutions can help a society to formulate its problems, to suggest solutions, to test these solutions and monitor their consequences, to propose alternatives and test those – and so on. The formulation of problems requires the ability to conceptualize and to develop alternative ideas about a situation. The suggestion of solutions requires some understanding of what has been tried before elsewhere and with what consequences. The testing of policies and the monitoring of institutions may call upon the insights and techniques of many disciplines. None of society's institutions is potentially so full of these capacities as is the education service, even though that service has been tardy in making them available in the past.

Making society and its institutions more competent is only one aspect of this task of the education service. The other is to make individuals competent in the whole range of personal and social activity. I believe, for example, that people can be helped to be competent in personal affairs, to understand themselves and their strengths and weaknesses, to develop the ability to build on strength and to remedy weakness. People can become more conscious, not only of their capacities but of their motives and emotions. In doing so they can become more effective people. Similarly they can become more competent in social relations, learning how to make their personal contacts with others more fruitful and harmonious. They can be helped to understand their own prejudices and those of others and in doing so to transcend them.

Democracy requires political competence of a high order. Nobody ever took seriously Robert Lowe's aphorism that 'we must educate our masters'. Anyone can draw a cross on a ballot. But if democracy is not to be merely oligarchy tempered by electoral defeat, people need to know how to run democratic institutions. If power is to be shared, people need to know how to use it. They need to know how social institutions work and how they can be changed.

Consider, for example, the kinds of services that exist in Britain to meet family needs, the kind of use that is made of them and extension of them that seems called for. There are family doctors, health visitors, social workers, family planning clinics – all offer help and advice, yet all fall short of the comprehensive *educational* service that is required, if people's needs are to be met. Or take the needs which arise when people determine to do something about their environment: the need for political understanding and skills, the need for legal understanding, the need for organizing ability, the need to assimilate facts, policy, decisions and regulations. This sort of competence has to be learned.

The most familiar version of competence is economic: the ability to earn a living and to maintain oneself and one's family. But vocational training has usually been conceived so narrowly as to amount almost to an academic discipline. It has been assumed that the training of an electrician can consist chiefly of the theory and practice of electrification. But it is clear to anyone who has a man in to do some wiring that the skill is the least difficult part of the business, which requires that the technician knows how to manage his work, to soothe his customers, to get on with his colleagues, to manage his superiors so that he gets the supplies he wants – and so on. Vocational competence must also include a knowledge of how an enterprise works and how an individual can get the most out of it, either singly or in concert with others.

Perhaps most people would accept, as Western society struggles with depression, that economic competence is most urgent. As I understand it the difficulty of the poor in advanced economies, especially the United States and increasingly in Western Europe, is that the pattern of jobs is changing, often quite fast. At the turn of the century most of the labour force was engaged in manual work. The early development of technology – railways, building, factories – required vast amounts of unskilled labour. Given a high demand the working man could usually find someone to buy his labour even though he might not get much in return for it.

Today the situation has changed. The labour force has a quite different appearance, so that in the United States white collar workers outnumber blue collar workers. Farm workers who at the turn of the century accounted for one worker in every three, now account for only 5 per cent of the work force. There is also projected a general net decline in unskilled work, as part of the overall change in the nature of work. What we are seeing is a tremendous growth in technology and human services – in health, welfare, education and recreation. It has become a highly professionalized work world with little opportunity for the unskilled and the uneducated.

In other words, one of the most obvious characteristics of advanced industrial societies is that the number of jobs requiring no skill diminishes and the fastest growing areas of employment are in government and social service which require education and training. The plight of the negro in an urban community in the United States is precisely that the jobs he could do are disappearing and the jobs available are not for the ill-educated. This fate awaits the children of manual workers in Britain unless we can readily alter the bias of our education system.

There is a final element of competence which many readers will feel is stretching the meaning of the word: I refer to recreational competence. I do not share the cant view that we shall all be a leisured class before we know where we are, desperate for something to do. I see no evidence that this is at all likely. I do not believe in 'education for leisure'. This is a concept which accompanies the patronizing view that for most people work must be a boring and mechanical necessity offering them no satisfaction of any kind. Certainly it looks as though the most repetitive jobs which can be better done by machines are being taken over by machines, and a good thing too. But what the displaced workers need is not leisure but another, and better, job. Preparation for this must be part of an increased vocational competence. But all of us have spare time, and we all of us feel that we might use it better. Provision for the arts, hobbies, sports and even spectator activities seem to me to be a legitimate part of any further education service.

This is merely a shortlist of the kinds of competence which an education service could help to develop. To some it may sound almost impossibly utopian. They may be comforted to know that the bones of it already exist, in Britain at any rate, in the further education institutions we already have. Patchy though it is, inadequately housed and staffed, subject always to the sneers of left-wingers about 'mere' vocational education or 'ballroom dancing and flower arranging', our further education institutions are the places, so far the only places, where people go for courses which help them to understand themselves and society about them, which give them vocational training, which introduce them to the methods of political and social action – and which enable them to pursue their multifarious hobbies and other interests. The service tradition is not only of long standing, it is visibly at work.

If education were even better organized to help people to be competent, there could be no complaint about the content or level of work required. Academics who strayed into courses provided for these purposes might be tempted to describe them in terms of the familiar disciplines of economics, sociology, political science, public administration, psychology, mathematics, statistics and the like. And courses such as I have described would be a better introduction to scientific method than most existing degree courses in physics, chemistry and biology. As for level, a person who manages to master the complexities of laws and official regulations and to discover what kinds of action and assistance these make possible will have been operating on at least the level of a postgraduate course in research methodology. It is my experience that people who could not conceivably imagine themselves on such a course as these exist at the moment, will in practice attain as high a degree of sophistication in knowledge and method when their own homes or children are affected.

What, then, is a course of education if it is not a syllabus or a curriculum in the traditional sense – if its purpose is not to study a subject, cover the ground, understand physics or learn a certain amount of history? It may be that we are now ready to offer an answer to this question – since it is clear that such an answer must begin not from the needs or structure of a subject but from the needs of the student. What is it that he hopes to get out of the course? How should an institution set about planning to provide it?

The first thing is obviously to formulate the student's problems. He has come to the institution in the first place because he wants help that he cannot get elsewhere. What is it that he wants to be able to do when the course is finished that he could not do before it started? There are innumerable answers to this question. It may be that he wants to get a job, or a better job than the one he has. He may want to do his present job better. He may want to get some control over his own immediate circumstances, through doing something himself, combining with others or by pressurizing those responsible. He may want to perfect a skill or deepen understanding. Human beings are likely to express many goals, and some will want to achieve more than one at a time. The definition of these goals is a serious business, needing time and (for people who are not used to doing it) help. At present it takes place, if at all, in ways that are both hurried and desultory. And some of the methods proposed to remedy these defects are simply breathtaking. For example, the much praised 'foundation year' at Keele University is admired because of the chance it gives to students to change their courses, and its success is measured by the fact that numerous students do this. Only an autonomous institution could be happy at spending a *year* of someone's life in such a process, whatever other advantages the 'foundation' might offer. So long as educators imagine they have all the time in the world they will remain useless to most people. The challenge before them is to find speedy sure ways of helping people to determine their objectives and the ways in which they will attain them.

What a student wants to do at the end of the course is not the whole story. He needs to know what he is like at the beginning. This may sound crass – but in fact very few of us understand ourselves very well, and perhaps most people have a poor idea of their own strengths and weaknesses. The second priority for the student, therefore, is to know what he himself brings to the course. This, too, is a serious business, though there will be some temptation in educational circles to over-elaborate it. It should not at this stage be necessary to go in for in-depth exploratory sessions, T-groups or group dynamics: all of which are ways of prolonging the process past the patience or practical situation of most people. All that is needed is that the students are brought to realize what it is they have and lack – so far as their goals are concerned. Of these two areas, it is important to emphasize what they have, because it is upon this that they will build. The skill for the educator resides in helping a student to see what characteristics he possesses to enable him to get what he wants. It is also important (and more usual in education) to reveal weaknesses, so that the student can be helped to remedy them or minimize their effect. But perhaps the guiding principle here is the immortal sentence of Dr Spock (with which *Baby and Child Care* opens): 'You know more than you think you do.'

This definition of the student's capacities is important for another reason: it questions the purpose of 'requirements' which educational institutions lay down for potential students. We shall return to this again: enough for the moment to point out that the practice of building on a student's strengths and seeking to remedy his weaknesses is quite different, in approach and effect, from telling him that he has to have achieved something before he can start. To say that before embarking on post-school education one must have reached a certain standard is for most people like telling a man who asks the way to Norwich that if you wanted to get to Norwich you would not start from here. It is the business of educational establishments to devise ways for people to get to where they want to go from where they are now.

This, in essence, is what a course should be. We know the student's present situation and circumstances, his character and abilities. We know what his goals are. A course is simply the means by which he gets from one to the other. This poses problems for the student and the institution, and although these problems look similar and are discussed in similar terms, they are in fact rather different. For the student the problem is how he himself is to proceed. The problem for the institution is planning, because the institution wants to serve large numbers of different people. The more the institution tries to treat each student as an individual, the more complicated the planning will threaten to become. Its response to the demands of students will depend on its success in predicting (but not prescribing) what these will be. But perhaps it is now time to see what such predictions would amount to in practice.

Part Four: Independent Study – An example

At the North East London Polytechnic my colleagues and I have created a new programme of higher education. Our opportunity arose with a report by a Government inquiry into the education and training of teachers (James, 1972), though by the end both we and the Government had moved away from the simple concern with teacher training. The essence of the James Committee's proposal was for a two-year course of higher education of a general rather than a specific nature which involved no irreversible commitment to a vocation or a subject specialization. Its successful completion would attract the award of a new diploma – the

Diploma of Higher Education, which would represent a substantial step towards alternative vocational or academic goals including professional qualification as a teacher and the award of a degree.

By the end of 1972 the Government had announced (White Paper, 1972) that it was committed to the idea of the new diploma but said specifically that its proposals were 'designed to serve a wider purpose than that envisaged in (the James) report'. The new diploma was to have six characteristics: it was to be no less demanding intellectually than the first two years of a degree course and the normal minimum entry qualification was to be the same as degree or comparable courses. It was to be a new option in both public and autonomous sectors of higher education and covering both general and specialized courses. The new award was to be made generally acceptable as a terminal qualification and in particular as giving access to employment. It should be seen as a foundation for further study and should be designed to earn credit towards other qualifications including degrees and the requirements of professional bodies. It should be validated by existing degree-awarding bodies, like the Council for National Academic Awards and the universities. Students working for the diploma would qualify for mandatory awards.

Long before the White Paper, and indeed as soon as the James Committee reported, the Director of our polytechnic set up a working party of seven to make proposals for a programme leading to the new diploma. The members of the working party were anxious to use the James recommendations as an occasion and the basis for a substantial innovation in higher education. In our initial planning we consciously followed the James proposals even to the extent of adopting the James terminology. We were also conscious that our work in the polytechnic was itself a contribution to the national discussion about the Diploma of Higher Education. We believed that it was important to try to work out the broad proposals for the new award in the context of the policies and circumstances of a particular institution.

The North East London Polytechnic is unusually self-conscious among British institutions of higher education about its policies and objectives. An important principle of its policy is to design courses round the needs of prospective students rather than to seek students to fit the courses that the polytechnic would like to run. It has sought to attract those who would be 'likely to benefit' from its courses rather than selecting those who, on the evidence of some formal entry requirement, might be predicted to succeed. It also has an established commitment to the people of its locality: the polytechnic's buildings are spread through three East London boroughs, and two of these have the lowest take-up of higher education in the country.

The working party took, as a basic planning principle, a somewhat crude 'systems' approach. We started by considering the students who were likely to come into the programme, and we then considered the qualities and capacities we wished them to display at the end of it. The problem for us, then, was to design a programme which would get them from where they were to where they wanted to be. Of course we did not imagine that our descriptions, either of entrants or of leavers, would be complete. We did not try to describe them in detail at either stage, but concentrated on those characteristics which seemed relevant to our planning, so our description of entrants was in terms of stereotypes and of leavers in terms of general characteristics. For example, we expected that the entrants would be both men and women, but since nothing in our planning was to depend upon this distinction this characteristic did not form part of the stereotypes.

We believed that in planning the programme we should give priority for those who were either unattracted by existing higher education or for those who had hitherto settled for a course of teacher training. In the end, the stereotypes of entrants were as follows:

The school-leaver who is inclined to a career in school teaching or work with children but is not quite sure about this and has no wish for a conventional academic course;

The school-leaver who is content to continue with the subjects studied in the sixth form but has no strong commitment to them – a type of student who hitherto has often proceeded into general arts or science degree courses;

The school-leaver who expresses a (frequently vague) desire to pursue studies and career that 'have something to do with people' – a type of student who hitherto has often applied somewhat indiscriminately for admission to courses in sociology, psychology, social work;

The student in his early twenties who has not established himself in a career and has developed a desire to return to full-time education to prepare for a career, but has no clearly formulated objective;

The older student who has established himself in a career, has decided upon a clean break and wishes to raise his standard of education prior to the pursuit of a new career (NELP, 1974).

In considering the entrants, we were immediately faced with the problem of entry requirements. The James Report had recommended that 'The normal requirement for entry to Dip.H.E. courses should be the possession of two A levels in the G.C.E., but there should be generous provision for the exceptions in the case of mature entrants and those applicants who, although possessing different formal qualifications, are strongly motivated to teaching and give promise of becoming effective teachers.' As we have seen, the White Paper too asserted that the normal minimum entry qualification should be the same as for degrees. These requirements presented us with some difficulty. We regarded the James formulation as a brave rationalization of the existing position where two A levels (with three O levels) were generally accepted as the minimum entry qualification for degree courses and where something less than this was acceptable for a course of teacher training. Thus A level was held to be some guarantee of academic standard or of general education for which strong motivation was in part an acceptable substitute. We ourselves doubted the significance of two passes at A level as an indicator of a standard of general education. Existing courses in higher education varied in the extent to which they demanded achievement in particular subjects at A level as a prerequisite. Clearly a programme of general education, open to all students with two A levels of any kind, could presume no subject knowledge or skill which had been developed by all students to that level. We wished, too, to give more weight than was usual in degree courses to those qualifications which were attained in further education colleges, like Ordinary National Certificates and Diploma, which were recognized as in some way comparable with A level. And we particularly wished to take advantage of the James Report's acceptance of motivation as a substitute for formal qualifications particularly in mature students. We thus initially laid down minimum entry requirements as follows:

Passes in two subjects in G.C.E. at A level, together with passes in three other subjects at O level or C.S.E. grades 1 or 2 in three other subjects or;

Pass in O.N.C. or O.N.D. or;

Pass in Intermediate examination of a recognized professional body (on a list to be prepared) or;

Formal qualifications (e.g. of overseas examining bodies) equivalent to the above.

We added:

Generous provision for exceptional admission should be made for applicants who produce evidence of strong motivation to further education. Such applicants who are under the age of 21 should have completed 7 years of secondary education or its equivalent in full time and part time education.

In the matter of entry requirements we were assisted by a study group set up by the CNAA and the UGC to establish 'guidelines' for the Diploma of Higher Education. In its guidelines the study group accepted the White Paper formulation for entry requirements and added:

Institutions offering the diploma should be willing to accept a wide range of qualifications and/or experience as equivalent to the above G.C.E. attainments. This would include such qualifications as O.N.C. and O.N.D., or evidence of appropriate attainment in such fields as art, music, drama or physical education.

Institutions should exercise their discretion in waiving normal entry requirements in the case of mature students who have appropriate experience or alternative qualifications.   (Guidelines, 1973)

We regarded this second paragraph as being especially important, and said in our final submission that we would indeed waive formal entry requirements for strongly motivated applicants.

We realized that our stereotypes of entrants, quoted earlier, referred both to their characteristics and their objectives. Our description of the characteristics of leavers from the programme was consequently rather general. We expected them to go into careers in which a general education was highly valued and which did not require specialist technical expertise. We thought there would be four major career areas: in business and public administration; teaching; social work; and communications. We did not intend the Dip.H.E. to be an adequate terminal qualification for careers in these fields, nor did we think these were the only ones for which our Dip.H.E. would give an adequate general education. But we found it helpful to have these career areas in mind when we discussed the more detailed objectives of students. We particularly hoped that our programme would contribute significantly to the provision of highly skilled recruits for employment in North East London.

In deriving more precise objectives for the course from these general potential areas, our working party decided that all these jobs required identifiable skills. It was central to our approach that these skills were definable, necessary and teachable. We conceived the student's objectives in our programme as those of a general education defined in terms of skills relevant to his ultimate vocational goals. We assumed that there was a wide range of skills which could be defined and assessed and which constituted a common base for employment or further education and training.

We said that we expected that these skills would include the following:

Competence in basic skills so as to:
1. read, write, speak and use mathematical methods;
2. use techniques, like graphic presentation and typewriting, audio taping, electro/mechanical calculating, filing.

Competence in particular skills, separately and in appropriate combination, enabling him to:
1. identify, from a variety of sources of information, which particular sources are relevant to a defined need;
2. find, select and use written graphical and oral material appropriate to this defined need;
3. create and organize such material;
4. organize and involve himself in both formal and informal group activities such as committees, seminars and work teams;
5. use mathematical and statistical tools and methods of logic as aids to thought and analysis.

Competence in general skills, separately and in appropriate combination so as to:
1. formulate and agree problems, propose alternative solutions and test them;
2. generate, implement and evaluate programmes of action involving others;
3. identify in given situations, problems of personal and social values, judgements and decisions;
4. relate his thinking to established bodies of thought and knowledge and thereby to make use of these;
5. identify for any course of action and for separate elements in it the evidence which would indicate failure.

Competence in the ability to:
1. consider, select and define a field of special interest and then pursue this interest for a period of at least twelve months;
2. relate his special interest studies to the body of existing knowledge in that area;
3. recognize and characterize the subject methodologies involved in that area;
4. relate theoretical approaches in his area of special interest to current practices in the field;
5. characterize and distinguish between the likely approaches to a given situation or set of problems, taken by:
    philosophers, sociologists, psychologists, economists, technologists, scientists, designers, artists, etc.;
6. where appropriate – read, write and speak in a language other than English (NELP, 1974).

In order to pursue these objectives we saw it as our duty to create a programme which would offer specific tuitition to enable the student to develop his competence; the means to practise the coordination and transferability of skills in action; an intellectual environment to foster competence in the student to act decisively and rationally in a variety of open situations; a framework for guidance to help the student to define, direct and develop his own studies; a work context where each student could act effectively as an individual and in groups; and a range of provision to help the student to work towards vocational and academic goals.

As our discussion proceeded a number of changes occurred in our proposals which were reflected in their final formulation. We had begun by taking over the idea of general and specialist studies directly from the James Report. The more we discussed these, and even more when we came to put our ideas into practice, the more we found ourselves agreeing that general or central studies would best be pursued in groups of students with different specialisms, interests and career goals, and that specialist studies would best be pursued individually, alongside our colleagues in other parts of the polytechnic. In other words some features of the students' education were best accommodated centrally, involving the staff and students on the Dip.H.E. programme itself, and some would be better arranged by calling on the individual help of the staff of the polytechnic as a whole. The division was not absolute of course: many skills would be fostered in both modes of study. What occurred, however, was that a formulation taken over as a matter of expediency from the James Report soon began to be worked out in rather different terms in the course of serious educational planning. The consequences of this will be seen later.

Another development was even more important. We started, it is true, from a systems approach to course planning. We established our stereotypes of entrants and the characteristics of leavers, and we began to plan a programme by which the students would go from one to the other. Over a considerable period of time, and after many false starts, we realized that to do this was to fall into a logical difficulty. If we were to provide for the development of students from where they were to where they wanted to be, was there not some inconsistency in determining the programme in advance? Surely what we should do was to provide the student with the means by which he himself could determine seriously both his present situation and his future goals, and then create his own programme which would take him from one to the other. From a fairly conventional desire to create a new course we moved imperceptibly to the idea of providing opportunity for independent study. What we had to do, as planning staff, was to *predict* the range of provision which students would want us to make, not to prescribe the courses they should take.

To this end we decided that our programme should begin with a planning period, lasting for a total of six weeks. This was particularly important because we had to assume that whatever their backgrounds the entrants would have a view of what educational programmes were like which was quite different from our own. Whatever we could say in an initial interview, they would still half expect to find that the essence of their 'course' would be a stated syllabus leading to a written examination. Their experience of such examinations would lead them to suppose that the questions would be reasonably predictable in form if not in content. We assumed, therefore, that the entrants would have had no experience of creating a programme for themselves.

We hoped that they would be astonished both by the amount and the kind of work expected of them. We asserted that this would in itself have an important effect on morale and would help them to become accustomed in a short time to the methods we proposed. The central principle of the planning period was that the students should accept responsibility for their own activity. Everything that they agreed to do was to carry with it an obligation to note their own activity and progress and to seek critical assessment of it from staff and peers.

With the first entrants we gave the most general indications of what we intended, confining ourselves largely to descriptions of our approach to planning and insisting, if anything, upon making clear the view of knowledge and learning that was implicit in it. By the second year we had come to feel that this was being less than fair to students. In our desire not to prescribe, we were in danger of being both unhelpful and misleading. We therefore created a draft form of statement which made explicit the logic of the planning process through which the students were to go. They were to state first of all what they took to be their present qualifications, experience, capacities, skills, strengths and weaknesses. We hoped that they would be able to see this as an opportunity to reveal positively to themselves and their colleagues what it was they brought to the programme and which gave them the promise of being able to proceed. They were then to outline their personal, academic and vocational plans after gaining the diploma – and then to translate these into a statement of the skills, knowledge, capacities and qualities that they would need by the time the programme ended to accomplish these plans. The next step was to persuade the students to formulate the problems which arose from their desire to get from where they described themselves to be to where they wanted to be. Their outline solution to these problems in effect was to constitute their programme for attaining the diploma.

In addition to this the statement had to include the criteria by which the student's performance could be tested for qualifying assessment and a more detailed statement of a programme of activities for the remainder of the first term. It concluded with a note that the statement itself could be varied, with the agreement of tutors, provided that the variations and reasons for them were made explicit and were set out in a similar form to the initial statement. The student had to gain the assent of two tutors to this statement.

In common with other polytechnics, new programmes of higher education at North East London are validated by the Council for National Academic Awards, an independent validating body whose operations are described in more detail in the next chapter. Normally the Council requires as a basis for its validation not only a statement of purpose and philosophy of aims and objections, but an outline of the proposed course in some detail. It is used to studying curricula, syllabuses and timetables – knowing, in other words, with some precision what the students will be doing on the course as it proceeds. We were clearly unable to offer any such outline. It is true that we drew up examples of the kind of thing that we expected students to do, and we felt obliged to show how any such demands could practically be met by the arrangements we proposed both in the School for Independent Study and in the Polytechnic as a whole. But we had to say, of course, that these were purely hypothetical outlines. Our problem was to find some way of assuring the Council in advance that the individual programmes of students would be acceptable without acting in such a way as to prescribe what those programmes were to be. The device we hit upon was an external validating board whose job it would be to act as a check upon the nature and quality of the students' proposals. It is important to realize that the Validating Board was to be concerned with the student's *planning*, not with his performance. The latter task was to be assessed in the normal way and the assessment moderated by external examiners. In the event the Validating Board has been extremely influential. Its existence ensures real seriousness in the planning period. The students know that they have to meet the Board and that their own individual programme may be discussed with a member of it at length and in detail. This means that the planning process is itself under outside scrutiny. In the first year, both we and the Board were feeling our way towards some effective procedures. By the second year we had been able to arrange that every single student met a member of the Board on the day of their visit, if only together with a group of his peers. A quarter of the students were seen individually by a Board member. The Validating Board has been able to say that in its view the capacity of our students to understand, to explain and to defend the educational task they were undertaking and the programmes they were creating, is far more extended than is usual even in the later years of higher education.

The second task which the Board undertook was to help to keep open the genuine possibility of independent study through the creation of programmes which may differ radically from that which we ourselves had predicted. In this they were to act as a kind of court of appeal, before which a student could defend a unique proposal. The possibility was to remain open for students to convince the Board of the validity of a programme for which they have not managed to gain the agreement of staff. This situation has in fact arisen.

As explained earlier, we gradually came to the view that most students would find, in their planning, that they would require two modes of study. The first was in what we began by calling 'central studies' and came increasingly to refer to as 'group work'. Here the students, together, in large or small groups plan a programme of activities, all of which are vehicles for the solution of individual problems. Each activity has two outcomes, one of them a group product, the other the individual student's report upon it. The object of group work is to enable the students to gain and demonstrate the capacity for the joint planning and implementing of educational proposals. The scale of the projects may vary from a small group working on a limited topic for one or two days to an elaborately planned exercise by a group of eight or more lasting for half a term.

The second mode of study was what we began by calling 'special interest' work and have increasingly come to call 'individual work'. Here the students find members of staff elsewhere in the Polytechnic who are ready to accept them as individuals and to create for them some form of tutorial relationship.

The relationship varies greatly. Some students assist staff in a way that is more familiar with research students. Others arrange simply a weekly or fortnightly supervision period at which their work is presented and discussed. Others embark upon a guided course through existing lecture or seminar programmes. What is common to all of them is that by the end of their two years they are capable of creating and presenting for assessment a piece of independent work.

Few people in higher education have any difficulty in accepting that such a piece of work, call it a project or thesis, is acceptable as a basis for qualifying assessment. Our other form of qualifying assessment is less familiar. In it we seek to judge the student's capacity to organize the work with others and in particular to use the skills he has acquired in new and unfamiliar circumstances. The whole of group work in the last term is therefore devoted to a 'set situation' in which students are placed in unfamiliar groups of five and are required to formulate a problem or problems, to propose solutions and to say how they will be tested. The acceptability of the problem formulated is judged on a number of criteria. It must enable each individual to demonstrate his achievement of his own agreed objects within the group activity; it must be open to solution in the form of a group project within the stated time; it must have its origins in or relevance to the local community of the Polytechnic and be demonstrated to be socially useful; it must include a technical or scientific perspective; and it must require students to seek, collect and analyse data from a library and field sources. It is on the basis of this set situation and the individual work project that qualifying assessment is made.

As this book was being written two intakes of students had begun the diploma programme. Of the seventy-three entrants in the first year and one hundred and one in the second, forty-five had the normal university qualifications, one-hundred and six were mature students – that is they were over twenty-one but without the normal qualifications – and twenty-three were neither mature nor normally qualified. We have been unable to distinguish, in their subsequent progress, any significant difference in aptitude or performance between these three groups. As part of our object was to encourage people from the locality to apply to us we have been particularly pleased that of the first entry 7 per cent have come from our three local boroughs and from the second year 18 per cent. The proportion of all our students from Greater London is 70 per cent.

This description has been brief, but I hope that it has been sufficient to suggest that it is possible to enable students to create their own programmes of higher education, to offer this opportunity to most people whether or not they have done well in the education service in the past, and to be, in short, a genuine service to the community. The programme differs from others in higher education in that it is based, not upon subject disciplines or upon combinations of subjects, but upon the logic of learning. It is this which gives the programme its coherence and the students an assurance of its value. I have no doubt that there are other ways of achieving the same ends, and I trust that there are many better ways. But I hope our programme has shown that the task now is to look for such improvement, because alternatives to the traditional system are clearly possible.

Part Five: The task of the 'teacher' in independent study

The reaction of many of our colleagues and others to the notion of independent study, in which students create their own programmes of academic work, is – where does this leave the staff? Some cynically believe we are taking our wages for nothing. Others even more cynically assume that we do not mean what we say, but are teaching away like mad, just like everyone else, while publicly pretending not to do so. Some go even further and say we are deluding ourselves – that we must have a 'hidden curriculum', just as restrictive as a subject discipline and all the more dangerous for being unacknowledged. When I assert that teaching and learning are opposing activities, and that one precludes the other, I am met either with incredulity or with attempts to neutralize what I am saying by a discussion of what I mean by teaching. Without making too heavy weather of it, we are under some obligation to say what the staff are for. The rigorous auto-didact is rare: what is it that other learners need to make their learning more effective? I think this can be summed up as confidence, access and criticism, and this section offers some examples of each.

The first thing learners need is confidence. Learning simple skills, like riding a bicycle or swimming, is almost wholly a matter of confidence. Anyone who will get on to a bike and pedal off will learn to ride it without any instruction at all, and some people do in fact learn it in this way. For more complex operations, like creating and following a programme of education, confidence is needed both to start and to persevere. So much is an educational truism, and many are the injunctions to teachers to respond positively to the work of pupils or students before they begin to judge it. For independent study we have to go even further. Our students have to have enough confidence to welcome failure. This is because it is through failure, properly used, that we learn. The educative function of practice and experience is that we learn to do things well by first doing things badly and then doing them better. The world is unhappily full of people who fear to fail, and thus fail to learn. Students must be confident enough to fail, to face failure and to use it.

It is the experience of most people in education that makes them fear failure. In their experience failure has carried penalties, even punishments. It may have closed doors for them for life. Failure has meant their learning less, not more. No wonder they fear to venture and need their confidence restored.

Facing failure means accepting explicit criticism from others and developing self-criticism. The way to do better is to find out what can be improved and to improve it. We need to seek out shortcomings, not conceal or ignore them. Criticism is to be welcomed. But again most people have learned to resent criticism and to expect it to be resented. The ability to accept and act on it is enormously liberating, and comes from confidence.

Most important of all, we are asking the students to plan their own programmes. To do so, they must start from themselves: they are what they have got; they do not start with someone else. So they need to estimate accurately their own abilities and have confidence in them. They need to be clear about their weaknesses and have the confidence to face and remedy them.

Methods of creating confidence are legion – from appearing in battle-dress and beret and uttering clipped sentences from the top of a tank to the display of infinite wisdom and understanding. In education the teacher tries to judge which of the reactions available to him will work with a particular student or group of students. The disparity of activities engaged in by students studying independently makes the creation of confidence a matter of judgement that can impose very serious demands.

But organization can help. In the early stages of a programme the activities proposed must be nicely judged to offer the necessary element of safe risk, so that students can venture and succeed enough to be ready to discuss failure. This means that teachers need to have at hand, not a ready-made programme of events, but a repertoire of activities from which they can respond, as necessary, to the needs of students.

But I suspect that more important even than this is a sense of control, not of the course (which is a contradiction) but of one's physical and intellectual material. Students, like armies, need to be sure of their supply lines: otherwise they plunder the countryside. They need to know what is available to them, and how they can get it. They need to know what is to happen and when. They are justified in requiring that announced events take place, at the time and place stated, and that it is physically possible for them to meet the educational demands made upon them. (If it is not, the demands must be changed.) The enemy of morale is muddle. All this sounds trite – but people outside education would be astonished to know with what frequency and insouciance courses are changed, lectures cancelled and required work (like essays) neglected.

Students also need to be sure that the staff know what they are doing – and can give a coherent and convincing account of it. No two teachers will agree about everything, but all those responsible for a programme need to be clear what it is they do agree about, and what gives intellectual coherence to their actions. Students are not fools, and sooner or later even the most apathetic of them will ask what a teacher thinks he's up to. He needs a good, clear statement in reply. Quite as many students lose heart through the intellectual muddle and vagueness of their teachers as through the incompetence of academic organization.

Allied to intellectual coherence is intellectual honesty. Students need to know that we have standards, and to know what these standards are. There are some teachers who fear that criticism will undermine a student's confidence, or who simply fear to offend. I am sure this is mistaken. It has usually the reverse effect from that intended. The student soon comes to worry at the lack of reaction, and to distrust his own judgement and the capacity of his teacher. The task is to help a student to take criticism, not to shield him from it.

Finally, there is nothing so conducive to confidence as being treated seriously as an individual, valued for oneself and respected for the contribution one makes. Again, there seems to be no method that will not have this effect in some circumstances: the problem of judgement is a delicate one. I have seen students blossom from being simply listened to (perhaps for the first time in their lives), and others grow through vigorous, even venomous, argument.

The second task of the teacher is giving access to learning. What we seek here are the simplest keys which will unlock the fullest cupboards. For example, Ruth Beard found (Beard, 1970) that *graduates* did not know how to use the index of a book (did not even know where it was) and were unable to 'skim' books to gain the information they required. My own experience is that very few graduates have any idea at all of how to tackle, independently, a new sphere of interest. Students do need help in learning how to learn – even though much of the instruction in this is of a very modest sort. It includes hints and practice in how to read, to gut a substantial work, to explore a new field, to use a library, to construct one's own personal system of retrieving information. Most graduates leave their degree courses with a heap of material, and with no means of finding anything in it ever again. Presumably their teachers hold the view that they can never need it again.

In independent study, the students need more than this. They need practice, and hints, in planning work on a small and a large scale, in collaborating with others, in gaining the interest and help of specialists, in organizing their material, in writing – notes, essays and research reports – and in knowing how far they are failing. This offering of lifelong access to information and technique is often claimed as a consequence of higher education. But attempts to ensure that it is effective are commonly regarded by academics with suspicion. No systematic attempt is made to ensure it, and most of the procedures of post-school education hinder it. Potentially, the most junior librarian is more educative than the subject specialist – and happy the student who discovers this early on.

But access is more than technique. Even the most independently competent and well motivated students will flag at times. Students get stuck, and need help in making progress. They change (something which is, after all, part of the purpose of their education) and lose their bearings. In all this a teacher can help to see that part of the present impasse which can become the basis of growth. The technique may even be somewhat ignoble. It is to watch, in an hour of depression and boredom, for the sign that movement is possible – through a faint wish to get something right rather than wrong, to finish rather than prevaricate, to think through a difficulty rather than remain baffled, to sneer at the performance of others or his own, to gain pleasure from his success or envy at that of others. The teacher is the person (the responsible person, though contemporaries can be equally effective) who should see what it is in the student that will give him access to further study.

It is the role of example to give access. We should not desire that our students become or act like ourselves (that arrogance is well judged by students who calculate what the examiners this year would like to hear). Instead we should hope that in looking at our own competence, students will be tempted to become competent themselves and surpass rather than emulate us. I often feel that this is the function of the lecture *tour de force*. No-one supposes that being at such a lecture teaches a student how to give one. I myself do not believe that much is directly learned from such lectures either: students tend to remember the occasion rather than the content. But they seem to set a standard of intellectual performance which reinforces a student's intelligence and ambition.

A fourth example of access is to offer a clue to mastery. I have spoken earlier of teaching being a matter of hints and suggestions. It is a common teaching failing to try to give too much. If a student finds that for one part of his work he needs access to some part of economic theory, it is irresponsible to point to the whole of economics. What he needs is access to economics, and particularly that part of the discipline that is of direct use to him. He may of course go on to master the rest, and indeed invent an entirely new economics for himself – but that can safely be left to come later. As it is, there are graduates who to my certain knowledge have spent three years and more at economics without ever discovering that the so-called laws of supply and demand involve a relationship around *price* – and later cause untold bother and inconvenience to central and local government which employs them by insisting on applying economic concepts in situations where no visible price exists. All they needed was someone whose job it was to see that they did not miss the point.

With the final example of access we are back near the first: this is to offer students ways of doing things, or methods, techniques or even tricks of the trade. There is a danger that this will turn out to be merely facile, and so it would be if technique were all. But the object is learning, and more effective learning at that. Perhaps methods are best thought of as systems of 'don'ts' – so as to avoid unnecessary hindrance, waste, muddle or disaster. They are safest thought of in that way too: to be told a dozen things that go to make a bad report leaves a student still with an infinite number of ways of writing a decent one, each free from at least a dozen faults.

The third task of the teacher is criticism. This function, too, is much misunderstood in education. In the practice of most schools and colleges it is a matter of judgement rather than criticism. A student writes an essay and gets B+, with a few comments if he is lucky. This is a travesty. There is academic vulgarity at its very worst in that B+. It assumes that the correct response to a serious piece of work is a label. What the student needs is not an estimate (of what, God knows) but shrewd critical comment. If a teacher cannot offer that, he had better not offer anything.

The function of criticism is to help the student to improve. He needs it when he first begins to plan a programme, so that the programme can be improved. He needs it as he produces work, so that he is forced to consider how far his programme is doing what he wants of it, and he needs it at the end to tell him how far he has failed. He needs the assurance of standards, that what he has produced has to some extent withstood the worst that can be said about it, and that where it has not it can be mended. Little learning takes place when anything goes.

Of course, in being critical the teacher seeks to increase the student's self-criticism. This will help to increase his independence. But even the most self-critical of us need outside criticism too, because it will almost certainly find flaws that we ourselves have missed.

Nor need the teacher's criticism be offered from on high, on authority. Anyone can criticize, and there is no project that cannot be improved by the criticism of those less expert than its authors. Other students can often be as much help in this as a teacher. What we expect from the teacher is that he will criticize effectively. To do this he has to choose what to attend to at any one time. To criticize everything is to be of very little help. It requires judgement to know what it is most important for the student to know he is getting or doing wrong at this particular stage in his programme.

The notion of criticism of a student's work by a master is very common in the education and training of artists. Here it is clear that the student is taking the initiative: he is not being 'taught' to play that Beethoven sonata, he is playing it. And his teacher is pouncing on errors and being merciless to flaws. It is something of this kind that the good teacher achieves with his students in post-school education.

Again, his techniques may vary enormously. There are those who are coldly formal, cloyingly polite or witheringly sarcastic: be sure there will be some student somewhere who will respond to the most unpromising of attitudes. But on the whole, since criticism is the object, it pays to be courteous with it. Temptations

165

to self-indulgence should be resisted: the important thing is not that the teacher should feel good, but that the student should do better.

There are times when the student himself will want the criticism of an expert. No teacher can claim to know everything, and those who defend the primacy of specialization on the ground that one cannot teach what one does not know are perforce limiting the students to their own knowledge. Nor is it possible for all teachers to become adequate in criticizing the structure and organization of a piece of work, even in an alien field. But the student may also want criticism of his understanding of it. In such a case it is very important to have the work considered by another teacher competent to criticize its substance, and arranging such scrutiny is a prime task for a teacher.

These, then, are the functions of the teacher when we cease to regard him as a repository of accumulated facts or acquired techniques. The focus of his attention is the student – but the student acting in certain well-understood ways, in formulating problems, proposing solutions and testing them. He will want to give the student the confidence to spend time and energy in the formulation stage, to create bold and imaginative solutions and to accept the toughest criticism. He will want to offer the student access to the means for following these processes, and he has the duty firmly to say when he thinks any of the student's procedures are mistaken.

Again, it would be wrong to claim that these activities are unknown in post-school education. None of them were invented overnight for the purposes of a particular form of independent study. They have been used by many teachers in many disciplines and many kinds of institutions. What is new is our determination to put them explicitly to work in a framework of post-school education where they are particularly apt, because its epistemology is consistent with the logic of learning.

By this point in an explanation of what teachers do for independent study, the cynical reactions recorded at the beginning of this section have somewhat changed. Now, the reaction is, of course, it will work only if you have very good teachers. And indeed it does appear as if one is asking for paragons. They need

166

to know what it is to do independent work of their own, they need great sensitivity to the needs of others, the readiness to respond to students' demands and the flexibility to do so successfully, they must *know* a very great deal about existing disciplines and methods of work. They must be people of order and judgement, and they must be ready to face substantial intellectual demands.

There are two ways in which these requirements are in fact met. The first is that, in my experience, people can approach this sort of capacity, once they realize that it is necessary and determine to do so – and once they have the chance to stop trying to teach people things. It is astonishing what mental, emotional and practical changes follow the abandonment of instruction into a body of knowledge. People find wholly unexpected capacities. But this is not the whole answer. Of course, no one teacher is ever going to be the kind of Renaissance Man described above. But a group of teachers, even a small group, can aspire to it. It then becomes a question not of creating perfect individuals but of organizing the accessibility of a group. I believe that the spread of a service, like education, to accommodate most people, cannot await the production of ever better teachers. We have to use the teachers we have. But they can be used well or ill. It is the argument of this section that independent study enables them too to be more effective.

CHAPTER FIVE

Who does what?

WE are now in a position to say how education after school is to be planned and organized. Such planning and organization should follow from a view of what and whom post-school education is for and what it consists of. I hope it is now clear that I think that it should accommodate a rational balance between the service and autonomous traditions, that the service should be for everyone and should reflect the logic of learning. This is a plurality of purposes and needs, some of which may be mutually incompatible, so a system of post-school education is likely to be more successful if it is a plural system, with structures of organization and control which differently reflect its different activities. It was part of my argument in the last chapter that post-school education has been too conforming, for all its surface diversity.

As we saw at the beginning of this book, it is somewhat eccentric to leave organization to the last chapter. Most people seem to start with it. The watchword of educational planners seems to be 'Planning first, purpose afterwards'. They believe that education systems and institutional structures can and should be set up before anyone discusses what they are for. This is one explanation for the resilience of academic drift. Governments may have all kinds of aspirations, and institutions may seek all manner of innovation, but they typically try to achieve their ends through inappropriate means. They establish a new institution (a college or a department or 'school') with most of the features of a traditional model to do a new job, without asking whether these features are apt for the new purpose. So innovation falters, and original intentions are neglected or even reversed. Often administrators make a virtue of purposelessness by claiming to be somehow 'neutral': 'What's best administered,' they seem to be saying, 'is best.' On this view good administration depends not so much on purpose as on objectivity. Unfortunately the claim to objectivity is spurious: even in the most high-minded civil services it is a cover and excuse for an unacknowledged point of view.

This chapter starts with the organization needed for those of all ages who have left compulsory schooling. (I call them 'students' for simplicity: I hope it is clear by now that I do not mean just the young.) We have to find ways of enabling people to formulate their own problems with the help of the education service, and of creating a service that accommodates their solutions.

Most educational plans go awry because of the neglect of this glimpse of the obvious. At all levels people are trying to solve problems, when the problems are not in fact theirs. This weakness afflicts those towards the top of any hierarchy more than those towards the bottom. To be specific, most educational planning, the world over, has been in difficulties because senior administrators and politicians have tried to meet, for example, the needs of industry. But they are ill-placed to know what these needs are. All these pinnacular people have to do is to decide that one of the jobs of the education service is to meet the needs of industry and provide the means for doing so. The definition of need can be left to industry itself, in collaboration with those institutions which are trying to be of service. The part of the education service that has to be involved is the individual college and the individual department or the individual member of staff. A responsive service of this kind is difficult to run if people who are not directly concerned keep trying to take decisions.

After all, it is their own problems that people are best able to define and manage. For example, a senior administrator may well have problems with a varied and diverse system or with an unsympathetic treasury, and he is well placed to define and solve these. But the problems of individual adults seeking education are quite different, as are the problems of individual teachers or institutions. The senior administrator may not understand these problems at all well, may not even know if there are any. (Senior British administrators, in my experience, know quite a lot about the education service, but they know little of what it is like to work in it or of how it actually does work.) His solutions, therefore, may indeed be directed to solving his problems. but at the cost of exacerbating those in colleges and schools. It may be obvious to an administrator (indeed it normally is) that rationalization and economy are eminently desirable – so Ministries of Education are constantly rationalizing. The British Ministry has a record of rationalizing post-school education once every five or six years. But this may (and usually does) inhibit innovation and restrict opportunity in schools and colleges. Even policies which purport to meet the needs of students and teachers may fail to do so because these needs have been imperfectly understood. More important, when administrators seek to determine the means through which their policies are to be implemented locally, they very frequently err. The consequence is that their own policies collapse despite all their best efforts. When, in 1966, the Secretary of State for Education and Science announced a very clear 'binary' policy for higher education he sought to carry it out by establishing thirty polytechnics, but these polytechnics were less apt for implementing the policy than for solving some of the senior administrators' problems of cost, rationalization and control. Whatever their success in any other direction, their contribution to the binary policy has been on the whole negative.

One reason for this offers another example of the same point. Once an institution is 'designated' to become a different kind of institution, it sees this transformation as its own major problem. It thus loses sight of other problems, including those which prompted its own designation.

The priority for administration is to determine where problems have to be formulated and decisions taken. There are some kinds of problems which can be formulated and solved at one particular point in the education service: others may require collaboration from elsewhere. For example, teachers no doubt see such questions as salaries, conditions of work and resources for books and equipment as among their own more pressing problems. These are obviously not to be solved by teachers alone but in continuing discussion and negotiation. In these cases the problem for administration is to be sure that everyone can hear and understand what it is that the various parties to the discussions are saying. (This further statement of the obvious would not seem so necessary if I had not seen salary negotiations in Britain where one side quite simply could not understand what the other was proposing.)

All this argues not for endless consultation and participation, for representative committees on this and consumer councils on that, but for a rational disposition of responsibility. Meetings without purpose, committees without responsibility, discussions without consequences are all simply ways of maximizing frustration, apathy and thoughtless grumbling. We need instead two characteristics of democracy. The first is to give initiative at the appropriate level, and preferably as low in any hierarchy as possible. The neatest comment on this kind of discussion occurs in *Up the Organization*: 'All decisions should be made as low as possible in the organization. The Charge of the Light Brigade was ordered by an officer who wasn't there . . .' (Townsend, 1971). The second is to see that these initiatives are open to criticism. In all administration, in short, there are two questions to be answered. The first is 'Who should do what?' The second, no less important, is 'To whom should he be accountable?' The first raises questions of responsibility and initiative, and the proper distribution of powers and duties. The second raises the problem of control. In a democracy it is not enough to decide the first question alone – however democratic the body to whom responsibility is given. The second question is the beginning of safeguards against irresponsibility, tyranny and scandal.

Students

All educational planning and organization should start from the individual student. Whatever is done must be best for him. This, of course, is the reverse of normal practice. Usually it is governments which decide the shape of the education system, allocating duties to regional or local authorities and determining the framework in which institutions operate. They may seek to do all this on the basis of some view of manpower needs or social demand; but they do it nonetheless, and students have to take what they can from what is offered. This sort of planning 'from the top down' is fundamentally misconceived. It places responsibility where it is least well exercised. I propose, therefore, to discuss planning 'from the bottom up'.

It will be seen from Chapter 4 that I think the student should be responsible for planning his own programme. Without this, academic freedom is a very thin concept: as we shall see later, discussions of it seldom encompass the academic freedom of students. But the argument of this chapter does not depend on a general change to 'independent study'. Our own schemes for this are not the best or only ways possible. Indeed I hope that many better ways will be found. Nor do I underestimate the extent to which the student already takes initiative in choosing an educational institution, or a course, or from among options within a course. If we start with the student, it is clear that we need a plural system, with different kinds of institutions and courses, different modes of study, different traditions of education. And we need to see that this variety is accessible to him, physically, practically and psychologically. But once on his course, to whom is he accountable? Normally, he is so in two ways. The first is to any grant-giving authority (or his parents) for the proper use of the money. The principle holds even when the student is self-supporting: he is making a claim on resources which he ought to be prepared to justify. There has to be a way of convincing those supporting him that he is being diligent. At present institutions in England are, quite rightly, required to confirm this to grant-giving authorities. The second way in which a student is accountable is to his tutors and external examiners through the examination system. Students very often scorn the examinations commonly met with in post-school education and question their validity. But none of this criticism can alter the need for the student to be accountable for what he has done. If examinations are to be replaced, their successors must fulfil this function of making students accountable.

In our own programme of independent study, the students are accountable from the beginning – for planning what they do in the first six weeks. These plans are available for scrutiny by an external validating board. If the practice of planning one's own programme spreads, this function will almost certainly be borne by institutions themselves, if only for want of sufficient public-spirited people from outside. Again, students, like Secretaries of State, must accept that the greater the responsibility, the greater the need for them to be publicly accountable.

Staff

The contribution of staff to planning and organization has in the past been discussed almost wholly in terms of academic freedom, in terms of the protection of academics rather than their responsibility or initiative.

Normally when people discuss academic freedom they have in fact a whole complex of freedoms in mind. In the first place there is the freedom of academics: the absence of discrimination on grounds of colour, sex, religion or politics; the right to teach according to one's own conception of fact and truth; the right to publish; and the right to pursue personal studies or research. In the second place there is the freedom of institutions, meaning the freedom to make appointments, to admit students, to determine curricula and standards, to make a balance between teaching and research and to decide the shape of future developments. These two aspects of freedom, personal and institutional, have been the common currency of academic discussion in democracies (see Robbins, 1963). It has normally been assumed that the second helps to guarantee the first. Since the late 1960s, however, there has been an increasing demand for internal democracy in institutions, for staff and students to share in their government. This is because institutional freedom in the matter of curricula or the balance between teaching and research was found to be compatible with something not far from tyranny for junior staff. This is why the consciousness of freedom among vice-chancellors, professors and heads of department was not universally shared among lecturers, many of whom took the view that academic freedom should include the freedom to determine academic relationships among staff and between staff and students. Nor is the traditional notion of freedom much help outside an institution which carries the autonomous tradition into the very detail of its workings. To teach according to one's own conception of fact and truth is acceptable if it is agreed that one's teaching is itself autonomous, bearing no relation to anything else in the institution. On this view, one would lecture on one's chosen subject whether or not any student wanted to hear and whether or not it plausibly contributed to any programme of education. Once

173

the attempt is made to create a programme of study in which many staff share, the individual's freedom is circumscribed by his responsibility to his colleagues and to the programme.

The cardinal rule is that programmes should be created by those who will carry them out. This is not so much an extension of freedom as an acceptance of efficiency. Programmes are best implemented by those who have created them. Our framework for independent study was implemented by a group of staff who had helped to devise it. In so far as students do not themselves create programmes of study, these should be the responsibility of staff. This may seem obvious in England, where the independence of the individual teacher is prized in primary and secondary schools as well as in post-school education. It would be revolutionary in most other parts of the world. And even in England, there is the constant battle to fend off 'external' examining bodies of all kinds, which see their task as the creation of syllabuses and examinations.

A similar objection attends the traditional formulation about freedom to do research. This again seems more appropriate to the single scholar writing away in his attic. Today research is more often a matter of teamwork, and in some disciplines requires enormously expensive equipment. Here again we need not so much a right to pursue the truth and to publish (rights without responsibility are empty), but recognized conventions which stop (for example) professors publishing the insights of research assistants under the professor's name.

How, then, do we make academics accountable for their teaching and research without robbing them of initiative and responsibility? Fortunately, in Britain, there is an instrument ready to hand for this purpose, the Council for National Academic Awards. This body does not itself create syllabuses or set and mark examinations. That is the job of staff in individual institutions. What the Council does is to consider the proposals, and approve (or reject) courses and examinations leading to the award of its degrees. If a college wishes to create a course it draws up a detailed submission, covering not only the educational purposes and principles behind it but also the detailed way in which these are worked out, together with essential if mundane matters of staffing, accommodation, equipment and so on. These submissions are solid documents, and they demand concentrated effort from a great many people. The Council treats them very seriously. Each submission it studies, not just in the Council's office, but through a 'visit' to the college, lasting a whole day or more, by one of its committees. At these visits the whole college comes under scrutiny, as well as the course itself and the group which has prepared it. Everyone concerned knows that he is to be questioned minutely on any part of the proposal by people who are extremely experienced in picking the weak spots in educational theory and practice. And many of the 'visitors' will be more eminent in the particular field of study than those who have prepared the course.

It is important to grasp what is actually happening here. It is generally assumed in academic life that at the level of higher education good teaching rests upon independence. As the Robbins Report put it,

It is fundamental that an institution should be able to prescribe the requirements of its own courses and the combinations permitted. We know of no argument that would justify the imposition of external control from the centre in this respect ... Liberty to experiment with content and method is one of the surest guarantees of efficiency and discovery.

All this is also true of the maintenance of standards. Of course standards vary to some extent: such variations are in the nature of things. But an autonomous institution should be free to establish and maintain its own standards of competence without reference to any central authority. The habit of appointing external examiners from other universities and the obvious incentive to maintain a high place in public esteem provide in our judgement a sufficient safeguard against any serious abuse of this liberty (Robbins, 1963).

From the discussion itself, it is clear that the committee assumed that the alternative to independence was central control, and it was specifically arguing against the latter. It even recommended the creation of the CNAA (out of the ashes of a technological predecessor) to offer degrees to non-autonomous colleges. But it is also clear from the rest of the report that the committee regarded such colleges as anomalies in higher education – colleges which were beginning to take up advanced work and could expect to become autonomous when the volume of such work was great enough. A device like the CNAA could not, in the committee's view, be a permanent feature of an established sector of higher education. Indeed members of the committee, including Lord Robbins, have since argued that the use to which the CNAA has been put amounts to a perversion.

I believe the Robbins Committee was unjustified in this, because it overlooked the need to strengthen independent initiative with external criticism. My hunch is that in education people are more likely to innovate if they have to face external validation. Most of us are not highly innovating people. Left to ourselves we should in designing a new course be content to reproduce what we know best. We should naturally expect to make changes here or there to suit local circumstances or particular staff, but we should probably act within the context of our own experience and be ill-placed to go beyond it.

Our situation is quite different if we know that we are required to defend our proposals to a body of people at least as knowledgeable as we are. We cannot proceed on this basis of our assumptions: we have first to make our assumptions clear. In doing so, we may be led to question them. The need to defend our proposals forces us to make clear not only the fundamental problems but the coherence of our solutions. And it is out of this greater understanding that most of us can be persuaded to innovate.

The experience of the new universities, quoted in Chapter 4, illustrates these points very clearly. Set up to innovate, they have largely failed to remain flexible or to resist a backsliding to departmentalism. Autonomy does not lead to continuing innovation.

We may contrast this with experience in the non-autonomous sector. When in 1956 those colleges of advanced technology which had been preparing their students for internal and external London degrees came to submit proposals for the CNAA's predecessor (the National Council for Technological Awards), many found themselves rejected, because they had submitted the old schemes without thought: they were forced to be more creative. More important, many of them found that they could not submit the old schemes at all, because they could not defend them with understanding and conviction. Courses had to be created from the beginning, and this led to innovation.

It is important to realize that the benefits of innovation derive from an institution like the NCTA or CNAA, regardless of the composition of those bodies. People in the colleges often complain that the members of visiting committees are themselves hidebound, unimaginative and even incompetent, and they imagine that they would be more radical if they were freed from this academic supervision. But in this they delude themselves. A radical course or a new approach which has passed the scrutiny of conservatives is likely to be very much stronger than one which has escaped it. It is very hard to argue that traditionalism in the CNAA has managed to keep a good course down for long. One of the most productive uses to which conservatives can be put is the testing and validation of reform. It is the *process* that is important. A programme is a solution to some problem of education. Its preparation demands that it be defensible against the most rigorous criticism possible. This very circumstance rids many programmes of grievous error long before a CNAA visit. It does not eliminate all, nor does the CNAA always spot the ones remaining. But the programmes are immeasurably improved.

This kind of process should be mandatory for all programmes of an avowedly educational purpose, in all post-school institutions in Britain. It is already normal in advanced further education, and should be extended to non-advanced work in colleges, to schools with post-compulsory programmes and to universities. For the schools and colleges it would be greatly liberating, especially from the tedious vulgarities of external examinations. (Oddly enough the schools have a similar device at a lower level, in Mode 3 of the Certificate of Secondary Education.) For the universities (as for the CATs earlier) it would come as a shock, but a salutary one, and one filled with the promise of successful innovation.

Another important feature of the CNAA is that it contributes to the necessary plurality of control in education, by separating the validation of programmes from the provision of resources. This gives increased guarantees of academic freedom, first by separating the functions of pipe player and tune caller, and second by making it possible to claim increased resources as a result of a CNAA criticism of provision.

There is no precisely similar means of accountability for staff in their research work. Traditionally, research has been a major part of the job of British academics: they report that they spend half of their academic time upon it. The staff of the Dip.H.E. programme described earlier give it either a quarter or a fifth of their academic time to it, and this is probably generous for further education. (The doubt arises because some of my colleagues count educational planning as administration, others as academic work!) In most places, there is no systematic check on the quality of this work, or indeed on whether it is done at all. There are two unsystematic ones. The first is that publication, if not research, is taken as a criterion for promotion, which serves as a check on quantity. And publication itself, with the attendant scrutiny by referees, offers the work to the judgement of peers, which serves as a check on quality. Probably these two checks are enough: a systematic attempt to monitor individual research would undoubtedly lead to more bureaucracy and would probably not lead to any more or better research. The question of the amount of time an academic should spend upon it is one for himself and his institution, though presumably the national funding of universities and colleges must take some account of global figures: otherwise the expansion of student numbers leads automatically to an expansion of time for research, without the latter's having been defended in any other way.

The funding of substantial research work, particularly team research, is normally a matter, in Britain, for research councils and private foundations. I think the way they at present make grants should cause serious concern. They are none of them so open and serious in their procedures as is the CNAA. They are open to charges of arbitrariness, cronyism and conformism. The chief difficulty is that an application for a research grant tends to be treated 'in confidence'. The application may be sent by the council or foundation to a referee, and the decision on it made by a committee in the light of the referee's report. This means that the applicant is usually told only that his application has succeeded or failed. He does not have the benefit either of criticism or of the chance to reply to it. Neither the applicant nor those considering his application are subject to the discipline of an open statement which is openly challengeable.

If the research councils and foundations were to become more open they would need to be organized along the lines of the CNAA. In a report to a major international foundation (Burgess and Pratt, 1972) I have argued that foundations in particular should do this as a way of avoiding the temptations of grandeur which are associated with the establishment of large central offices creating 'policy' which pervert research initiatives and stifle innovation. Foundations, on the contrary, exist to give away money. They have to advertise the availability of funds and decide which applications should be turned down. For this purpose the foundation itself could be very small: there is not very much routine administration involved, and its size would bear some relation to the amount of money available and the number of grant applications processed. The vetting of applications, however, is beyond the scope of a small administrative office and should be undertaken by a council or committee of people meeting for the purpose, on a part-time basis. The applications should not simply be processed privately. The short-listed application should be defended by its proposer before the award-making committee or a sub-committee of this. The reasons for making or not making the award should be given in full to the applicant.

The applications would be judged on two main grounds. The first is internal to the application itself: is the problem in the proposed project well formulated and does the project itself offer a plausible solution and the means of testing it? Foundations should be content with relatively vague policies, so as to encourage the widest possible submission of applications. The important thing is to diversify the search for solutions.

Another function of foundations largely neglected at present is that of checking that the successful projects are going ahead, keeping to their timetables and making the expected contribution. The foundation cannot perform this function itself either. It needs to find ways of building into every project measures of evaluation, so that it can tell at a glance how things are going. It needs thought as a substitute for bureacracy.

179

A foundation such as this implies a small group of highly sensitive and knowledgeable people whose job it is to encourage the submission of projects. Its office would be equipped to process applications and to arrange the confrontations between the awarding committees and applicants.

Many foundations are more ambitious. They acquire a large and high powered staff, who develop the need to have a centrally directed policy. They feel that their activities should be consistent and add up to a coherent programme, or that efforts should be concentrated on problems rather than upon people or institutions, or that dispersed efforts can easily run to waste: what is needed is a heavy concentration of resources on one particular problem. But all these arguments have to do with the needs of the foundation (for consistency and coherence) rather than of the recipients. They presuppose the existence of solutions – which, on the contrary, it is the job of research to seek.

A centrally directed foundation robs itself of many potential benefits. If initiative lies with the applicants, the foundation's role is one of assessment and criticism. Proposals come from the initiators, while the foundation is well placed to mount a formidable assessment. The reverse process, where policy is made at the centre, means that the initiative is remote from the problems and is open to criticism only from those whose position, as applicants, may inhibit them or reduce their effectiveness.

In other words, foundations do not need the services of very high-powered staffs at headquarters, all brimming with ideas and policies. What they need is dedicated bureaucrats with a flair for gaining the interest and services of the best possible part-time members of assessing committees. The most appropriate qualities for officials are those not of the missionary but of an entrepreneur.

So far I have discussed the ways in which staffs of institutions can be responsible and accountable for their educational and research work. The key is that they should retain the initiative in making proposals, but that there should be an external body whose assent they must gain. There would be different bodies for different purposes: a CNAA for educational programmes and awards; the research councils, private foundations, firms and government departments for research. Staff will act, on their own or in groups

180

for the creation and running of educational and research programmes. At present, these groups are rather rigidly organized,
in subject departments and faculties, but I do not think this is the
most rational solution, even from the point of view of discipline-
based studies. It seems to me to be a mistake to make educational
organization the basis for administrative control. Many of the ills
of present subject departments, from the tyranny of professors
onwards, stem from it. Academic organization should arise from
academic activity. If a congeries of groups of staff decide they have
something to gain from a common organization, then they can
form one and call it a department or faculty. To establish
faculties first and then create activities to fit is mere job-making.
The secret of rational senior appointments in institutions is function, not post. Unfortunately, one never sees functions advertised
– only posts, with at best a platitudinous 'job description'.

Colleges

Staff and students working on a particular course or in a particular
department are not, of course, working in isolation. They are
working in the context of an institution. It is now time to consider
what the role of the institution ought to be. In my view, it has two
elements. The first is to offer a service through which staff and
students can gain what they need to do their job. This service is
largely concerned with the administration of resources. Again,
the usual practice is for this relationship to be turned on its head,
so that the administration carries all the power and thinks of itself
as writing all manner of instructions and procedures which take
priority over educational needs. A more creative role for the administration is to learn how to use external constraints and internal
organization to assist the main task of the institution, which is
education. If innovation is proposed, the usual response of administration is to seek reasons why it cannot be done. This is
demeaning to itself and to the whole institution. Its real job is to
display a creative opportunism to enable the innovation to go
forward as quickly as possible. The second task of the institution
is to establish its own broad educational policy. This should not
be a very elaborate matter. Indeed, if the institution is to have any
common sense of identity and purpose, what it needs is a coherent

set of well-chosen platitudes, expressing the general direction in which the institution has determined to go. For example it should say clearly to what extent it sees itself as being in the autonomous or the service tradition. To the extent that it is in the service tradition, whom has it primarily decided to serve – employers or employees; the local community or an élite of the nation; all adults or those capable of benefiting from its programmes? It is the job of academic boards of colleges to establish broad principles such as these. Most of them fail to do so and spend their time instead grumbling and wrangling about detail. This leaves them powerless to judge and to influence the actions of administrators because they have no agreed criteria against which these actions can be set. This is why such devices as committees of academic boards become somewhat clumsy instruments of administration rather than what they should be – a check by the board upon administration itself.

Many staff fear the existence of institutional policy. They do not realize that the lack of it very seldom means an increase in freedom for them as individuals or as members of a team. More often it means that they have to argue cases individually with all manner of 'powers' – heads of department, treasurers, administrators of all kinds. And in this situation it is the staff member, not the powers that be, who is in a position of weakness. And in schools or colleges with no educational policy, the pupils and students are at the whim of individual teachers. There are many parents who have found that teachers may decide that their child may not follow a particular course, not as part of a settled policy which is announced, understood and accepted, but at random and for reasons of expediency. Freedom depends on knowing where one stands and in having some means of controlling circumstances. It does not derive from avoiding overt statements of policy and letting the strongest powers prevail.

There is a similar danger from outside pressures. Here, too, the absence of a policy from those required to have one does not mean freedom for everyone else. It merely means they are bound by something which is more arbitrary and capricious. To take an obvious example, the curriculum in the sixth forms of British secondary schools is not laid down by the Government, but this does not mean that the schools are free to do what they think best. The examinations for the General Certificate of Education, at advanced level, are in the hands of GCE boards which are in effect accountable only to themselves. The curricula of British sixth forms do differ partly because the individual boards have different syllabuses, but they do not differ very much. And of course they differ most for pupils who will not be taking A level examinations. Changing the requirements and attitudes of the boards is so hopelessly difficult that new secondary school examinations are being evolved (under pressure from the Government) to create the necessary diversity and to give more pupils the chance of a curriculum appropriate to their needs and some recognition of success in pursuing it. The schools could have been very much more help in this if they themselves had worked out their broad educational goals in terms other than subservience to the existing examination system.

Although the general educational policy of an institution should not specify too much detail, it should certainly be couched in terms of the institution's development. It will be very surprising if the institution measures up in all respects to its own aspirations, so it needs some statement of how it is to get from where it is to where it wants to be. Such broad development plans are especially important because if the colleges themselves do not create them, educational discussion and decision will go by default. In educational policies, as in other public policy, those responsible for framing and implementing it tend to concentrate upon matters of administration and organization. There are good reasons for this, the chief one being that politicians and administrators are not best placed to deal with anything else. In British education, the division of function is clear and almost unquestioningly accepted. The authorities are responsible for providing and administering; they are not responsible for 'education'. Authorities put up buildings and pay teachers; they make regulations about class sizes and standards of accommodation. They fix hours and times of attendance. But it is the schools and colleges themselves which are responsible for curricula, methods, and indeed educational objectives. Of course, the educational institutions are not entirely free, but the educational constraints under which they work are

183

provided by independent examining bodies rather than by central and local authorities. Even the inspectorate, which might be supposed to be an instrument for transmitting specifically educational policies from the authorities to institutions, does not in practice act in this way. The inspectors tend to see their job in terms of assisting and advising individuals. Their independence is something they themselves value. It must be said at once that in further education the inspectors have been more inclined to act as spokesmen of the DES, but they have done so in administrative terms. There has been little central educational guidance for them to offer.

All this leads the central and local authorities to overlook the importance of educational development as a contribution to policy. After all, what goes on inside educational institutions can powerfully affect the attainment of policy objectives. For example the reorganization of British secondary education is designed to set a framework to achieve educational and social objectives, like the extension of opportunity. But it is clear that even when reorganization is complete, the practice of individual schools will determine how far these objectives are met. Nor is it possible for the authorities to be neutral. It may seem that by neglecting educational development they are remaining so: in fact they are ensuring the perpetuation of existing objectives and practices which may or may not be in line with their policies.

In arguing that the authorities should interest themselves in educational development, I do not mean that directions about curricula, examinations and methods should be handed down from the centre. On the contrary, it is essential that the staff of individual institutions are encouraged to create the context in which they are working. The authorities' responsibility is for the framing of national policy and the determining of the place of a particular institution in the national and local pattern. It is right that they should explain the policy, the pattern and the institution's place to the staffs of institutions. Occasionally the institutions themselves do respond by considering their educational development in the light of this knowledge. Normally, however, they will do this seriously only if it is required of them.

Indeed, unless individual institutions are required to plan their

184

own educational development in the context of national policy, they are unlikely fully to understand what the policy is. It is a familiar educational principle that we learn best by solving problems. If a government has a policy for higher education in the public sector, it needs to be sure that the institutions through which it is working understand what the policy is and that their work is compatible with it. The best way of ensuring this is by requiring them to undertake educational development planning.

These plans should start from the colleges' formulation of problems and the means for solving them: should start, in other words, from educational proposals and then go on to say what these imply for staffing, accommodation, laboratories, libraries and so on. In this way the colleges will understand their place in the whole education system, will contribute creatively to policy and will gain self-confidence in their dealings with the authorities, the universities and the world outside. Those institutions which are gathered together in groups of disparate colleges are in special need of some such exercise. Otherwise they will remain monuments only for expediency. Indeed this kind of academic planning need not stop at individual colleges. Each should be required to collaborate with other local colleges and decide how they would work together. Indeed, this might make it possible to create a more rational way of agreeing the growth and distribution of courses than the horse-trading of the Regional Advisory Councils.

That this is not normally required of institutions offers a marked contrast to the establishment of the new universities such as Sussex and York in the 1960s. When these were set up, each had an academic planning board which set out in general terms the way the new university ought to go. Albert Sloman, the Vice-Chancellor of the University of Essex, claimed in his Reith Lectures that 'it would be hard to over-emphasize the influence of the Academic Planning Board . . .' (Sloman, 1964). Yet the new universities were operating within a well-understood academic tradition, and to those who were founding them and working in them their purposes and practices were relatively clear. The service tradition, on the other hand, is always required to attempt something new. It has to resist age-old pressures and so it needs serious academic planning even more urgently than the new universities. Normally what happens is that the Government seeks from the local authorities an outline of future plans implied in existing accommodation and that known to be coming into use. In other words, it tries to encourage not the creation of new institutions, but a rationalization of current developments – which had evolved out of the piecemeal approvals and the fragmented course structures of the past education. To produce real change, something more than this is required.

The point is that existing institutions have staff in post. Academic planning therefore has to be done by the staff (rather than a planning board), and that it should be so is part of the purpose of the exercise. On the other hand, some guarantee is needed that the job has been well done. Some body is needed to assess the development plans of post-school institutions. The body should be locally based, but it should be established by, rather than identical with, the local authority. It might include respected academic and public figures who are in sympathy with the post-school policy. It would be a College Assessment Board. The board would discuss and make public a fairly detailed list of issues which an academic development plan should take into account. These would be largely questions of academic policy and balance – for example the relation between full-time and part-time students, between advanced and non-advanced work, between teaching and research, between the polytechnics and other colleges. The board might also give general advice about the production of plans, and in particular how proposals for buildings and staffing should be shown to arise out of educational objectives. The object would be not just to produce a list of courses but to plan a complete institution. In other words, the board would not tell the colleges what sort of institution to organize but would give guidance on how to produce plans.

As the colleges produced their plans, the board would study them, visit the institutions (perhaps by means of sub-committees), and make certain that the plans were consistent with the policy and that the physical proposals were adequate to meet educational requirements. Once satisfied, the board would say so to the regional or local authority or to the Secretary of State. This process should take place before the formal commitment of resources – so that the creation of an educational plan could be a condition of development. The final decision, of course, would rest with the Secretary of State working with and through the local authorities.

Nor should this process go on for each institution in isolation. It needs to be aware of what other institutions are doing and to take this into account. Each college, whether a university, a polytechnic, a college of education, a technical college or whatever, should be faced with the need to assert what it considers its contribution to post-school education locally to be. It should then have to discover how far this squares with the aspirations of other colleges and should collaborate with them in putting forward to the responsible authority (whether single, or a joint education committee) an agreed set of outline proposals for development. I would in other words leave with the Government the determination of policy but would remove from it the initiative of deciding who does what. The Government is not particularly good at deciding the best means of achieving its own objectives. I believe the colleges would do better.

There are two objections to this kind of procedure. The first is that it would lead to very different arrangements from one part of the country to another. I regard this as an advantage. If many people are seeking solutions to the same problem, we are much more likely to hit upon good ones.

The more serious objection is that the colleges may simply not be up to the job. This is like the argument about self-government for colonies. The colleges (colonies) will be 'ready' for self-development (self-government) in so many years' time, if they are given it now: if they are not they will never be ready. But in any case, I do not believe the argument carries very much force. The technical colleges and the polytechnics have shown themselves quite capable of substantial educational development by meeting the exacting requirements of the Council for National Academic Awards. Of course, some of them fail, but the failure is itself educative and leads to improvement. It is similarly possible that particular colleges will make unrealistic 'bids' for development, or will reveal that they do not understand the overall policy to which they are being asked to contribute. But there will be sufficient checks against the first of these possibilities: the other colleges in the area constitute one; the local authority or joint education committee another; the DES the third. In any case it will be the essence of individual and joint development plans that they are couched in terms which show what share of available resources is for this. The second possibility is again an advantage, not a disaster. To have it revealed that a particular college does not know what it is doing must be wholly to the good.

The importance of calling for development plans in this way is that it gives the individual colleges the greatest possible freedom to determine their own development, within the context of national policy and the available resources. It can only encourage innovation and realism. The submission of these plans to the local authorities or joint committees will give the latter an understanding of the institutions they maintain and of the stake which they themselves have in them. The authorities may find the development plans unacceptable (or a single authority may believe itself to be particularly hard done by). In such a circumstance the authorities should be free to put up their own alternatives, and ultimately the matter will be decided by the Secretary of State. And it is the submission of development plans to the Secretary of State which will give the Government its cue as to the final distribution of resources.

In the earlier discussion of the CNAA I made it clear that I do not regard external validation as in any way calling in question the competence, the standards or the good faith of institutions, but as a vital instrument of educational development in its own right. It is a way of ensuring thought and innovation. It is for this reason that I believe that if colleges are asked to produce educational development plans there could well be a body to which they could submit them if they wished. None of the existing agencies can do this job. The CNAA is concerned with courses, and in any case is heavily overextended. The local authorities and the regional advisory councils are not equipped for it; and Her Majesty's Inspectors are unhappily inadequate. There is a great need to offer the colleges, especially groups of colleges, the chance of working together to produce educational proposals which they will then need to cooperate in defending before sceptical peers. There can be little doubt in my view that the proposals would be greatly improved.

In short, we need to find ways of giving to the colleges the responsibility for their own development, singly and together, and of securing their accountability, both academic and administrative. The bodies to whom they should be accountable, in a country the size of Britain, are elected local authorities, and it is to these bodies that we must now turn.

Local authorities

In England and Wales post-school education, except for the universities, is the responsibility of local education authorities. They have the duty to offer full-time and part-time education for those over compulsory school age together with leisure-time occupation for such people in cultural and recreative activities. This general duty has led to an extraordinary diversity. Large numbers of pupils stay on at school, in the 'sixth forms' of secondary schools, after the compulsory school age of sixteen. Traditionally such pupils have worked for the advanced level of the General Certificate of Education which gives access to institutions of higher education. But increasingly the schools are offering other courses. Pupils who leave school at sixteen may still decide to stay in full-time education taking either academic or overtly vocational courses in colleges of further education, technical colleges and the like. Most young people remaining in touch with the education service do so part time, either in the evening or with some release from work, in these same technical and other colleges. Most adults remaining in contact with the service do so in evening institutes which offer a bewildering complexity of academic, vocational, cultural and recreational courses at all levels wherever a sufficient number of people can be enticed to take an interest. Included in the local authority provision are polytechnics, which offer chiefly courses at first-degree level, colleges of education which train teachers and a variety of other institutions which combine the functions of these two institutions with a commitment to lower-level work. The question is, what is the role of the local education authorities in the organization which is described

189

in this chapter? If educational planning is to be done in the institution, and if institutions are to collaborate in what they provide,
what is the role for the local education authority? The importance of the authority is that it is directly elected. It is the
point at which education becomes accountable to the general
public and to ratepayers and taxpayers. What measure of responsibility should go with this accountability?

At present the local authorities are rather restive about their
role in post-school education. I believe that this role is of enormous
value. Local authority administration has served the service
tradition well. Experience suggests that the tradition is neglected
the further an institution gets from local authority control. The
local authorities, however, have shown themselves to be dis-
satisfied with the way in which post-school education has been
financed and controlled. Some of their representatives have urged
that they give up responsibility for it altogether. In my view this
would be a mistake, and an urgent task of the Government is to
persuade the local authorities that they have a role and give them
the means to fulfil it.

The dissatisfaction has had three main sources. The first lies in
the fact that although polytechnics and other colleges doing
advanced full-time work are the responsibility of individual local
authorities, they tend to serve the people of more than one
authority. This means that the relationship between the authorities and the institutions is far less straightforward than that
between the authorities and their schools. Authorities without
colleges tend to feel that they have no say in what goes on in
higher education: authorities with colleges believe they are carrying a burden for their colleagues with very little direct return to
themselves. Both feelings are exacerbated by the second source of
dissatisfaction: the way in which advanced further education is
currently financed. It is not just that individual local authorities
may feel hard done by, justly or unjustly as the case may be; it is
rather that the authorities again believe that although they are a
major source of finance, are the channel for the rest – and have
nominal responsibility – the whole of advanced further education
is actually outside their control.

With new arrangements for college government, this feeling has intensified and is the third ground for dissatisfaction. If the colleges are to be so independent, what precisely is the role of the local authority? If it is to be that of a post office or bank, it is small wonder that many local authority representatives would far rather get shot of the job. I believe that it is a perversion of the local authorities' role to reduce it in this way: the authorities represent the legitimate public interest and they have a place in any public system of higher education.

These feelings of dissatisfaction have recently come to a head in a number of ways. There was first of all the idea of a 'polytechnics grants committee' which would distribute resources to the polytechnics in the same way as the University Grants Committee distribute resources to the universities (see the next section). This idea foundered on the evident differences in the two cases. The universities are autonomous, the polytechnics are not: an independent committee acting as a buffer between Government and individual university makes sense, but there is no obvious place for such a committee for the polytechnics. Where would it be placed: between the Government and the local authorities, between the authorities and the institutions, or between the Government and the institutions – and if the last of these, where would the local authorities be then? One answer was given straight away (by the Association of Municipal Corporations); they would be on the PGC! But this merely points up the differences again. The UGC is composed of academics and staffed by civil servants and is acceptable to the universities for this reason. It would not be in the least satisfactory to the polytechnics to have resources channelled to them, not by their local authorities, but by representatives of these and other authorities sitting on an ad hoc committee. Nor would it be satisfactory to the Government – or to a number of local authorities themselves. What has emerged, therefore, is a committee of local authorities (the Local Authorities' Higher Education Committee) whose role is to be an advisory one in planning. Some of its members feel it should be given control of resources, but this is unlikely. The importance of the committee, however, does not lie in what it might do or claim to do, but as evidence of LEA frustration.

What, then, can be done about that? The first step is to involve

191

the local authorities themselves (not just their chosen representatives) in the planning of their sector of post-school education
locally. Basically this means deciding how the public interest is
to be best represented in its finance and administration. I suggest
that the way to do this is for the Secretary of State (after all the
appropriate consultations) to issue a circular which requests local
authorities, either singly or in groups, to prepare proposals for the
administration of post-school education in their areas. Such proposals should include the arrangements for the submission of
development plans for institutions and groups of institutions,
though the actual submissions would come later. I should expect
that this would lead to consultation among adjacent local authorities, arising out of their particular circumstances, and the extent
of collaboration might vary. This exercise is not one to determine
the role of individual institutions or even to plan the development
of post-school education in an area. That comes later. Its purpose
is to ask the local authorities to solve their own problems of administration. They will know the objects of the policy for the
public sector, they will know that their job is to reflect the local
public interest in this. The question is how this is to be done. In
some places the authorities might decide to leave things much as
they are, with individual authorities responsible for their 'own'
institutions, with recoupment through the 'pool' for advanced
work. In others they might decide to set up joint education committees to administer the institution or institutions which serve
their joint areas. One problem would be to decide the proportionate representation of authorities on these joint committees.

I believe that a process of this kind is greatly preferable to
existing arrangements, whether these are the inchoate LAHEC, or
the Regional Advisory Councils. The latter serve somewhat irrational and artificial areas, they make decisions which they are ill-
equipped to make and the rationalization they afford is quite
spurious. My proposal gives the initiative to the local authorities
in the areas they know best, in control and administration. It
places upon them the responsibility of working out the democratic administration of post-school education in their areas.

In most places the authorities will do this without trouble.
Occasionally there will be strife, and this may be irreconcilable.

In some places a dominant authority may be simply uncooperative. For this reason, the authorities' arrangements should be subject to the approval of the Secretary of State. It is in any case right that local proposals should be nationally acceptable – provided that the initiative for them has been a local one.

Once the local authorities have determined how they propose to carry out their responsibilities for higher education in the public sector, they in turn can be asked to call for educational development plans from the colleges in their areas. Such development plans are long overdue, especially in the wake of the Government's White Paper. In the past, educational planning from the DES has normally meant that the Government has not only stated its general objectives but has then announced what it proposes to do to achieve them. So we have had designations of colleges, guidance about institutional government – and so on. What I now propose is something rather different. I believe that it is right that a government should lay down national policy for various sectors of education: that is what governments are for. I accept that governments also make decisions about the overall distribution of resources. Certainly governments need to be sure that the administration is likely to be satisfactory – that, after all, is what the Education Act 1944 was largely about, and a very fruitful piece of legislation that has turned out to be. But I do not believe that governments are best placed to settle detail, and that efforts to do so have normally been self-defeating. For one thing, the Department is simply not adequately staffed to do a detailed job properly. This is why I have suggested making a reality of the 'partnership' with local authorities by giving the latter an outline of the job they are required to do and requiring them to agree how to do it. Consultation about administrative forms is not enough.

It may be objected that the negotiations between local authorities would produce different patterns of administration for post-school education in different parts of the country. This would be their chief merit. There is no reason why an authority or a form of collaboration which suits rural Wales would be equally apt for metropolitan Manchester. Local government has recently been reorganized in Britain, after a Royal Commission but from the centre, and the resulting patterns, consistent and tidy though they are, are widely recognized to be a disaster. What the local authorities need to do, singly or together, is to formulate the particular problems in their areas which post-school education is expected to solve, to create in broad terms the kinds of institutions that seem plausible means to their solution, and to hold these institutions accountable for what they then do. The authorities in turn will be directly accountable for their actions to their electorates.

The Grants Committee Principle

In Britain, the autonomous tradition has been recognized and protected by a remarkable administrative device. The universities, whose autonomy is enshrined in their individual charters, get most of their income from the Government, yet their claims for resources are made to the Government, and Government grants are distributed to individual universities, through an independent body, the University Grants Committee. The committee is composed largely of academics, and is staffed by civil servants. It has had a dual task: first to advise the Government on the total money provision to be made for the universities; second, to allocate the total provision between the universities. In carrying out the first of these functions the committee is advisory in the strictest sense: the decisions are taken by the Government in the light of the committee's advice. In the second function, however, the UGC is only formally advisory, because the convention has been established that the Government does not inquire into or question the committee's recommendations about allocation between universities.

Two principles governing the UGC's work have been established from its earliest days. The first is the principle of a quinquennial settlement and the second is that of a block grant. This combinations of principles is held to facilitate the planning of academic development and give the universities a great measure of financial autonomy and responsibility. It reduces the need for constant examination and review which would be implied to a system of annual estimates. The Government knows its obligations for a number of years ahead. The disadvantages of the quinquennial block grants are, first that the planning process becomes increasingly short-term as the quinquennium proceeds; second, inflation could have an eroding effect on the allocations; and third, new and unpredictable developments are hard to accommodate and this inhibits the universities' responsiveness to change.

It is the block grant principle which was said to be the main bastion of autonomy. Any other system would imply a detailed control over academic matters in individual universities which the UGC has always resisted. Of course, the quinquennial allocations were based on estimates and development plans submitted by the universities, and the UGC makes its views on these known. Major departures from the lines of development laid down in the plans were first cleared with the UGC, and in any case developments were conditioned by building programmes which had to be agreed in advance. And behind all this the universities were aware that developments which were unacceptable to the UGC might prejudice their claims in the next quinquennium.

Increasingly, too, the UGC accepted a duty to give the universities as much information as possible on national needs, including changes in potential student numbers and in the need for graduates in particular fields; on developments in non-university institutions; and on its own thoughts about university education. Even so, this still left the individual universities free to plan their own development within the national pattern in the light of their own circumstances.

The object of all this was to establish the UGC as a 'buffer' between the state and individual universities. In recent years the principle has been somewhat eroded, and it is possible to trace this process in the development of the UGC's procedures first for recurrent and second for capital grants.

It has become almost customary for chairmen of the University Grants Committee to use the UGC's quinquennial report as an occasion for discussing the whole role of the committee. Sir John Wolfenden's contribution in the report for 1962 to 1967 was to articulate the rapidly changing relationships which in the universities themselves were noticed but not fully understood. Sir John Wolfenden traced the use of the concept of a 'buffer' to describe the activities of the UGC, from a conversation between Hugh Dalton and an earlier chairman, Sir Walter Moberly, in 1948, to a statement in the House of Commons by Anthony Crosland in

1967. The defence of the buffer concept was that it relieved the Government of direct responsibility for the universities and it safeguarded the universities from political interference. It was regarded as 'an earnest of the Government's willingness to provide money for the universities "without strings", and it enabled the universities to enjoy public funds without the fear that the gift might turn out to be a Greek one'.

Sir John also recorded that the 'apparently passive function' of the UGC as a buffer was changing. The Robbins Committee had noticed that the UGC was not passive in regard to the policies of particular universities. Even the block grants were given to universities after an examination and discussion in each of a background of regional needs. And if a university spent its grant in a way contrary to these needs, the UGC might well give it less next time. With capital grants, the UGC was even less passive. Building programmes were evolved and discussed in detail with the committee. In a period of expansion the general policy of universities depends more on capital grants than on any others, and in these the role of the UGC was central. In its developing role, the UGC had therefore evolved increasingly formal procedures for dealing with issues which might formerly have been settled on a more gentlemanly and ad hoc basis (Robbins, 1963).

An example of the latter was the Memorandum of General Guidance sent out in November 1967 (UGC, 1967). This was not the first time that the UGC had sent out general guidance. The chairman had written to vice-chancellors on 20 December 1966. But the Memorandum was the first formal document in which the UGC sought to tell the universities about 'various factors' which they had considered in deciding about university development in general. The factors were divided into three groups: background factors, earmarked and 'indicated' grants, and particular academic activities. The background factors included total numbers, of undergraduates and postgraduate students; unit costs; collaboration with industry, between universities and with other sectors of higher education; the use of capital resources and income from non-UGC sources. The UGC assumptions about student numbers derived directly from Government policy. The Secretary of State had announced a target for the number of places by 1971 to 1972 and had promised the financial resources to meet it. Within the total numbers, the UGC cautiously took the view first that under-graduate numbers were a genuine priority and second that in the light of the current A level trend the major increase here must be in arts-based rather than science-based courses. The effect of these decisions on postgraduate numbers was that the latter were smaller than the universities had wished, and the UGC set out its reasons for this.

On unit costs, the committee decided to act on the basis of information before it from the quinquennial submissions about the range of costs between universities. Its object here was to bring similarity into the costs of universities by the simple expedient of assuming that costs were similar in making the allocations. It was left to the universities which had got more or less than they had hoped to manoeuvre as they thought fit within their new financial constraints.

Of more fundamental importance was the UGC's decision to make clear its attitude to the development of particular academic activities. It decided that undergraduate teaching in agriculture should be discontinued at three universities in order to concentrate resources into fewer schools, although it did not intend to reduce the total provision for agricultural education. It thought a similar concentration would be appropriate in agricultural economics and hoped that no further developments would be undertaken in this subject. That was the only area in which the committee had decided to stop an existing activity in individual universities. In other areas it decided that there should be no further proliferation. For example, though there was to be a substantial increase in the numbers of students in existing schools of architecture, the com-mittee thought that more such schools were unnecessary. Univer-sities contemplating the incorporation of existing non-university schools would have to do so within the allocations made to them. In the arts, the committee decided against small departments. It sought to strengthen selected departments and to limit expansion elsewhere. In biological sciences, too, the committee did not think that more schools were desirable and would prefer to see further development taking place selectively in existing schools. Further funds for oriental, Slavonic, Eastern European, Latin American and African studies should be concentrated in existing centres. Development in existing centres was also proposed in town and country planning and veterinary science. In certain technological fields (particularly metallurgy), student demand already fell short of available places, and the UGC said that no further courses were needed.

The committee's decision about management studies and social studies, though in line with those in other areas, had particularly serious side effects. In management studies the committee hoped for a further substantial expansion in the quinquennium but considered that this would best be concentrated in existing centres. It added that 'universities should be cautious in establishing new courses until there is greater evidence of the type and duration of courses which can usefully be added to the great variety of existing offerings in this field'. Further undergraduates in particular were not encouraged, though an exception was made for such courses in which an element of management studies was combined with some other subject, such as engineering. Equally, in social studies the UGC believed it would be a more efficient use of resources to accommodate the large increase in student numbers at universities where this subject was already strongly established. Priority, it thought, should be given to economics, law and statistics.

This decision was being taken as ten former Colleges of Advanced Technology were attaining university status. At this time their management and social studies departments were struggling to become more than just 'service' departments for other disciplines. Although there were many teachers of more traditional technological subjects who viewed this development with impatience, it is probably fair to say that most staff in the CATs were convinced that a development into the social sciences was for them appropriate. Some of them believed that it would be possible to extend the 'sandwich' principle, which had proved itself in technology, into the social sciences. The effect of the UGC's decision was not only to balk the former CATs of an academic development which they wished to undertake (at precisely the moment when they became 'autonomous'); it also meant that the extension of the sandwich principle into the social sciences was

198

left largely to the polytechnics and other technical colleges. It has not taken place in universities.

In another field three of the former CATs gained from concentration. In providing for expansion of diploma courses in education, the UGC concentrated such courses especially designed for scientists and technologists in three universities: Bath, Brunel, and Chelsea College of Science and Technology.

In the middle of all this generally restrictive guidance the UGC was able to announce a small unqualified expansion in dentistry, medicine and mathematics.

When the Memorandum of Guidance was issued, there were many in the universities who saw it as yet another example of the extension of the power and influence of the state in university affairs. Though the words were not actually used in the Memorandum, the whole exercise seemed to be concerned with rationalization and cost-effectiveness – ideas which the universities associated more with bureaucracy than with academic life. Reality, however, was not quite so simple. The pressure to produce a Memorandum of Guidance seems to have come mostly from within the UGC itself, and indeed from individual universities. There was very little indication of pressure from the state.

The second example of the changing role of the UGC is seen in the control of capital spending. In March 1954 it began to devise a system of schedules, the first of which was to give it a clear picture of the accommodation a university was seeking to provide in its new building. This was to be, in effect, the instructions to be given to the architect, and the schedule of accommodation for a new teaching building would show the proposed number and size of rooms required for academic staff, lectures, seminars, laboratories, libraries, and so on. The UGC at this point would assess whether the accommodation requirements were too meagre or too lavish for the purpose of the building. This would be done by the UGC officers, with the advice of members of the committee or its sub-committees and after sometimes considerable discussion with the university concerned. The second schedule was prepared by the architect, giving precise information about areas allotted to particular purposes, details of finishes and so on, the total cost and the rate per cubic foot and square foot. These plans and specifications were scrutinized by the UGC officers and architects, and when they were approved the university was free to prepare working drawings and contract documents and prepare tenders.

In order to judge the reasonableness of the universities' first schedule proposals, the UGC found itself establishing cost limits. This took time. The committee had to build up norms in the form of scales of accommodation for various grades of academic staff, clerical staff, lecture theatres, drawing offices, laboratories, libraries, halls of residence and so on. These formed the basis of the 'usable areas' of a building, and an allowance was added to determine its gross area. There also had to be established standard square foot rates for various types of accommodation, costs of special services or special features, like excessive floor loads, unusual span or ceiling heights, radioactive shielding. With the small building programmes of the early 1950s, it was difficult to make progress quickly, but after 1957 the UGC was able to recruit a small department of architects and quantity surveyors to advise both on individual buildings and on a system of cost-analysis which would provide the norms. Provisional norms for some types of accommodation were established in 1957 and extended in 1960. Procedures for cost limits for halls of residence came in 1958 and for science buildings in 1960. These were later extended to other buildings. From 1960 universities were asked for their individual building requirements in terms of square feet, and the UGC can now fix cost limits for all projects submitted. Finally, the information on these building control procedures, on space standards and cost limits was gathered together in 'Non-recurrent Grants: Notes on Procedure', issued for the first time in 1963 (UGC, 1963).

It is clear that these procedures and controls accompanied the growth of Government spending on university building, and it is worth stating the truism that the universities could have avoided the procedures only at the cost of refusing the building. Those who found the controls irksome could at least ask themselves whether they were more restrictive than an absence of building would have been. It is also true that the UGC was greatly assisted in evolving its norms and procedures by the fact that a very similar exercise had already been taking place within the Ministry of Education so far as buildings for schools and further education were concerned. In this sense, the influence of the Department of State began to affect the practice of universities. And the influence has increased. In the mid 1960s the norms and standards of accommodation for higher education both inside and outside the universities were made comparable.

The upshot of all these developments is that the UGC has come to operate in ways that are indistinguishable from those of a Department of State. The controls which it is beginning to exercise resemble those of the Department of Education and Science in the public sector (Pratt, 1974). Many university people comfort themselves with the thought that since the committee is composed of academics, it must be intrinsically different from a Department of State; but it is not the composition of the committee which is significant, but the job it is required to do. A committee which operates as a bureaucracy will not cease to do so because it is not staffed by bureaucrats: indeed this may mean only that its bureaucratic activities are done less well. It seems clear that the crucial factor in changing the character of the UGC was not ill-will or imperialism on the part of the Government, still less any conscious intention to change in the UGC itself, but simply that the growth of the number of institutions for which it was responsible and of the amounts of money dispensed have rendered the old relationship impossible. This particular device for recognizing and preserving autonomous institutions is simply inappropriate if the number of institutions is very large. This has profound implications for the development of the autonomous tradition and for the size of the sector devoted to it, and these implications will be discussed in the next section.

The Government

We turn now, at last, to the Government. Those readers with suspicious minds will see that this section is a very long one and may be tempted to infer that for all my remarks about planning 'from the bottom up' I do after all regard the Government as the most important element in the administration of education. The only sense in which I do, and it accounts for the length of this section, is that hitherto Government has been the most intrusive and the most in error. Much of this section, therefore, deals with the common mistakes which people and Governments make about the role of Government in education. I begin with the ways in which Governments actually plan education.

In the last two decades there has been an enormous growth of new techniques of educational planning, some of them derived largely from the insights of economics. In these techniques planners have hoped to find more certain ground for their proposals, an 'objective' reason for doing one thing rather than another. Unfortunately the hope has been deferred. The situation has nowhere been better put than by one of the leading exponents of the economics of education, Mark Blaug. In an article in the *Economic Journal* of June 1967 he wrote:

Consider the curious predicament of an educational planner who consults the fast-growing literature on the economics of education for guidance in making policy decisions. On the one hand, he is told to gear the expansion of the educational system to quantitative forecasts of the demand for highly qualified man-power. On the other hand, he is urged to project what is quaintly called 'the social demand' for education, that is, the private consumers' demand, and to provide facilities accordingly. Finally, he is furnished with calculations of the rate of return on investment in education and advised to supply just enough schooling to equalize the yield of investment in human capital with the yield of investment in physical capital. Obviously, the three approaches may give different answers, and, strangely enough, the literature offers little assistance in reconciling different methods of educational planning. To add insult to injury, however, the advocates of man-power forecasting scoff at the assumptions underlying rate-of-return calculations while the proponents of rate-of-return analysis are equally scornful of the idea that man-power requirements can be predicted accurately. In the meantime, higher education is being expanded in many countries simply to accommodate the rising numbers of academically qualified applicants, apparently on the notion that something like Say's Law operates in markets for professional man-power, supply creating its own demand. All this is very confusing and in the circumstances we can hardly blame some educational planners who are beginning to doubt the value of the contribution of economists to educational decision-making (Blaug, 1967).

Let us look at these three approaches in a little more detail. The classic manpower forecast starts with a view about the development of the economy. Usually a government expects the economy to grow, indeed asserts that it should and clearly wants it to do so. This growth is inevitably to be accompanied and assisted by industrial development. This development is held to require increased numbers of people trained at various levels, and the manpower forecaster assumes that these skills are to be provided by the development of the education service. The whole process leads step by step from a view of a nation's economic future to proposals for the establishment and expansion of educational institutions. In recent years manpower forecasting has become very sophisticated, but it is important to realize that the sophistication has been in the techniques used to quantify rather than in the thought behind the method.

In fact, as a way of dealing with reality every single step in this sort of manpower forecast is absurd. We cannot forecast economic growth: this is not only technically impossible but logically impossible. Nor is there any ground for an inevitable association between economic growth and the need for educated people. There is a worldwide tendency for rich countries to have educated populations, but it is by no means clear whether this is because educated populations become rich or because rich populations can spend money on education. As far as growth is concerned the evidence is contradictory. In the United States the land grant colleges are held to have assisted economic development in the nineteenth century. But in Britain the Industrial Revolution took place without any help from an education system at all. The state in India with the most highly developed education system is Kerala, but it is industrially one of the least developed. In Pakistan, the development of large-scale industry has required trained people (though not very many): the development of small industries has taken place without any contribution from the education service; not only the workers but most of the owners and managers of these enterprises are illiterate. Manpower planning theoreticians have been able to link education with growth only by regarding education as the 'residual factor'. In other words, they assume education to effect growth because they cannot think of anything else which does.

Nor is there any established connection between levels of skill

203

required and particular kinds of education. In practice skills seem almost infinitely substitutable. Even the jump from an overall need for trained people to enrolments in particular institutions is logically and practically nonsensical. There is no reason to suppose that the education service, as it has developed in most countries, is the best vehicle for developing particular skills.

Many people who have become disillusioned with manpower forecasting on a national scale still believe it possible and right to forecast the demand for particular skills. Many countries prepare forecasts of the demand for scientists and engineers. Perhaps most prepare forecasts of demand for teachers and doctors. A favourite method of dealing with scientists and engineers is to inquire of industrialists what their 'need' for such people might be. The method has proved generally unreliable. It has also had disastrous educational consequences. The planner is forced to admit that his method gives him only general indications about the need for trained people. The development of relevant training institutions on the other hand requires some precision about the occupations into which their students will go. The planner knows he cannot provide this even in principle, so he is forced to argue that the training institutions should produce people with a broad general training, on the ground that they will then be able to adapt to a variety of jobs. In practice this means training people who are good for nothing in order to satisfy manpower demands.

Unfortunately, detailed manpower plans are as empty as overall ones. An expert paper on the demand for university trained engineers in the Netherlands (Ruiter, 1969) concluded that there were no satisfactory relationships between the demand for engineers and indicators of economic growth (production volume, productivity, investment). The factors determining demand for engineers remained obscure. Forecasting was based on the assumption 'that a reasonable development in the past, if continued, may be thought to give a reasonable assessment of what will be required in the future. The fact that a judgement to what extent the development in the past has been satisfactory is necessary, introduces an extra arbitrary element in the forecast.'

The weaknesses of manpower planning are now generally well

known. Normally in Britain governments have followed the Robbins Committee on higher education (Robbins, 1963) in deciding that manpower planning was simply 'impracticable'. The report added that 'while it is possible, for a number of professions and over a short time, to calculate with a fair degree of precision what the national need for recruits will be, we have found no reliable basis for reckoning the totality of such needs over a long term'. I was once present at a meeting in the Ministry of Education in Pakistan where a manpower planner mentioned his subject. The senior civil servant present said, without rancour, 'Oh that's quite exploded.' We at least know now that the solution to the problem of supplying an economy with needed skills is *not* to make a manpower forecast and design educational provision in the light of it. Unfortunately it still exerts a fascination for those who seek some kind of objective certainty to relieve them of the need for decision. Politicians and bureaucrats alike reach for it when otherwise baffled. For example, a British Minister of State said in 1975, '. . . the Government must do something more positive in the manpower planning field to guide its choices in the educational field . . .'.

What the Robbins Report did was to settle for the second method of educational planning, by 'considering what the demand for places in higher education is likely to be', and it asserted the guiding principle that 'all young persons qualified by ability and attainment to pursue a full time course in higher education should have the opportunity to do so'. In practice this meant projecting the trend of 'demand' from qualified school-leavers on the basis of certain assumptions. This exercise was more recently repeated by the Department of Education and Science and published in Education Planning Paper No 2: *Student Numbers in Higher Education in England and Wales*, HMSO, 1970. (There was a companion volume for Scotland.) The methods of the paper were no advance on those of the Robbins Report except that the latter's reference to 'social demand' was changed to 'private demand'. This private demand 'has . . . to be forecast mainly by projecting the aggregate demand pattern observed in the past, allowing for changes in numbers qualified to enter higher education'. The projection was made in a series of steps:

projections of the numbers in school, starting from the population figures from the General Register Office and the Government Actuary's Department;

projections of school-leavers with qualifications appropriate for entry to higher education, and projections of the corresponding output from further education establishments;

projections of entrants to higher education, based mainly on assumptions about the proportion of qualified leavers (and the corresponding output from further education) who will enter;

projections of places in higher education, based on assumptions about the length of course and postgraduate provision. (DES, 1970.)

This is the classic private or social demand forecast. The first thing to notice about it is the role which 'assumptions' play. The assumptions are in fact policies or points of view and it is possible to question all of them. For example writers at the time (Armitage and Crampin 1970) asserted that 'the neutral assumptions' about the secondary effects of raising the school-leaving age, the effect of secondary reorganization, the consequences of social changes like an increasing pressure for education from girls or the awakening of the backward north almost certainly led the Department to make very serious underestimates of demand. Some of the Department's assumptions, like those about the distribution of initial entrants to various sectors of higher education, were not even 'neutral': they were taken out of thin air. Nor was the paper entirely scrupulous in setting out its assumptions. The most startling example of this was that it ignored part-time students altogether. Projecting the number of full-time students without making any assumptions, implicit or explicit, about part-timers made the whole exercise meaningless.

But it is not only in its reliance on assumptions that this method of forecasting is discredited. More fundamentally objectionable is the projection of past trends. There is an implication here that the past offers a firm 'neutral' basis for projection. But what has happened in the past is not God-given. It is the result of past decisons and choices. To take an obvious example, the numbers getting into higher education do not represent a demand for higher education, but a satisfied demand. Even the numbers applying for higher education do not represent some neutral demand, but the demand under certain conditions of supply (of kind of courses available, of grants for students and so on). To make a time series of this so-called 'demand' and extrapolate it into the future cannot in the least be described as planning.

Unfortunately an exercise like this is more than vacuous; it is dangerous. Despite all the disclaimers about assumptions, work of this kind is in fact used to pencil in numbers for the future. For example, vice-chancellors, the University Grants Committee and others were asked in 1970 to address their minds to the possibility of accommodating something over 400,000 students in universities by the end of the decade. Advanced further education was asked to contemplate trebling its numbers in a similar period. These requests were consistent with the figures in the document, and it must be that they were already built into what is laughingly called the planning process.

However, if such figures are underestimates, as they could be on almost any other assumptions than those favoured by the Department, the result of expanding higher education in line with the paper would be the same as if a positive decision had been taken to restrict opportunity. The Government might just as well have said that it had decided not to meet any likely demand for places in higher education. It might equally well have added that any demand which it *did* meet would be accommodated haphazardly. As is clear from the fate of the Robbins recommendations, a structure of higher education and a balance between its sectors based upon unrealistic forecasts can never be put into effect. The system creaks and groans, and develops in all kinds of ways unforeseen at the beginning. It is then no good the Government or anyone else having a policy for higher education because there will be no way of implementing it. To follow private demand forecasts is to plan for inadequacy exacerbated by muddle.

Criticisms like these were made when the planning paper was first published in 1970. The reaction of the Department was interesting. It continued to use the same methods, but gave up publishing the assumptions on which it works and the forecasts which it makes. The result was the White Paper of December 1972, and I want to quote from this the whole of the discussion

207

about numbers, to convey fully its intellectual flavour. It was as follows:

The Government of 1963 endorsed the general principle, following the Report of the Robbins Committee, that courses of higher education should be available for all those who were qualified by ability and attainment to pursue them and who wished to do so. Successive Governments since have followed this principle and, despite the pressures of economic stringency and competing claims, higher education institutions have been enabled to grow and to keep pace broadly with the rising numbers of those qualified for and seeking higher education. The number of full-time and sandwich higher education students in Great Britain more than doubled from 192,000 in (academic year) 1961–62 to 463,000 in 1971–72; in the same period the number of part-time (day) students rose from 42,000 to 70,000.

The impetus of increasing staying-on in education to 18 will continue beyond the raising of the school leaving age; and the proportion of young people achieving qualifications at the Advanced level of the General Certificate of Education (or its equivalent) will also continue to increase. The planning of higher education provision must make allowances for this, as well as for the increasing size of these age groups over the next ten years. Much harder to foresee, however, is the likely trend in the attitudes and intentions of those young people towards higher education and their requirements within it.

The subsequent career patterns of some of those taking degrees or parallel higher education qualifications in future, for example, must be expected to differ significantly from those of their predecessors. The expansion of higher education provision has already reached the point where employers' requirements for such highly qualified people in the forms of employment they traditionally enter are, in the aggregate, largely being met. These patterns of employment are already changing and will continue to change as employers increasingly take the opportunity to enlarge the areas of work in which more highly educated and qualified recruits can be placed advantageously. Even so, there seems little doubt that the continuing expansion of higher education will more than match the likely expansion of graduate employment opportunities as these are understood today.

Opportunities for higher education are not however to be determined primarily by reference to broad estimates of the country's future need for highly qualified people; although attempts to relate supply to likely demand in certain specialized professions – and, particularly, at the postgraduate stage – will be no less important than before. The Government consider higher education valuable for its contribution to the personal development of those who pursue it; at the same time they value its continued expansion as an investment in the nation's human talent in a time of rapid social change and technological development. If these economic, personal and social aims are to be realized, within the limits of available resources and competing priorities, both the purposes and the nature of higher education, in all its diversity, must be critically and realistically examined. The continuously changing relationship between higher education and subsequent employment should be reflected both in the institutions and in individuals' choices. The Government hope that those who contemplate entering higher education – and those advising them – will the more carefully examine their motives and their requirements; and be sure that they form their judgement on a realistic assessment of its usefulness to their interests and career intentions.

The possibility of significant changes of this kind, alongside the uncertainties inherent in trying to predict matters of human behaviour some ten years ahead, makes it difficult to offer more than tentative estimates of the likely level of demand from qualified applicants for higher education places by the end of the decade. On a balanced judgement, however, the Government would expect to be providing by about 1981 for something of the order of 200,000 entrants annually from within Great Britain aged under 21. This would represent about 22 per cent of the age group then aged 18: compared with 7 per cent in 1961 and 15 per cent in 1971. Further uncertainty arises about the total number of places such an entry might imply. For example, the Government would not consider it justifiable to maintain, with so large an entry, the proportionate share that has been devoted to postgraduate work in recent years. And it is hard to know how many within the entry might choose a shorter course leading to the Diploma of Higher Education if these developed successfully on the lines indicated in the preceding section. Allowing also that provision for more mature entrants and for entrants from overseas would not grow proportionately so fast as that for young entrants, the Government consider that needs will be met within a total of 750,000 full-time and sandwich course higher education places in 1981. This figure has accordingly been adopted as the basis for the Government's longer-term planning in higher education (White Paper, 1972).

What this passage reveals most of all is embarrassment at the unsatisfactory nature of what the Government is itself doing. It hops from the notion of private demand to that of manpower planning and, finding the latter equally unhappy, back again. Buried in the figures is an exercise, detailed elsewhere in the White Paper, which involves cutting the intake to colleges of education by about a third on 'manpower' grounds. When all is done, the Government can do no better than a 'balanced judgement' based on unstated assumptions and unpublished forecasts. Again every stage of the process leading to the vacuities quoted above is absurd.

And since the White Paper, the combination of changes in 'demand' and a worsening of economic climate have caused Government to revise the number of places in higher education again and again. Their progress, over five years, has been 1970: 800,000; 1972: 750,000; 1976: 600,000. The results are as absurd as the process which led up to them.

All this leads us to wonder whether we might not be on safer ground in the economic certainties of rate of return analysis. In a sense rates of return are simply a summary statistic expressing, as Professor Blaug puts it, the prevailing relationship between the costs of more schooling and the earnings that may be more or less confidently expected to result from it. A rate of return analysis starts with a cross-tabulation of the labour force by age, education and earnings before and after tax. From these are constructed age earnings profiles by years of schooling; that is, cross-section data are used to project life-time earnings associated with additional education. If the costs of education are treated merely as negative earnings we can calculate the present value of the net earnings differentials associated with extra education at different discount rates. There is the difficulty that the earnings associated with additional education cannot be attributed to education alone. Individual earnings are also determined partly by native ability, family background, social class origins and so forth. Some American authorities have decided that about two-thirds of the observable earnings differentials associated with years of schooling are statistically attributable to differences in educational attainment. Professor Blaug concludes that 'the commonsense interpretation of the rates of return that have been calculated is that they represent something close to maximum-likelihood estimates of the average amounts of additional expenditures on education'.

Professor Blaug himself notices, however, that the rate of return approach is also vulnerable to objections. For example if there is no relationship between the relative earnings and the relative productivity of educated people, rate of return figures are economically meaningless. Equally if the supply of and demand for educated people change in the future, rates of return will differ from those calculated. And the approach ignores the non-monetary benefits of education and, more seriously, it ignores the monetary benefits other than those accruing directly to the individual. More important to my mind is the assumption that cross-sectional data are a good proxy for lifetime earnings. The most that rate of return analysis can do is to give very rough indications of the likely returns to particular kinds of education.

In many ways rate of return analysis has been the least popular of all the planning methods, perhaps because it challenges received opinion too openly. All the studies known to me show that the rate of return to part-time post-school education is higher, often much higher, than that to full-time education. This cheerful finding has been largely ignored. There is consistent pressure from the professions towards full-time courses, and this pressure is abetted by governments. The implications of it for some of the proposals in this book, however, are interesting. There is a higher rate of return on accommodating working-class students in the courses which attract them than in multiplying the courses which traditionally serve the middle classes.

It is something of a shock after discussing all these objections, many of which are faithfully noted by Professor Blaug, along with some others, to find him asking, 'Can we somehow combine all these approaches, or must we choose one in preference to the two others?' The more relevant question that occurs to most people, and particularly to busy administrators, is whether any of these approaches are of any use at all and if so how can they be used. I believe that all three approaches have a use but that success in using them depends on a proper understanding of what planning is.

The commonest failure of educational planning, exemplified in all these three approaches, is the attempt to derive policy from techniques. In every case the planner looks at the past and the present and then projects it into the future on the basis of a number of assumptions. Sometimes the planner himself can see no alternative. He believes that some numbers, however doubtful, are better than none at all, and he acknowledges that he will have to keep changing the numbers as different facts come to light and different assumptions are made. Sometimes the planner even believes that projections made in this way have the quality of inevitability. He believes that his projections are inescapable. More politically-minded planners may even welcome these methods because of this very air of inevitability. If policy emerges in this 'neutral' way the planner can disclaim responsibility for the consequences. The knockdown argument is 'What else can you do?' Perhaps this last remark reveals most clearly both the attraction of planning by projection and what is wrong with it.

There is indeed something else that can be done with these techniques of planning, even with present planning practices. As we have seen, they tend to be used because politicians and administrators want some neutral excuse for policies. Governments are full of policies: they fight elections upon them and they attack those of their opponents. Let us for the moment (but only for the moment) accept that the right place to start is with a policy. British Secretaries of State are entirely used to making statements of policy, as are the Opposition, independent commentators, educational organizations and so on. A Secretary of State might evolve a policy on a number of grounds. He might decide, as a matter of policy, that it would be right to offer places in third-level education to all those qualified and applying for them (Robbins, 1963), or to a certain percentage of the country's eighteen-year-olds by 1980. The proportion he chose would depend partly upon his own attitudes, on how ambitious, humane or philistine he might be, and also upon some estimate of the cost of alternative decisions. He might settle for something relatively modest, like a fifth of the age group by 1981 (which is roughly what the Government's White Paper implies), or he might decide that by the end of the decade English children should have similar opportunities available to them as Californian children ten years ago. He might even set out to create an education service which was designed to meet the needs and aspirations of all adults, however these might be expressed.

He might also decide what kinds of higher education should be offered. These have been discussed very fully in Chapter 2, where alternative traditions in higher education, the autonomous and the service, are described. The Secretary of State might well want to know the implications of accommodating the expansion mostly in universities or mostly in further education. He might wish to decide on what proportion of the expansion should be in part-time and full-time courses. He might even want to influence the proportion of courses leading recognizably to job qualifications. The Secretary of State, in short, would have a policy not only for expanding higher education but for determining in broad terms the balance between its sectors.

But of course it is open to the Secretary of State to start from different premises. He might wish to begin from the belief that the proportion of GNP devoted to higher education should increase, diminish or remain constant. He might want the rate of spending to grow faster or slower than GNP, or to keep in line with it. He might also decide, within this financial constraint, to accommodate as many or as few applicants as possible. Whatever the amount spent, he could choose between an élitist or a mass system. Different Secretaries of State would have different priorities and different policies. The point is that in evolving a policy he needs to know some of the implications and consequences of his decision before he takes it. It is at this point that the educational planner comes in. Ideally one would expect him to be able to tell the Secretary of State what the implications were for different policies and even to suggest ways of telling whether the policies were or were not likely to be successful. The Secretary of State needs to make his policy assumptions or value judgements explicit from the start. The planner would then be usefully employed, not in making more or less unwarranted assumptions about trends, but in predicting the unintended consequences of policy, in evolving measures of success or failure and in understanding different structures of costs.

If the planner is told (or tells himself) what policy is, he can say how likely it is to be achieved, what the difficulties are and what effort will be needed to overcome them. If a country has a policy for the expansion of higher education, the manpower planner can give a warning that at the rate the economy is growing and is likely to grow there will not be a comparable expansion of the jobs that graduates traditionally do. The Government might then decide to expand higher education on other grounds, but at least the manpower planner has been able to improve the basis on which the decision has been made. What he cannot do is to say how many graduates 'ought' to be produced from the point of view of manning the economy some years hence. Similarly, a Government may decide that a certain proportion of its people should get higher education. The 'private demand' planner can make clear how far the present education system is likely to produce the required result and how far extra or different effort is needed. And in the expansion of particular institutions and courses, the rate of return analyst can offer some indication of (among other things) the current 'need' for various kinds of graduates. The techniques described earlier are tests of policy, not autonomous methods of planning.

It must be added that reliance on technique is not only wrong-headed but damaging. To take 'social demand' as an example, its reliance on past trends inevitably (logically) produces a wholly unnecessary conservatism. Let us take the DES planning paper again as a basis. We shall have to make one additional assumption (no less warranted than those in the paper) about the cost of part-time advanced students in further education. This must be of the order of one-fifth of the cost of a full-timer in further education, but to be safe let us settle for a quarter.

Now let us suppose that the Secretary of State would like to see places available in some form of higher education, full-time or part-time, to some half of the eighteen-to-twenty-one age group by 1980. This is still a little way behind California 1960, but never mind. It implies something over 1,300,000 students. Let us also suppose that the Secretary of State is anxious that spending on higher education should be kept within the bounds set by the planning paper. What can we tell him?

In the first place, he will have to notice that according to his advisers the 'cost' of a university student is one and a half times as much as that of a full-time student in further education. We can therefore suggest that the universities expand more slowly than the planning paper allows, say a gentle rise to 250,000 places by 1980 (or about 60,000 less than Robbins suggested and 125,000 less than the 1972 White Paper provides). This gives us the equivalent of 125,000 university places to use elsewhere. We could get 188,000 places in full-time advanced further education for the same money. But let us not rush into this. Why not make just 50,000 of these places available, bringing the total in full-time FE up to 250,000 like the universities? The remaining places would allow us to accommodate 700,000 extra part-timers on advanced courses in FE. And the colleges of education could chime in with their 130,000, giving us 1,330,000 places in all. (Since this was written the Government has settled for some 80,000 places in colleges of education – the balance to be taken up by advanced FE.)

One has only to do a calculation of this kind to reveal the objections to what is now called 'planning'. Relying on 'trends', Ministers may be persuaded that they can offer opportunity to a fifth of the population. If they had a policy, they might accommodate nearly double the number. At all events, the real planning is still to be done.

This insistence on having a policy may sound trite, but the British Government is not alone in trying to do without one – or at least without one that is positively stated. Its recent White Paper was concerned with matters of scale, organization and cost (White Paper, 1972), and this indeed is what most governments mean when they talk about planning for post-school education. What we get by way of policy are various attempts at coordination, rationalization and regulation. (In other systems, where these tendencies have been traditional, the current vogue is for decentralization, democratization and participation – but the vacuity of the exercise is the same.)

The last 20 years have seen much coordinating and rationalizing in British post-school education. For example in 1956 further education was divided among 'local', 'area', 'regional' and 'national' colleges and colleges of advanced technology, the division being on the basis of levels of work. In 1966 advanced further education was to be concentrated in thirty 'polytechnics'. By 1976 further education, including the training of teachers, will be offered in most large cities by amalgamated 'institutes', but this policy differs from its predecessors in being much less overtly announced or discussed.

But if it is wrong for governments to start with techniques or with 'policies', where should they start? A policy is best thought of as a solution to some problem. A policy for rationalization is a solution to the problems of Ministers and bureaucrats. A policy for meeting social demand is a solution to the problem of winning the votes of sectors of the electorate. Good policies are attempts to solve a number of problems. There are two things a Government is uniquely placed to do – the first is to formulate problems on a national basis, the second is to distribute national resources. And it is these two things that it should concentrate on. It is not best placed to devise solutions to problems that are not political or administrative – that is problems of education, health, industry, poverty – and it should not try. But it can judge other people's solutions, and support those that are promising.

So the first steps in the Government's planning is to formulate the problems. It is astonishing how seldom this in fact takes place. Usually Governments, and those advising them, jump straight to solutions and come to regard as the chief problem the difficulty of implementing these. As a consequence much thought, energy and expense goes on trying to perfect solutions which are not at all apt for the problems which, though ill-formulated, remain to plague us. For example, the creation of thirty polytechnics in Britain in 1966 did meet the need for bureaucratic rationalization, but the educational and social problems which the 'binary policy' was meant to tackle were not clearly formulated. The policy itself was arguably apt for some of these, but the creation of the polytechnics worked against their solution. This tendency to start with solutions actually reduces the potential for new ideas. The solutions which most readily come to hand are old ones. They are no longer apt, if indeed they ever were.

The kinds of problems which Governments express will be problems of social engineering: how do we get from the present state of affairs to a different, improved, one? Such problems are best formulated in negative terms, to give them greater precision. There is no limit to our positive desires, but we cannot do everything – so what are we determined not to put up with any longer? At the compulsory stages of education, for example, we can formulate the problem of 'producing the full man' – the cultivated citizen. Educational goals are frequently expressed in these sorts of terms. But they are empty because they are unlimited. On the other hand, if we say that the problem is to end illiteracy among eight-year-olds, the problem becomes precise enough to invite solutions. We know, for a start, that our present solutions are inadequate because large numbers of eight-year-olds are in fact illiterate. (If eight is too ambitious an age for such a formulation, take any other: the point remains. Indeed the abolition of illiteracy in adults is a necessary task of post-school education to which our present arrangements make little contribution.)

The formulation of problems, then, is the first and most difficult task. Of course Governments will not do this on their own. They will need the help both of the professionals in the field and of the public at large.

One admirable device for doing this would be the departmental committee. At present such committees are tempted into solution-mongering, but even so their potential is clear. Even now people often misunderstand the purpose of these committee's reports. They complain that there is nothing new in them, or that they are not particularly radical documents. This is true; but the committees' chief importance is that they make possible progress by consent. What happens is that a committee is asked to study a particular subject, like non-vocational adult education (Russell, 1973). At once, organizations and individuals start putting in 'evidence'. A large-scale public debate is initiated. The issues begin to be clarified and aired. Research is commissioned. At the end of it all, almost unnoticed, the conventional wisdom has become quite different from what it was at the beginning of the process. The committee's report stakes out the new frontiers of *acceptable* advance. More radical spirits are, of course, already far away over the horizon: their achievement will become generalized through the next report. The committee does not attempt revolution: it is an agent of democratic change.

One can think of two inquiries, one an example, the other an awful warning – both from higher education. The great and accepted achievement of the Robbins Committee was to make acceptable the idea of expansion to an academic community which had been more than reluctant to contemplate it (Robbins, 1963). This achievement rested much less upon the actual report, even with all those appendices, than it did on the fact that the argument went on for the two years in which the committee sat, and the expansionist case could be clearly seen to be the better.

Compare this with the work of the Prices and Incomes Board on academic salaries. Here, too, the objective of the Board was to change university attitudes, particularly to notions of productivity. Its members were expert and they worked quickly. They reported twice. On the issues they themselves regarded as important they carried no conviction and commanded no assent. This is quite simply because the people concerned had no share in the formulation of the issues and in the creation of consensus (PIB, 1968).

Since the formulation of problems is unfamiliar and difficult, it would be the task of such departmental committees to concentrate the mind of the service upon it. The terms of reference of one of them might be something like this: 'To review the education service for those between sixteen and nineteen, by formulating problems, removing impediments to the search for solutions and establishing tests for such solutions.' All the processes of consultation by Governments should be on similar lines. Again, at present, Governments consult, if at all, only on their own proposed solutions. They exclude, at the most important stage, the help of those best placed to give it, and they reduce the very process of consultation to a charade.

I have said earlier that Governments are ill-placed to evolve solutions, except to political and administrative problems. This is why they, and any committees which advise them, should concentrate on making solutions possible, not try to impose their own. Of course, they may have a bright idea, and if they do, they should see that it is tried somewhere; but they are highly unlikely to find the complete or final answer. And if they do, it will not last for long. What Governments find hard to understand is that there are national problems, in educational and other social fields, but no national solutions. Panaceas are uncommon.

We need alternatives. The best we can do is to proceed by trial and error, learning from the mistakes of one attempted solution, and applying the lessons to others. The best we have done hitherto is somewhat less than this. Lessons from many attempts to solve social problems go unheeded, because politicians, civil servants and educators have a vested interest in being right and successful. Where Governments propose solutions, particularly on a national scale, they cannot admit error, so similar solutions are tried over and over again. This makes it hard to improve. We need instead many alternative solutions, so that we can judge which are most promising. We need in particular the two essential characteristics of post-school education – the flexibility and responsiveness to demand that arise from a spontaneous and unsystematic provision. We must avoid the attempt to prescribe in detail a national pattern of institutional provision. A policy has to be expressed in different terms. It must ensure that institutions develop naturally as the need for them arises. There is no logic in supposing that a single pattern of institutions will be appropriate for all parts of the country, for all industries or for all types of students.

This is not as eccentric a view as it might seem. It has already been accepted quite explicitly in the establishment of the Council for National Academic Awards. Here is a national decision to make degree awards available to colleges outside the universities (as part of a solution to social problems), to release the colleges from external university courses, and to ensure that the standards of these awards are nationally recognized and comparable with those at the established universities. No attempt is made to prescribe national curricula and syllabuses. The same principle should apply in the establishing and financing of institutions.

This view of the role of Government, as a formulator of national problems, may seem an unfamiliar one to most people. It will certainly surprise many people in education and other social services, who are used to dealing with Government policies all the time. But it is one which is entirely consistent with the Education Act 1944, where the Secretary of State has a general duty 'to promote the education of the people ... and the progressive development of institutions devoted to that purpose, and to secure the effective execution by local authorities, under his control and direction, of the national policy for providing a varied and comprehensive educational service in every area'. The extent of his direction and control is spelled out in later sections of the Act, and is confined largely to a regulatory and appeal function. In the past, Secretaries of State have acted in this spirit, too. When the time came to reorganize secondary education so as to abolish the folly and injustice of selection at eleven plus (in line, as we have seen, with developments in most other countries) the Secretary of State requested local authorities to prepare development plans. This is surely the way for him to act in the future. For example, if Britain is to meet the problems of young people through reorganizing what other countries call 'second-level' education – that is for those from sixteen to nineteen or twenty – incorporating a variety of existing and new institutions, the question for the Secretary of State is not how, in detail, is this to be done? Rather it is, who should be given the responsibility for doing it? The answer lies in the Education Act 1944, which lays upon local authorities the duty to secure the provision of further education, and in particular to prepare and submit schemes of further education.

It may be that we are not yet ready, even for this. Perhaps seriously monitored experiment, both in the curriculum and in organization, is first required. There have been many innovations in schools, FE colleges, industrial training and elsewhere, some of which have been promising, while others are known to have failed. All these experiments should be generally known and seriously evaluated, and further innovation should be sponsored and monitored. On this basis, more general schemes of post-school education could be framed. The Government is in a good position to establish a body to monitor existing experience and to sponsor new initiatives, and such a body might itself then prepare recommendations for general schemes. Its terms of reference would be to support, encourage and monitor innovation and to learn from experience. For this purpose it would need some 'pump-priming' funds, but it would have the merit of being otherwise very inexpensive.

A similar initiative could be taken with organization. For this a selected number of local authorities could be asked either to prepare proposals themselves or to encourage groups of institutions – schools and colleges – to collaborate in preparing plans through which they would together provide for the needs of young people in the age group.

There may be other problems that might better be tackled, not by local authorities, but by individual institutions. Perhaps the best method for the Secretary of State is to say what the problems are and then invite 'bids' to attempt solutions.

Although the formulation of problems is a basic function of Governments, there are in fact two others of scarcely less importance. The first is the overall distribution of national resources, and the second is the scrutiny of solutions. The distribution of resources follows naturally from problem formulation. The announcement that the Government saw a particular problem would be accompanied by the determination to do something about it. It is at this point, in current practice, that things begin to go wrong, because Governments (and Oppositions) feel they have to have solutions to put to the electorate. Instead they should announce a shift in priorities: more resources would go to the problem areas than hitherto, if necessary at the expense of other things. In a really tight corner, they might even put a figure to the resources. Up to a point British political parties do this already. What they need is the courage of their convictions, and the sense to make a virtue of giving the responsibility of reform to those best placed to make it. (I have spoken on enough political platforms to know that this kind of commitment is a perfectly easy one to defend. It raises less scepticism than more grandiose solutions and has the added advantage of reducing cynicism about political promises.)

Usually shifts of resources in any one year would be marginal, but this need not always be so. Up to a point, the allocation of resources would need to await 'bids' from those authorities and institutions willing to tackle problems. But once the system became familiar, institutions and authorities would come to be able to respond more quickly, would begin to anticipate the Government's moves and would thus make it possible for really substantial shifts in priorities to be made quickly.

The need for speed in tackling problems underlines another weakness of the present arrangements. When Governments want to create national solutions they need, if they are democratic Governments, to consult endlessly and gain general agreement. For example, legislation in Britain, even DES circulars to local authorities, comes only after considerable discussion. The solution is then an inevitable compromise, which has taken sometimes years to reach. If the Government is not bound to impose a solution nationally, but instead asks for proposals for solving stated problems, no great consultation is necessary on the solutions at all. People who do not agree will not propose. Those who do propose will be binding no-one but themselves. The essence of this approach is responsibility not consultation.

The third job of Governments is the scrutiny of solutions and the regulation of standards of provision. In Britain the second of these is the job of the Secretary of State already. The first is scarcely attempted. It is essential, however, if we are ever to learn from experience. When problems have been clearly stated and solutions offered, we can judge how far the latter were appropriate and how far they were successful. A solution must be monitored. Its progress at all stages must be checked against the original problem. The conventional view of evaluation is that it is the sort of thing you do at the end of an exercise, whether in public policy or a course in mental arithmetic. In my view, for public policy at least, it is crucial that it is undertaken from the very start, otherwise it is too late. The conventional view, of course, conveniently accommodates most policies, because they are not explicitly related to problems, and thus all activity after their announcement can be considered successful. But it plays havoc with any hope of solving social, educational or other problems.

The monitoring of policy need not be a gigantic exercise. All bureaucracies have systems of routine data collection. What is usually lacking is not statistical and other material but its use. Data are available on virtually every characteristic of students, staff, courses, wastage, examination results and so on. Much of it is collected by the Government, and lies discarded on its shelves. Local authorities and the colleges themselves collect, and usually ignore, the rest. Such data, covering individual institutions and the sector as a whole, can serve as key indicators of the progress of the policy. It is worth asserting that tendencies towards the failure of policies can usually be detected very quickly. The majority of irreversible changes seem to occur in the formative years of institutions. The rate of change seems to decline over time rather than increase. It is during these early years only that there is opportunity to exercise control over their development. If monitoring of policy is not undertaken until, say, five years after its initial statement, most of the development of the institutions will have already taken place. Since it has been unmonitored the development will almost certainly be other than that required.

There is one place where monitoring cannot be done by the Government: that is, the activities of its own bureaucracy. In regulating standards of provision, in negotiating nationally the salaries of teachers and in many other ways, the Department of Education and Science, though acting formally in the name of the Secretary of State, is inevitably a power in its own right. Often it has gone on acting as if the Government's policy was quite different from what it was. This is not out of ill-will or sabotage. It is just that the problem of consistent administration is a difficult one.

It points the need, however, for a check that the administrative acts of the Department do not hinder the solution of problems which it has itself assisted the Secretary of State in formulating. Existing pressures in the system – of resource distribution, salary structures, student grants, building programmes and other institutional structures – are very strong and will prevail if left unchecked. Newton's Laws apply to social institutions as well as apples. 'A body continues in the same state of motion until acted upon by a force' is a law to be engraved on every bureaucrat's desk. Educational institutions will follow the historical process of academic drift unless positive steps are taken to prevent it. The institutional structures that generate these pressures are the place where the attack has to be made. Understanding their role and their use in policy implementation would enable social change to take place far more effectively.

Let us take just three examples of this from British post-school education.

Salary scales for teachers in Britain depend upon the level of work in a college. This means that if a college or local authority decides that it would contribute to a solution of some problem (of the access of workers, for example) that institutions should be comprehensive, the staff should not be penalized for achieving it. Under present arrangements the rewards go to those institutions which are the least comprehensive. Institutions which are meant to accommodate students at various levels should not have their establishments and staff salaries determined on the basis of levels of work. To avoid this would upset not only long-standing practice of teachers' salary negotiations but a whole socio-educational tradition. But this is precisely what the problem may require.

A similar point concerns part-timers. These students are conventionally expressed, for resource purposes, in terms of their full-time equivalence. This is odd from many points of view. In the first place it is mere convention. In the second, the convention counts the majority of students in the public sector (the part-timers) in terms of the minority (the full-timers). Third, it is so ungenerous as to discourage colleges from accommodating part-timers. If the expansion of part-time places would be a solution, then it would need different, and more generous, conventions about the resources available for them. These 'no less important' students, as the 1966 White Paper called them, might then find themselves welcome in prestigious colleges instead of shunned as opportunity arises.

The third example concerns student grants. At present grants are 'mandatory' if a student is on a recognized full-time course of higher education. If he is on any other kind of course the grant is 'discretionary'. Again those 'no less important' students who are on courses below degree level or who are studying part-time need new administrative arrangements if they are to be accommodated.

In the past, the three instruments mentioned here have been divisive as well as destructive of policy. They discriminated between staff and institutions on an irrational basis, causing friction and inhibiting cooperation. They seemed to set a value on certain kinds of students as against others. Yet they are regarded by most people as 'neutral'. A Government wishing to tackle problems through post-school education will court failure unless it ensures that all these 'neutral' rules and conventions are altered to activities to accommodate the solutions it seeks.

It is precisely here that the Government, in the person of the Secretary of State for Education and Science, is least well placed to monitor its own activities, especially those undertaken on its behalf by the Civil Service. Part of the difficulty lies in the fact that Secretaries of State, like most Ministers, are moved to other jobs after only a short period in education. Part seems to lie in the relationships between Secretaries of State and the DES. Secretaries of State have a number of functions, of which the formulation of policy is only one. They have to defend the Department and its concerns in the Cabinet and the House of Commons. They have to represent the interests of education in the country at large. They have to take responsibility for the way the Department is administered. This means that they identify with the Department and are not well placed to check that its proposals and day-to-day activities are well designed to implement their policies.

The difficulty is not one which is confined to education alone, nor to any particular government. Ministers of all governments and all departments quite commonly assert that they have been 'captured' by the Civil Service. Many add that despite their best efforts their clearly stated policies have not been put into effect. This has nothing to do with a conspiracy of civil servants or with ill-will on their part. It is inevitable in the circumstances, since it is the administrative machine that does the work and there is a constitutional convention that Ministers are responsible for (and thus have to defend) what the machine does.

The notion of the helplessness of Ministers is not new, but many of the proposals for dealing with it are unconvincing. For example, I do not believe that importing 'experts' into the Department has had any very profound consequences. There has been no shortage of experts in the DES itself. Nor does the solution lie in giving each Minister a political private office. There seems no reason to believe that the recent widespread introduction of political advisers has had the desired consequence of strengthening Ministers in thier dealings with their departments.

What is required quite simply is the application to the activities of the Department of the principle on which the CNNA validates the courses of polytechnics and other colleges. In other words the

Secretary of State needs a group of people (differently composed, perhaps, for different areas of his responsibility) who will scrutinize seriously the proposals which the Department is agreeing for formulating problems and implementing solutions.

The group would also require an analysis of existing activities which bear upon the problems and their proposed solutions, asking how far the existing activities are failing and what grounds there are for believing that the proposed ones would be more effective. Similarly they should be able to investigate all the instruments at the disposal of the Department for carrying out the stated policy – not only those which are identified by the Department but also those other instruments and activities which may affect its outcome.

Finally, the group must satisfy itself that all proposals have, built into their structure, the means for assessing their effectiveness. They need to be certain that the grounds on which the proposals can be said to have failed are known and stated at the beginning, and appropriate means are found for measuring the extent of this failure. In particular it is important to know the time at which evidence might begin to become available that the proposals are failing to meet their objectives.

It is important to set up the process formally. In bureaucracies, unless somebody is given a particular job to do, the job does not get done. So long as the process is established it is probably less important to worry about who should be involved. Certainly Ministers should be there (probably the Secretary of State and the junior ministers), so should senior civil servants, but the bulk of the group should be outsiders predominantly from education and from politics – and fortunately there are many people who combine these interests.

Who does what?

It should now be obvious how post-school education should be organized. Administration should derive from purpose. The object of providing post-school education is to offer a service to all adults, to help them to tackle their own problems. Most post-school education, in my view, should be in the service tradition. In so far as it is educational (as distinct from 'research'), it should undoubtedly be administered as a service, since responsibility to students and the public as a whole demands accountability.

We should accept with gratitude the chief virtues of the service tradition and build upon them and recognize what it is in the tradition which enables institutions to do all those things (like responding to social needs and educating the workers) which would spread post-school education. Administratively the foremost of these virtues is flexibility, or as some unkindly put it, muddle. It is precisely the fact that certain courses appear where nobody expected them that constitutes responsiveness. It is the existence of different levels of work and modes of study in the same institution that both attracts students to further achievement and provides some chance of qualification even for those who fail. Attempts to rationalize this flexibility end by destroying it, especially where the attempt is made through the designation of institutions. Instead the strategy should be to state, clearly, the problems which post-school education is asked to solve, so that the Government, the local authorities and individual institutions exercise their powers and duties in such a way that development will be easiest and most profitable if it contributes to solutions. I suspect that we shall need to create for this purpose 'comprehensive academic communities' of post-school education offering, either singly or together, the variety, flexibility, responsiveness, innovation and concern for the deprived which have characterized the service tradition.

The duty of the Secretary of State will be to formulate those national problems to which post-graduate education might offer a solution. He will distribute national resources in accordance with this formulation. He will finance those institutions charged with the task of proposing solutions, whether these are the local authorities, the research councils, the University Grants Committee or individual institutions. He will monitor their solutions and regulate their standards of provision. He will make certain that these very regulations do not inhibit possible solutions. The local authorities will be responsible, singly or jointly, for the development of institutions in their areas. They will settle the general pattern of post-school education and the place of each individual institution. They will require the institutions to prepare academic development plans and to be accountable to them for resources.

The institutions will create the framework in which their students and staffs can create programmes or education and research. In doing so the institutions and their members will act in the context of the Secretary of State's formulation and the local authorities' general direction about their place locally. They will have access to a plurality of funding, from the Secretary of State, the local authorities, the research councils and from other foundations and Government departments. This plurality is the most helpful guarantee of innovation and responsibility. All these institutions at whatever level are accountable for what they do. Such a system would make it possible for the development which is most urgently needed in post-school education – that is, of opportunities for independent study for all students.

This kind of system is appropriate, I believe, for all education, at least to degree level. In particular it would be as apt for universities in Britain as for further education colleges. The autonomous tradition is not appropriate for education, because it inhibits responsibility to and for students. The change I propose for the universities would be less than the universities think. With the multiplication of universities, the 'autonomous' arrangements through the UGC have largely broken down. The UGC acts like a Government Department and lays down, not regulations, but norms, which have the same effect. For individuals in universities the changes I propose would be greatly liberating.

Is there then to be no autonomous sector at all? I think there should be one – because we should retain the reality of different systems, the possibility of comparison, the development of alternatives. The advantages of autonomy are not negligible. But the sector should be small, so that it can be genuinely autonomous. It should be supported in the same way as we support museums, art galleries, opera and the theatre – for its own sake. We must not ask autonomous institutions to put forward arguments for their existence, or bids for resources. That would be to undermine their nature. The judgement about the size of the sector would be for the Secretary of State, as part of his judgement about resources, but I should guess that no more than six universities, mainly postgraduate, would be about right, together with some autonomous units attached to other institutions.

Changing Public Policy

The proposals made here for the organization of post-school
education raise this very serious question: can public policy be
rationally conceived and judged? Probably most people believe
that it cannot. They say politics is the art of the possible, not of the
rational. Public policies and their criticism are both subjectively
based and depend on value judgements. What happens in human
affairs depends on human nature: it is the motive or a decision of
an individual or the dynamics of a group that 'really' determines
what is done. The controlled experiment – the core of scientific
rationality – is impossible in social and political affairs, so certainty in these matters must always elude us. It is these characteristics of public and social policy which resist the logic that lies
behind the physical sciences, so we must put up with our hunches
and our unresolved arguments.

I believe this view is both wrong and dangerous. It is wrong
about what science is, and it is dangerous in that it undermines
the democratic control of affairs.

Let us start with the problem of objectivity. There are some
people who suppose that in science it all depends upon the objectivity of the individual scientist. They can never have heard or
read about two scientists quarrelling. Objectivity is not secured
by the impartiality of the individual but by the 'public' nature of
science. A hypothesis remains subjective while it is private to its
creator; it aspires to objectivity and becomes of scientific importance when it is tested by experience and can be seen to stand up
to tests – when it has become public. In this social theories, or
public policies, are no more subjective than theories about the
physical world – though the tests employed may be very different.

Nor is social science or politics unique in looking at things
from a particular point of view. Science is not just a body of facts,
somehow 'objectively' collected. Indeed, what distinguishes
science from pre-science is that facts are selected for a purpose, to
test a hypothesis. In the natural sciences, theory determines the
point of view – as it does in the social sciences. Description will
depend not only on the facts described but on our point of view,
which is bound up with the hypothesis we wish to test.

Even people who accept this description of the natural as well as the social sciences may still object that so much in the latter – and in politics – depends upon value judgements. There is a sense of course in which the value judgement is simply another name for a policy: it is what ought to be done. But this does not mean that one cannot treat one's policies scientifically. We can say, for example, that *if* such and such was our policy, what would tell us whether it had succeeded or failed. We can apply to it tests which are generally acceptable. To take an example from higher education in Britain, we can say that the policy of concentrating advanced-level work in ten colleges of advanced technology after 1956 could be said to have failed if the growth of advanced work was greater outside them – as indeed it was. More important, we can make predictions (hypotheses) about the consequences of a policy and test them as they develop. So long as we have made the predictions (or developed the hypothesis) it is astonishing how quickly they can be tested – or how soon one knows whether the policy is going to succeed or fail.

Nor are we helpless when faced with the value judgements themselves. For example, there may be room for argument whether it is right to try to eliminate barriers to the further education of working-class people. In the end somebody has to decide. But it is entirely possible to introduce greater rationality into the decision by describing alternative policies and by predicting their consequences, particularly their possible unintended consequences. Value judgements are in fact of great importance. Objectivity rests not in denying their existence (which is dishonest) or seeking to eliminate them (which is impossible) but in making explicit what they are and testing them. Value judgements (policies) are the hypotheses of social science: we cannot make progress without them.

A third version of the claim that social science is subjective rests upon the assumption that in the natural sciences, we achieve certainty or finality. But this is not so. Scientific theories are overthrown because a better one comes along, and we can discover whether or not a new hypothesis is better than an old one. If they are different they will lead to different predictions which can be tested experimentally; on the basis of the experiment we may find that the new theory leads to a satisfactory result where the old one breaks down. Scientific certainty has been replaced by scientific progress. In all this the social sciences are not different from the natural sciences.

People's motives need not detain us very long either. In science a man may advance a hypothesis out of ambition, envy, greed or emotional disturbance. A piece of work may depend for its success upon the personal relations of the members of a team. But we do not think of judging the hypothesis or the work by reference to character or togetherness. Nor should we in social affairs. Yet too often we accept goodwill or the quality of collaboration instead of effectiveness. If we can get used to judging outcomes rather than effort, we shall find people readier to modify their own and joint behaviour in the interests of achievement. The practice of requiring results, rather than seeking to modify behaviour directly, is more promising and less arrogant.

The attractive notion that social questions are all a matter of human nature boils down to the assertion that only one of the social sciences, psychology, or perhaps social psychology, is of relevance. Of course our institutions and traditions are man-made. They are the results of human action and decisions. But this does not mean that they are all consciously defined and explicable in terms of needs, hopes or motives. Even consciously and successfully designed institutions do not turn out according to plan because of their unintended social repercussions. Thus, their creation affects not only other social institutions but also 'human nature' – the hopes, fears and ambitions both of those immediately involved and later of other members of society.

The trouble with the insights of pscyhology is that, from the point of view of policy, they are vacuous. A good example of this is the permanent controversy about the effects of heredity and environment. The enormous amount of heat and energy devoted to the argument about which of these is more important must be of purely academic interest. It cannot tell us what measures should be taken to improve intelligence: it does not even tell us what measures *can* be taken. We can discover how to improve intelligence not by knowing the relative contribution of many generations and of powerful economic pressures, but by trying one or two ideas and seeing if they fail.

There is a similar difficulty about sociology. The most familiar fact about British social life, illustrated time and again by Government inquiry and endless academic research, is that working-class children do less well academically than middle-class children. As J. W. B. Douglas puts it very clearly in *All Our Future*, 'the middle class pupils have retained almost intact their historic advantage over the manual working class' (Douglas 1968). The establishment of this fact is not enough – we need to know what to do about it; yet as C. D. Darlington said (in a contribution to the nature-nurture debate), 'sociology is a descriptive science, and sociologists are more apt to offer explanations than to test them with experiments'.

As for the controlled experiment, this is clearly not central to science – or we would have no science called astronomy and no scientific study of the weather. What we have to do, in public affairs and astronomy alike, is to recognize experience as our impartial arbiter. Moreover the experience must be of a 'public' character, like observation and experiment, not 'private', like aesthetic or religious experience.

The task for the social and natural scientist is one of trial and error of inventing hypotheses which can be practically tested and of submitting them to these tests. In most current practice the trial is unmonitored, the error explained away. Existing social science is more interested in describing and explaining than in testing the explanations. What we need is a way out of the anecdotal and taxonomic prison in which public affairs and their attendant social sciences find themselves.

I believe that such a way out exists. We can begin by accepting Karl Popper's formulation of the continuous process by which intellectual progress is made. The process begins with the formulation of a problem; for this we propose a trial solution; to this solution we apply tests to eliminate error; all of which leads us to a new situation with the possibility of new problems. In this process the most often neglected step is the first – the formulation of problems. In politics and social affairs generally we are all too ready to leap to a solution, and we often persist in the solution, regardless of its irrelevance to our pressing problems.

Hardly less neglected is the third step – that of testing our proposed solutions. Public affairs are littered with policies and 'experiments' which are successful only to the extent that activity equals success. We do not normally test or monitor our solutions, or even wonder what tests might be appropriate. But the task of creating apt tests is as difficult and important as that of formulating problems. One consequence of our neglect is that our attempts at the second step – of proposing solutions – remains at an unacceptably humdrum level. Most of our 'solutions' have in fact been tried before, and have scarcely ever met the case. Only when we know that the first thoughts off the tops of our heads are either unrelated to our deepest problems or unlikely to offer solutions to them shall we be tempted into the bold and imaginative proposals that our present social catastrophe demands.

The heart of the matter is the demarcation which Popper makes between science and non-science, that is, his notion of falsifiability. A scientific statement is one which can be falsified: not verified – because no amount of verification can give us the assurance of truth. One falseification, however, can give us the assurance of error. This is why our testing in stage three of the process sketched above is the elimination of error, not the confirmation of truth. It is also why it is mistaken to contrast the certainty of the natural sciences with the uncertainties of the social sciences: all knowledge is provisional, and we make use of one hypothesis until a better one comes along.

But the bolder our hypotheses the more vulnerable they are to refutation. This is their value: if they survive our best efforts to refute them, they have got us further. Popper has destroyed scientific certainty and replaced it with scientific progress, but progress is possible only if people formulate real problems, propose imaginative solutions and test them to destruction.

This approach is directly relevant to public policy: we can and should study policy scientifically. In politics, our hypotheses are policies. They are proposed solutions to particular problems. We have to decide what would tell us that the hypothesis was wrong; that is, that the policy had failed. It is failure that we have to look for. This would of itself add rigour to our proposed solution and would help us to predict the consequences of policy and test our predictions. We should be alert for unintended consequences and well poised to learn from mistakes.

Above all, we need this rigour to enable us to move quickly. In social affairs we are dealing with people, so to persist in error is especially irresponsible. We need, in short, the quickest means, consistent with reliability, of knowing that things have gone off the rails. It is more important to find apt tests, even crude ones, than to accumulate sophisticated data. It is this process of formulating social problems, creating solutions and testing them which properly constitutes social science.

Of course, policies do not exist in a vacuum: they are implemented through social institutions. Creating these institutions can be thought of as a social technology. We have to ask of institutions, as we do of machines, whether they are fit for the purpose. If they are not, we need to decide whether to tinker with them or scrap them. This is no separation of theory and practice, for the practice is an important aid to theory and rationality. Indeed social theory cannot long remain rational if divorced from social practice.

I hope it is now clear that such an approach is essential in a democracy. It is by the rigorous testing of policies that we can hope to hold a government accountable. If we cannot decide what would tell us that a government had failed in its policies, we have no ground but whim for turning it out, and no ground for protesting that it has been arbitrary and capricious. Criticism is the spur of science and democracy alike. There is no proposal that cannot be improved by the criticism of those less expert than its authors.

Democratic governments seek to remedy abuses, relieve misery or reduce barriers to opportunity and self-fulfilment by changes in policies. They do this all the time, fitting new institutions into the framework of existing ones and adjusting them if they do not work. These governments, and their societies, can make mistakes and learn from them without risking a disaster that would dissuade them from further reform. They can make repeated experiments and continuous adjustments. But if this is how governments are to act, we must have a scientific approach to public policy.

Otherwise our reforms will be in vain, our mistakes unnoticed and our aspirations frustrated.

There is nothing new in the techniques we have to use: indeed some of them are crude in the extreme. What we must do is use the techniques to some purpose, and that purpose is the testing of public policy. In short, I believe that there can be an objective social science, that public policy and administration can be ordered scientifically.

It is important to realize that this kind of study of policy and the means by which it is implemented is not to be confined simply to the activities of governments. Nor need the testing involve infinitely elaborate exercises, though no doubt academics will seek to make them as complicated as possible and will continue to use the techniques evolved largely for their own sake. Usually we want to know quickly whether a policy is failing or not: we cannot wait for the length of time a 'research' programme usually takes. The problem for social and political scientists is to determine what crude, simple and cheap tests would give the information required. My colleague, John Pratt, and I have suggested such a test, which would be one way of telling whether our own institution (and others like it) was failing in its purpose.

It is an example of how seemingly small things can make all the difference. We were interested in the development of polytechnics. These institutions were designated with a degree of self-conscious-ness unusual in British higher education. They were to be part of a well and fully expressed 'binary policy' – which has been con-tinued under two governments. The essence of the policy has been stated earlier: it was to maintain and enhance a 'public' sector of higher education consisting of 'open' institutions responsive to social and industrial demand, concerned with vocational and pro-fessional education and thus attractive to working people and their children. At the apex of this sector there were to be thirty polytechnics, established as 'comprehensive academic commun-ities' offering opportunities at honours-degree level and below by all modes of study – full-time, part-time, sandwich, block release, day release and the rest.

But it is not enough to have a policy: you have to be sure of the means chosen to implement it. Were the polytechnics a good instrument for securing the goals expressed in ministerial speeches and in the White Paper of 1966? A certain amount of doubt about this was expressed at the time, and the doubts have been growing. Chief among them was the hunch that the polytechnics would 'go the way of the CATS' – that is, they would seek to become like universities and in the process would drop their technical college traditions. The consequence of this would be that, policy or no policy, a number of them would soon form themselves into a waiting list for university status and would stop accommodating precisely those students for whom they were intended. They would in particular cease to be comprehensive academic communities.

Of course, there may be room for doubt about the original policies. The point is arguable. But there is surely no argument for having a policy and then watching it disintegrate. It would be no good Ministers asserting their determination to press on east towards the new dawn if the system were actually going west. The astonishing thing is that no steps whatever were taken to discover as a matter of routine what direction the polytechnics were going in. The experience of those concerned, the odd research project here and there and the statements of some polytechnic directors combine to suggest that the policy has collapsed. But nobody really knew, so it was possible for the aspirations of Ministers and the assertions of the polytechnics' defenders to be quite different from reality.

Yet the facts could have been made available quite simply. All we needed was a group of 'key indicators' of polytechnic development. For example, we needed to know what sorts of people were applying to polytechnics and for what sorts of courses – and what sorts of people were being accepted. A study of student enrolments would have told us most of what we wanted to know about the balance of different kinds and levels of work. Some of the information about enrolments was already collected as a matter of routine and as gobbled up by the DES computer, but it was not very useful for policy without comparable information about applicants and without additional information about such things as social class and previous education.

236

The requirements for planning were surely obvious. What we needed to know about students was their age, sex, home address, educational qualifications and background, father's (and own) occupation, course applied or enrolled for (its subject, level and mode of study). There should have been no difficulty in evolving compatible application and enrolment forms which gathered this information as a matter of pure routine. If it had been collected, the country would have known whether the policy was or was not being served by the polytechnics. Individual polytechnics would have known how far they were meeting not only their own object- ives but also the objectives implied by national policy. (The poly- technics might also have been able to fend off isolated and time-consuming inquiries from outside researchers.) The fact is that without this sort of information regularly and routinely collected and published it was – and is – impossible to take seriously the polytechnics' protestations or claims; and there is a very important sense in which neither the Government nor the polytechnics know where the latter are going. The design of an application form may seem a detail, but what was at stake was the rational conduct of public policy.

In our own research John Pratt and I sought to apply this kind of test to the binary policy as announced. Our book *Polytechnics: A Report* (Pratt and Burgess, 1974) was a modest, faltering and incomplete attempt to present our findings. We asked ourselves what problems was the Secretary of State, Anthony Crosland, trying to solve; what solutions he proposed; and what would tell us that these solutions had failed. What instruments were available to him; how did he use them; and were there unused alternatives? In pure helpfulness we offered explanations for our findings, which are themselves in the nature of hypotheses, and some recommendations for the future, which are clearly alternative policies.

Anthony Crosland's problems were of many kinds, at many levels, and not all of them were openly acknowledged. For example one problem that he formulated privately with his officials was that the Robbins Committee just over a year earlier had produced a report on higher education which was bulky, prestigious and wrong. It represented the high water mark of the university reform of the late nineteenth century but it had little relation to the needs of actual or potential students, teachers, institutions or society. Indeed it did not discuss these at all seriously. Nor did it understand the provision for higher education the country actually possessed. Its recommendations were thus vacuous. It was essential for the Minister and department responsible for higher education to begin the destruction of the Robbins Report. This Anthony Crosland did with his Woolwich speech in 1965, and it is a measure of his achievement that not one of Robbins's major recommendations has survived.

It is a good example of how aspirations can be untested that most people, including most Ministers, still talk as if our present and future patterns of higher education are somehow in line with Robbins. Unhappily, although the report's specific recommendations have been dropped, the spirit behind them survives – in the polytechnics as elsewhere. So we may conclude that as a solution to the 'Robbins problem' the plan for polytechnics was only partially a failure.

Another problem, this time announced by Anthony Crosland, was that of the neglect of professional and vocational (or socially responsive) education at the highest levels. Anthony Crosland was quite explicit about this. He identified a further problem, which John Pratt and I have called 'academic drift', that in a unitary, hierarchical system the public institutions ape the universities at a cost to diversity and (if institutions are regularly 'promoted') morale in the public colleges. The plan for polytechnics was meant to be a solution for this problem.

It is hard to argue that 'apeing' has ceased. There are polytechnics with professors. The committee of their directors flirts with a 'polytechnic grants committee', quinquennial settlements and the end of local authority control. Their staffs hanker for a professional association divorced from that of their colleagues in further education.

There is widespread restiveness with the Council for National Academic Awards, mainly for 'status' reasons. Their students (see below) are little distinguished from university students. Nobody seriously denies that 'apeing' is rife. John Pratt and I argue that 'designating' thirty polytechnics made it more likely, and we offer several ways in which it could have been, and still could be, countered.

The third example concerns the polytechnics' students. Again, Anthony Crosland explicitly identified provision for sub-degree level work and for 'tens of thousands of part-time students' as a problem his policy sought to solve. John Pratt and I felt that this policy could be said to have failed if the polytechnics accommodated a smaller proportion of such students than their constituent colleges had done.

We showed that, even before they were designated, the proportion of part-time advanced students fell from 60 to 50 per cent and the proportion of sub-degree-level work from 78 to 71 per cent. This was discoverable at the time from the returns to the Department of Education and Science, and if it had been found, Ministers might have been alerted to the disappointment of their hopes. Today, it appears from the figures of the polytechnic directors (THES, 3 March 1974), the proportions are about 50 per cent in each case. And as the polytechnic directors pointed out, the growth areas are still in first- and higher-degree work. Numbers in sub-degree work and on part-time courses have alike declined since last year. These findings were not challenged. Instead large numbers of people working in polytechnics (mainly directors) who were prepared to claim 'undoubted success' for their institutions accused us roundly of being determined to describe the polytechnics as failures. But of course the idea of failure is meaningless unless it is set against intention, and it is this that we tried to do. It is true that we looked for evidence of failure: that is the essence of the process. I have just given three examples of the way in which we sought to take seriously the policy-hypotheses of ministers and to test them. No doubt the job could have been done better. It must be done better, over the whole realm of public policy, if our democracy is to be adequate for its problems.

Postscript

The attentive reader may have noticed that as this book has developed, the amount of foreign examples has diminished. This is largely because in all the literature from the last five years that I have read and in the various visits I have made, I have not found even now very much fundamental questioning of the purposes and practices of post-school education. By the time I come to contemplate such education as a service to all, I have left the world behind. Just to make plain, however, that this is not to be thought of as an idle vision, let me end by quoting the one official report I know which gives ground for believing that these issues will shortly be practical politics. It is from the draft report of the commission on post-secondary education in Ontario:

The educational goal of post-secondary education is to prepare citizens for life and work. This, in turn, breaks down into two subsidiary categories of educational goals. One, the general and traditional aims of education: to transmit knowledge, to create and transmit new knowledge, and to stimulate the development of critical attitudes – habits of mind – in students. Second, equally traditional and admixed with the first one, is the preparation for a career through training.

In our survey of current as well as historical literature we have not found any other educational goals or any more concise expression of them. We accept these as an accurate, though general, expression of educational purposes.

What gives meaning and life to these general goals is how they are accomplished and how they continue adjusting to changes in society. We have formulated a set of principles by which we believe these goals should be accomplished in our society; our recommendations, as well as our criticisms, are based on these principles.

1. *Universal accessibility*: We have accepted the need for universal accessibility to post-secondary education at all ages as our first principle. This principle must be reflected in a broad range of financial as well as academic policies. Hence our recommendations in this area stress the encouragement of lifelong education, part-time school attendance, and new ways of delivering educational services.

2. *Openness*: We have adopted the principle that all educational services should be more and more open to the public and, indeed, integrated within the general cultural and educational activities of the community. Institutions such as public libraries, museums, art galleries, and science centres should be treated as part of the community's educational services.

3. *Diversity*: As lifelong opportunity for education becomes more of a reality, there will be a need for even greater diversity of educational services than we have at present – diversity not only of institutions but of admission standards, programmes, length of courses, and so forth. This principle is far easier to announce than to guarantee. As part of the

240

public sector, post-secondary education is vulnerable to the pressures of homogenization and uniformity. We therefore offer recommendations which would safeguard the present diversity and introduce additional forms of educational services and alternatives.

4. *Flexibility*: There is simply no way anybody can establish firm and definitive guidelines for future educational services in an open and democratic society. Even if it were possible, it would be antithetical to the very ideals of openness and democracy. We must, therefore, have a post-secondary educational system which is sufficiently responsive to new social demands yet is also prepared to abandon those that are no longer deemed necessary.

One cannot plan for innovation, but incentives can be provided that would, when innovation and new social demands appear, allow and support such developments. Our recommendations on financing offer one such incentive, and those regarding the role of government and of institutional administration reflect the same orientation.

5. *Transferability*: We are convinced that, even if wide accessibility and even diversity were achieved, our purpose would be defeated if there were insufficient opportunities for transfers from institution to institution, from programme to programme, from profession to pro-profession. We are, therefore, offering recommendations designed to break down the licensing and educational links (one of the chief causes of rigidity), and also to provide orderly procedures for transfers of abilities, aptitudes, and skills (not just formal credits) from one post-secondary enterprise to another and, indeed, from any relevant activity in one's life to the educational process. We are advocating an 'accessible hierarchy' of educational services.

6. *Public accountability*: Both political principles and reality demand that we recognize the public nature of post-secondary education. The fact that practically all the direct costs of education are borne by taxpayers is alone a forceful argument for public accountability. What makes the acceptance of it necessary is, and must be, our faith in our democratic political institutions.

Public accountability must not be confused with detailed bureaucratic controls and meddling. Both as individual citizens and as members of the Commission, we have come to view the increased bureaucratization of our lives as one of the main problems of our society. In post-secondary education, bureaucratization endangers the very values we cherish and hope to pass on to succeeding generations; it also makes the exploration and search for understanding more difficult. The result can only undermine all the rest of our educational goals.

(Ontario, 1972.)

Bibliography

Aitken, 1966: *Administration of a University*, Robert Aitken, University of London Press.

Armitage and Crampin, 1970: 'The Pressure of Numbers: Speculation for the Seventies', Peter Armitage and Alice Crampin, *Higher Education Review*, Spring 1970.

Beard, 1970: *Teaching and Learning in Higher Education*, Ruth Beard Penguin.

Blaug, 1967: 'Approaches to Educational Planning', Mark Blaug, *The Economic Journal*, June 1967.

Bloom, 1956: *Taxonomy of Educational Objectives I: Cognitive Domain*, ed. B. S. Bloom; *II: Affective Domain*, B. S. Bloom et. al., David McKay.

Boston, 1971: 'The Students: A Slow Burning Fuse', Richard Boston, *Sunday Times Magazine*, 13 June 1971.

Bowles, 1962: 'Access to Education – A Global View', Frank Bowles, *College Board Review No. 48*, Autumn 1962. The full report appears as Bowles, 1963.

Bowles, 1963: *Access to Higher Education*, Frank Bowles, Unesco and the International Association of Universities.

Burgess and Pratt, 1970: *Policy and Practice: The College of Advanced Technology*, Tyrrell Burgess and John Pratt, Allen Lane.

Burgess and Pratt, 1971: *Innovation in Higher Education: Technical Education in the United Kingdom*, Tyrrell Burgess and John Pratt, OECD.

Burgess and Pratt, 1972: *Polytechnics in Pakistan: A Report for the Ford Foundation*, Tyrrell Burgess and John Pratt, North East London Polytechnic.

Carnegie, 1973: *Priorities for Action: Final Report of the Carnegie Commission in Higher Education*, McGraw-Hill.

Corcoran, 1963: 'The Admission Process in the 1960s', Mary Corcoran, Appendix A to Bowles, 1963.

Crosland, 1965: Speech by the Secretary of State for Education and Science, Rt. Hon. Anthony Crosland MP, at Woolwich Polytechnic, 27 April 1965, reproduced in Pratt and Burgess, 1974.

Crosland, 1967: Speech by the Secretary of State for Education and

Science, Rt Hon. Anthony Crosland MP, at Lancaster University, 20 January 1967, reproduced in Pratt and Burgess, 1974.

Crowther, 1959: *15–18*, report of a committee under the Chairmanship of Sir Geoffrey Crowther, HMSO.

DES, 1970: *Student Numbers in Higher Education in England and Wales*, Education Planning Paper No. 2, HMSO.

Douglas, 1968: *All our Future*, J. W. B. Douglas, Peter Davies.

Fischer, 1972: Background Paper, Jurgen Fischer, *Problems of Integrated Higher Education: An International Case Study of the Gesamthochschule*, International Association of Universities.

Grant, 1964: *Soviet Education*, Nigel Grant, Penguin.

Guidelines, 1973: Guidelines for Diplomas of Higher Education, report of a study group established by the CNAA and the UGC under the chairmanship of Sir Walter Perry.

Henniker-Heaton, 1964: *Day Release*, report of a committee under the Chairmanship of C. Henniker-Heaton, HMSO.

India, 1966. *Education and National Development, Report of the Education Commission 1964–1966*, Ministry of Education, Government of India.

James, 1972; *Teacher Education and Training*, report of a committee under the chairmanship of Lord James of Rusholme, HMSO.

Jencks, 1968: *The Academic Revolution*, Christopher Jencks and David Riesman, Doubleday.

Jessel, 1971: 'Idea of Working Class Chances at University Blighted by Statistics', Stephen Jessel, *The Times*, 6 October 1971.

Lohmann, 1968: *Report on Evaluation of Advisory Services OSU – Pakistan Technical Education Project*, M. R. Lohmann, Oklahoma State University.

McCarthy, 1968: *The Employment of Highly Specialized Graduates: a comparative study in the U.K. and the U.S.A.*, M. C. McCarthy, Science Policy Studies No. 3, HMSO.

Magee, 1958: *Go West Young Man*, Bryan Magee, Eyre & Spottiswoode.

Manpower, 1968: *The Flow into Employment of Scientists, Engineers and Technologists*, report of a working group of the Committee on Manpower Resources for Science and Technology, HMSO.

Mountford, 1966; *British Universities*, James Mountford, Oxford University Press.

NELP, 1974: *Diploma of Higher Education*, a submission to the Council for National Academic Awards, North East London Polytechnic.

Newsom, 1963: *Half our Future*, a report of the Central Advisory Council for Education, England, under the chairmanship of Sir John Newsom, HMSO.

243

OECD, 1972: *Interdisciplinary*: a report of a seminar organized by the Centre for Educational Research and Innovations and the French Ministry of Education, OECD.

Ontario, 1972: *Draft Report* of the Commission on Post Secondary Education, The Queen's Printer, Toronto.

Perkins, 1969: *Innovation in Higher Education: New Universities in the United Kingdom*, H. J. Perkins, OECD.

PIB, 1968: *Standing Reference on the Pay of University Teachers in Great Britain, First Report*, National Board for Prices and Incomes Report No. 98, HMSO.

Popper, 1959: *The Logic of Scientific Discovery*, Karl R. Popper, Hutchinson.

Popper, 1976: *Unended Quest: An Intellectual Autobiography*, Karl R. Popper, Fontana.

Pratt, 1970: 'What about the Workers', John Pratt, *New Society*, 26 March 1970.

Pratt, 1975: 'The UGC Department', John Pratt, *Higher Education Review*, Spring 1975.

Pratt and Burgess, 1974: *Polytechnics: A Report*, John Pratt and Tyrrell Burgess, Pitman.

Robbins, 1963: *Higher Education: Report of the Committee Appointed by the Prime Minister under the Chairmanship of Lord Robbins*, cmnd 2154, HMSO.

Ruiter, 1969: 'The Demand for University-Trained Engineers in the Netherlands', R. Ruiter, *Some Problems of the Development of Higher Education in Europe*, OECD.

Russell, 1973: *Adult Education: A Plan for Development*, report of a committee under the chairmanship of Sir Lionel Russell, HMSO.

Sloman, 1964: *A University in the Making*, Albert Sloman, BBC.

Townsend, 1971: *Up the Organization*, Robert Townsend, Coronet Books.

UGC, 1963: *Non-Recurrent Grants: Notes on Procedures*, University Grants Committee.

UGC, 1967: *Memorandum of General Guidance*, University Grants Committee.

Unesco, 1971: *World Survey of Education Vol. V: Educational Policy, Legislation and Administration*, Unesco.

U.S.S.R., 1961: *Statute on the Higher Schools of U.S.S.R., 1961* quoted in Grant, 1964.

White Paper, 1972: *Education: A Framework for Expansion*, cmnd 5174 HMSO.

Index

Academic drift, characteristics, 31–2; a world-wide phenomenon, 32–4; influence on student recruitment, 35–6; cause of, 36; reversing the tendency, 46; unquestioned by Robbins, 80; Crosland and, 83, 238; resilience, 168, 223

Academic profession, methods of self-protection, 67, 102, 182; anti-expansionist in universities, 79; conformity among PhDs, 96–7; and the subject department and discipline, 97, 98–9, 100, 102, 109–10, 115–16; reaction to advances in knowledge, 99, 100; and possibility of change, 101–2; responsibilities in single-subject honours degree, 106; immunity to criticism, 114, 116; authoritarianism, 115–16, 126–7; unexamined assumptions about education, 117, 124; and the results of their teaching, 124–6; need to defend its present practices, 132; concept of academic freedom (personal and institutional), 173, 182; accountability for teaching and research, 174, 180–81; promotion as a result of publication, 178; rationalization of senior appointments, 181; weak position in bargaining situation, 182; essential involvement in educational planning, 184, 186; *see also* Teachers

Administration, administrators, spurious claims to objectivity, 168–9; failure to supply the needs of industry, 169; and the needs of individuals, 169; belief in rationalization and economics, 169–70; interference in policy implementation, 170; priorities, 170–71; response to attempts at innovation, 181; should derive from purpose, 226

Africa, 65; European colonization, 93; educational institutions, 94

Aitken, Sir Robert, on the University Charter, 97, 98

Artisan's Club, Artisan's Institute, 22

Asia, 65; European colonization, 93

Association of Municipal Corporations, 191

Association of Principals in Technical Institutions, 60

Association of Teachers in Technical Institutions, 60

Austria, service tradition in technical colleges, 35

Beard, Ruth, and response to student complaint, 117; student access to knowledge, 162

Belgium, unspecified educational aims, 13

Blaug, Mark, on economics of education, 202, 210–11 (*Economic Journal*)

Bloom, Benjamin, taxonomy of educational aims, 125–6

Bowles, Frank, and admission process in HE, 64–6; nature of education, 66, 89; results of elimination process, 66–7; artificial restriction of places, 67, 68, 110; academic self-perpetuation, 67; preoccupation with standards, 77, 110

Education – *contd*
proach, 104–7; opening of entry to the unqualified, 109–10; concern with standards, 110; ignorance of its internal happenings, 117–18; authoritarianism, 126–7; implications of science, 127; consequences of logic of learning and of discovery, 134; method its chief concern, 134; to be open to student criticism, 134–5; criteria of what student can do, 135; should provide service for adults in need, 136–7; disparity between its evaluation and provisions, 141; role in modern society, 141–2; creation of competence, 142–5; failure to service the family, 142; to be based on needs of the student, 145; harmful results of failure, 160; function of criticism, 164–6; and plurality of control, 177; separation of programme validation from provision of resources, 177–8; LEA accountability, 190; unrelated to economic growth, 203–4; and development of special skills, 203–4; problems requiring formulation and solution, 217

Education, adult, neglect, 62–3, 84; vocational and non-vocational courses, 85, 144–5; government recommendations, 85; diversity in courses provided, 189

Education, further (FE), 27–8, 220; differentiated from university, 28; and professional and vocational needs, 28–9, 144; employer indifference, 63; number of students by method of study (Table), 75; provision of social and educational mobility, 82–3; cost per student compared with universities, 214–15; past efforts at coordination and rationalization, 215–16

Education, higher (HE), socio-cultural role, 15–16, 18; idea of study 'in depth', 21, 24–5; innovations due to FE colleges, 28–30; external validation of local initiative, 29; variation in routes to, 54–5, 64–6; expansion at loss to young workers, 63; who is it for?, 64; universal admission (examinations) process, 64–5; 'maintaining standards' theory, 66, 68; numbers entering (U.K.), 66–7, 68–9; regarded as a reward, 71; class composition of students, 71–3 (Table, 72), 74–6; suggested remedies, 73; Robbins/Crosland debate, 76, 84–5; invention of 'binary' policy, 78, 83, 233; expansion in non-university sectors, 80; élitism rather than mass provision, 85, 87–8; Western Europe/U.S./U.S.S.R. comparisons, 90–91; value of residence in college, 93; conflict between need to learn and to teach, 124; organization of subject departments, 131–2; Dip.H.E. content, 148; entry requirements, 150, 189; irrelevance of manpower forecasting, 202–5; dangers of social demand forecasts, 205; to be available to all qualified by ability and attainment, 208

Education, post-school (English), main issues, 11; viewed as a luxury, 12; its tasks, 12; official statement on its purpose, 14–18; autonomous and service traditions, 19–20, 44, 46, 168; precedes Open University entrance, 26; what is its purpose?, 44–5, 168; need to be socially responsive, 47; increasing cost, 48; differentiated from earlier stages, 49; importance for personal and economic development, 50, 137,

225; compulsory considerations, 50–51, 54; 'second' and 'tertiary' levels, 54, 69; national variations, 54–5; modes of attendance (Table), 56–7; discussions on day-release, 58–63; preference given to demands of society and the academic, 63–4, 87; small numbers benefiting from, 69, 86; should serve all adults, 86–7, 137, 168; continues to serve the relatively advantaged, 87; expansion of élite system, 87–8; need for universal provision, 88; variety of second-level forms, 89–90; subject hierarchy, 108; assumed intellectual gains, 125; application of Popper's theories, 127 ff.; should reflect the logic of learning, 168; periodical rationalization, 169–70; scrutiny process for educational programmes, 177; projected improvements in administration and finance, 191–4; policy decisions by Secretary of State (élitist or mass, proportion of GNP to be spent), 212–13; essential characteristics, 219; résumé of its organization, 227; implementation of author's proposals, 229; absence in overseas development, 239; China, 34; U.S.S.R., 32, 54

Educational, vocational, notion of levels of study, 108; student demand for relevance, 116; becomes a narrow academic discipline, 143; true requirement, 143

Education Act, 1918, provision for day-release, 59

Education Act, 1944, 193; non-mandatory 'county colleges', 59; and day-release, 60; spells out duties of Secretary of State, 219; LEA duties in FE, 220

Educational planning and organization, tries to solve irrelevant problems, 169; to begin with individual student, 171; from the bottom up, 171–3, 201; staff contribution, 173; Government method, 202, 207–9; new techniques, 202; manpower forecasting, 202–5, 213–14; social (private) demand, 202, 205–6, 214; return on investment, 202, 210–11, 214; role of assumptions, 206; projection of past trends, 206–7, 215; part-time/full-time rate of return, 211; attempt to derive policies from technique, 211–12, 214; point of entry into policy-making, 213–15; flexibility and responsiveness to need, 227

Educators, arrogant assumptions on school-leavers, 69; neglect needs of part-timers, 70; solutions to out-of-date knowledge, 134; reaction to families in need, 136; need to find quick ways of achieving objectives, 146; helping students to understand themselves, 146

EEC, equating degrees and professional qualifications, 111, 112

Employment, industrial need for mobility, 39; increasing needs for education, 143–4

England and Wales, development of post-school education, 20–23; university independence, 24; distinction between autonomous and service traditions in HE, 30–31; diverse second-level (after-school) education, 55 (Table), 56–7; academic and vocational courses, 58; accommodation of goals of educators, 58; statutory 'day-release', 58–9; eleven plus procedure, 68; nineteenth-century architectural 'renaissance', 93; individual teacher independence, 174; LEA responsibility for post-school education, 189

139, 140; and a fixed educational policy, 182

Pavlov, Ivan, conditioned reflex theory, 118, 129

Perkin, Prof, Harold, study of new universities, 100–101

Polytechnics, 22, 29; effect of academic drift, 31, 34; part of 'binary' policy for HE, 78, 83, 235; effect of Crosland's policy, 83, 236–7; variation in student numbers and 'precincts', 92; readiness for self-development, 187; first-degree-level courses, 189; idea of a 'grants committee', 191–2, 238; compared with universities, 191; 1966 establishments, 216; government policy, 223–4; failure to monitor its implementation, 236–8; planning requirements, 237; fall in proportion of part-time advanced students and sub-degree-level work, 239

Popper, Sir Karl, and the process of learning, 127, 129; schema for logic of scientific discovery, 127–8, 129; distinguishes three main types of learning, 128; application to human beings, 129; error elimination in theory testing (falsifiability), 130–31, 233; demarcation between science and non-science, 130, 233; nature of observation, 233; and the continuum of intellectual progress, 233; application of his theories to public policy, 233–4

Pratt, J., and Burgess, T., academic drift, 31, 238; simple policy-testing, 235; and 'binary' policy, 237; *Polytechnics: A Report*, 237

Prices and Incomes Board, and academic salaries, 218

Problem formulation, 129, 141; primacy over solutions, 129,

216, 232; a continuum of learning, 132–3, 232; dual characteristics, 133; intellectual requirements, 141; in student programme planning, 155–6, 158; Government characteristics, 216, 218, 221; and true educational needs, 217; suggested departmental committees, 217, 218; trial-and-error process in solution, 218–19, 232; to be followed by distribution of resources, 221; monitoring solutions, 222

Prussia, academic drift, 35

Regional Advisory Councils, 185, 188, 192

Research, 132; freedom to engage in, 174; teamwork and equipment needs, 174; absence of staff accountability, 178; funding, 178; application for grants, 179

Research Councils, 77, 178–9

Research foundations (private), 178–9

Robbins Report (1963), on aims of HE, 14–15; purpose, 18, 78; Committee set up, 24, 77; executive subjects, 25; generous implementation, 63; ensures continuance of élite system, 67, 76, 81, 84; equates HE with universities, 67–8, 76, 80; percentage of students with fathers in manual work, 71; and expansion of university places, 76–7; administrative proposals, 77–9; full-time/part-time division of HE, 78–9; minimum forecast of future demand for places, 79; failures and unconsidered areas, 80–81; concern with the 'clever', 86; and comparative standards, 110–11; on importance of independence in teaching, 175; view of non-autonomous colleges, 175–6; and UGC, 196; projecting (private) demand for places, 205–6, 207, 215;